D1451127

PERFORMANCE REQUIREMENTS
FOR
FOREIGN BUSINESS

PERFORMANCE REQUIREMENTS
FOR
FOREIGN
BUSINESS

U.S.
MANAGEMENT
RESPONSE

RICHARD D. ROBINSON

Assisted by
DAVID SHARP
CAROL A. ROBINSON
JOAN WYATT

PRAEGER SPECIAL STUDIES • PRAEGER SCIENTIFIC

Library of Congress Cataloging in Publication Data

Robinson, Richard D, 1921–
    Performance requirements for foreign business.

    Includes index.
    1. International business enterprises – Management.
2. Industry and state.   I. Title.
HD62.4.R62   1983   658'.049   82-22469
ISBN 0-03-062962-4

Published in 1983 by Praeger Publishers
CBS Educational and Professional Publishing
a Division of CBS Inc.
521 Fifth Avenue, New York, New York 10175, U.S.A.

© 1983 by Praeger Publishers

3456789   052   987654321

Printed in the United States of America

Contents

List of
Tables and Figures

x

Introduction

The purpose of this study, which encompassed 51 United States-based corporations, was to ascertain management response to the opportunities and problems created by government intervention in the international marketplace through the introduction of incentives and disincentives. The focus was primarily on developing countries but not exclusively. It was felt that one must view management reaction to government incentives and requirements in the context of the world economy, for many industrialized countries compete vigorously to attract foreign capital, management, and technology. This is a fact with which the developing countries must live and confront.

The central question we asked was: Did executives believe that what governments were doing influenced their decisions as to the direction and nature of corporate involvement in foreign markets? In making such a study, one comes away with a major worry. Is it possible for anyone to know other than those actually party to decisions at the time? And, if that be the case, how can an interview with one or two executives for two to three hours—and often several years after the event—provide a real understanding of what, in fact, influenced a corporate decision? One wonders if we were attempting the impossible. However, we reassured ourselves by realizing that what high-level corporate executives believed to have been the case was perhaps just as important—if not more so—than the objective reality. After all, it is the perceptions of managers that are important in shaping current and future decisions. From that point of view, perhaps this study does reveal an important level of reality.

In a sense, this research is the counterpart of earlier analysis of various government programs.* There are a few recent studies covering somewhat the same ground. Of perhaps greatest interest are Israel Frank's 1980 study, Foreign Enterprise in Developing Countries;† the 1981 statement by the Committee for

---

*Richard D. Robinson, National Control of Foreign Business; A Survey of Fifteen Countries (New York: Praeger Publishers, 1976), and Richard D. Robinson et al., Foreign Investment in the Third World; A Comparative Study of Selected Developing Countries Investment Promotion Programs (Washington, D.C.: International Division, Chamber of Commerce of the United States, 1980).

†Baltimore: Johns Hopkins Press, 1980.

Economic Development (CED), <u>Transnational Corporations and Developing Countries: New Policies for a Changing World Economy</u>;*
and the article by Ranjan Das entitled "Impact of Host Government Regulations on MNC Operations: Learning From Third World Countries."†

The present study is differentiated from these other works along several different dimensions. Only a small portion of the Frank volume is devoted to corporate response to host country investment policies. Even there, it deals with a much narrower range of issues, specifically incentives, transfer pricing and taxation, interest as a business expense, export requirements, Calvo doctrine and formula for compensation, renegotiation, and deterrent to investment. Not really analyzed at any length, if at all, are such matters as requirements (or commitments) to spin off ownership, management, and/or technology or to assume specific performance guarantees relative to local content, employment, investment, site, local research and development, production, and/or training. Finally, U.S. government policies are considered here in somewhat greater detail, such as investment guarantees, export credit facilities, illegal payments regulations, antitrust, export controls, and the impact of domestic regulation on the pattern of foreign trade and investment. Over all, Frank's work deals with a much more general subject matter. In contrast, the CED statement has to do with proscriptions for government and corporate behavior. It deals very little with corporate responses to specific government programs and policies. The Das article is targeted directly to the subject of this report but is limited to one country, India. It discusses, in some detail, multinational response to Indian government policies. However, the article is primarily descriptive. There is no material that takes one inside the thinking of individual managers; there are no direct quotes. His concluding paragraph, however, is worth bearing in mind as one reads the following pages:

> Cultural disparity between the parent and the affiliate will increase, with affiliates entering more and more into diverse businesses under environmental compulsion. The withdrawal of expatriate managers due to host government directive will hasten the process.‡

---

*Statement by the Research and Policy Committee, Washington, D.C., 1981.

†In <u>Columbia Journal of World Business</u> (Spring 1981):85-90.

‡Ibid., p. 90.

The very awareness of this process on the part of corporate managers influences their responses. It also increases the cost of maintaining a multinational corporate system, the nature of which is discussed in the following paragraphs.

Another relevant study is The Use of Investment Incentives and Performance Requirements by Foreign Governments,* published by the U.S. Department of Commerce. This analysis consists essentially of a tabulation of the frequency with which the foreign affiliates of U.S. firms had received incentives and were subject to performance requirements, by industry and country. The data were based on that collected in a 1977 statistical study.† On average, it was found that 26 percent of U.S. affiliates had received one or more investment incentives. Twenty percent had received tax concessions, 8 percent tariff concessions, 9 percent subsidies, and 5 percent other forms of incentives. The percentage receiving incentives was almost equally divided between the developing countries and the developed countries. As may be seen from Table 1.1, there was a wide range of frequency among countries. The same was true for the percentage of affiliates subject to performance requirements; although, in that case, the frequency was much greater in the developing countries. It was reported that of those firms surveyed, 14 percent of their overseas affiliates had been subjected to at least one performance requirement. Two percent had faced minimum export requirements, 3 percent maximum import levels, 8 percent a minimum local labor content requirement, and 6 percent a foreign equity limitation. The distribution of both incentives and performance requirements was fairly even across industries, with some minor exceptions (see Table I.2). Although all these statistics are useful and revealing, they are not directly relevant to the present study, which focuses on management reaction to incentives and performance requirements, which no one doubts exist with great frequency.

A recent study by Morris Sweet, Industrial Location Policy for Economic Revitalization: National and International Perspectives‡ analyzes policies and programs in Western Europe, Japan, and Canada with respect to the selection, control, and direction of

*Washington, D.C.: Office of International Investment, International Trade Administration, U.S. Department of Commerce, October 1981.

†Benchmark Study of US Direct Investment Abroad—1977 (Washington, D.C.: Bureau of Economic Analysis, U.S. Department of Commerce, 1978). The survey was based on information gathered from 23,641 U.S. nonbank affiliates of nonbank parents.

‡New York: Praeger, 1981.

TABLE I.1

Concentration of Low to Moderate Incentives
and Low Performance Requirements

Country	Percent of U.S. Affiliates Receiving Incentives	Percent of U.S. Affiliates Subject to Performance Requirements
Canada*	19	4
Belgium*	26	7
Denmark	28	2
France*	18	7
West Germany*	20	2
Italy*	29	6
Luxembourg	38	1
Netherlands*	29	2
United Kingdom*	32	3
Austria	25	4
Norway	11	7
Sweden	33	3
Switzerland*	12	7
Japan*	9	9
Australia*	37	8
South Africa	35	12
Argentina	31	13
Panama	21	15
Bahamas	16	10
Bermuda†	19	4
Netherlands Antilles	21	5
Liberia	21	15
Hong Kong	5	2
Singapore	24	11

*Countries are 10 of top 12 countries with the largest stock of U.S. foreign direct investment at the end of 1977. Only Brazil and Mexico of the top 12 are absent.

†Data for Bermuda were not disclosed for 1977. However, 1976 and 1978 U.S. direct investment position data indicate that for 1977 Bermuda would most likely place in the top 12 recipients of U.S. foreign direct investment.

Source: Calculations based on a special tabulation of data, gathered through the BE-10 Benchmark Survey of US Direct Investment Abroad—1977, provided by the International Investment Division of the U.S. Department of Commerce, Bureau of Economic Analysis. From Business America, November 2, 1981, p. 14.

TABLE I.2

Incentives and Performance Requirements by Industry

Industry	Percent of U.S. Affiliates Receiving Incentives	Percent of U.S. Affiliates Subject to Performance Requirements
Total	26	14
Mining	29	27
Petroleum	21	16
Manufacturing	41	19
Food products	46	21
Chemicals and allied products	42	19
Primary and fabricated metals	40	18
Nonelectrical machinery	37	14
Electrical machinery	48	21
Transportation equipment	45	27
Other	37	17
Trade	15	9
Finance, insurance, real estate	12	8
Other*	13	10

*Agriculture, forestry, fishing, construction, transportation, communications, public utilities, and services.

Source: Calculations based on a special tabulation of data, gathered through the BE-10 Benchmark Survey of US Direct Investment Abroad—1977, provided by the International Investment Division of the U.S. Department of Commerce, Bureau of Economic Analysis. From The Use of Incentives and Performance Requirements by Foreign Governments (Washington, D.C.: Office of International Investment, International Trade Administration, U.S. Department of Commerce, October 1981), p. 16.

foreign investment. He concludes that the experience of Canada and France indicates that foreign enterprise can live comfortably with controls. However, the evidence he introduces is not persuasive. So much depends upon the nature of the controls, the fairness and honesty of their application, degree of adaption to specific situations, and the extent and attractiveness of the associated incentives. There is abundant evidence in the following pages that controls in both France and Canada have, in fact, discouraged a significant flow of foreign investment and, indeed, we found that those two countries were often singled out by executives as being unduly nationalistic and hostile to U.S. business on a discriminatory basis. Certainly, foreign enterprises can live with controls, but how? It all depends on the particular situation. Japan was another case; so, likewise, the United Kingdom. Generalizations across countries are dangerous.

Despite the misgivings one may have about the accuracy of international trade and investment statistics, there is a good deal of evidence that the flow of direct foreign investment, as a percentage of the total international flow of commercial resources, is declining. What appears to be growing most rapidly are the flows of services, skills, technology, and proprietary rights under contract. Indeed, at least one executive in the companies in which interviews were conducted specifically stated that, in his opinion, the era during which direct foreign investment was of preeminent importance is over, that flows under contract were of greater significance.

It should be borne in mind, of course, that statistically the definition of what constitutes direct foreign investment is an arbitrary one and that the reporting of flows of intangibles under contract is done very inadequately by many countries. For purposes of statistical definition, an investment generally is termed "direct" if it constitutes more than 10 percent (sometimes 25 percent) of the equity of the enterprise in which the investment is made. Technically, though, direct investment is an investment made with the intent of exercising some control and assuming some degree of participation in management. The 10 percent (or 25 percent) definition is a purely arbitrary device. An investment may be "direct" even though the equity held by the investor is less than a given percent; it depends upon how the rest of the equity is distributed. An investment of over a given percent may not lead to control or management participation. Then there is the problem of control flowing from debt, not equity. That can happen if the debt/equity ratio is very high. Then there is the further problem of control arising out of a purely contractual relationship, whether that relationship be represented by a management contract, contracted manufacturing, or a restrictive license or technical assistance agreement of some sort.

An interesting question that arises, assuming that the international flows of commercially valuable goods and services under contract are starting to dominate, is what is causing the relative demise of direct foreign investment? Will the conditions and requirements being imposed on direct foreign investors by many governments erode equity-based control to such a degree as to discourage the direct foreign investor? How does a management justify the assumption of risk implicit in direct investment when "adequate" control is threatened at every turn? Increasingly, host governments are limiting managerial options with respect to plant location, choice of technology, level of employment, definition of target markets, changes in production, definition of the product mix, financial structure, ownership, appointment of key executives, legal form of organization, purchase decisions, and sourcing decisions. As the form and time of government intervention becomes less predictable, equity investors perceive heightened risk and uncertainty. The result is that they have to anticipate a very much higher level of earnings to overcome the higher rates by which they discount those earnings to the present. That swollen stream of earnings introduces even more political risk, and host political authorities may object. Remittance of earnings above a certain level may be blocked.

On the other hand, the underlying dynamics explaining the declining relative importance of direct foreign investment may lie with the massive balance-of-payment surpluses piled up by the oil-exporting countries and the recycling of these funds via Western financial intermediaries to the developing countries in the form of bank loans, that is, portfolio investment. Financial resources are thereby available to many countries from sources other than the direct foreign investors of the West, that is, from the large international, multinational, and transnational corporations. It may be of relevance to note that of the largest corporations in the world, those growing most rapidly are the large general trading companies and the large international service corporations, not those primarily in manufacturing. For these trading and service enterprises, direct foreign investment is only of marginal or transient interest, primarily as a strategy to develop a source of supply or a customer but to be spun off to local ownership as soon as practicable. Profit is derived largely from commissions and fees arising out of the international flows of goods and services, much less from dividends.

This study does not answer—and perhaps no study can at the moment—the two-pronged question suggested above: One, is direct foreign investment, in fact, declining relative to other international commercial flows, specifically those of skills, technology, information, proprietory rights? Two, is the underlying cause the intervention of governments or a shift in the source of financial resources, or both? One suspects that the answer is both, and a third possible explanation may be contributing to the apparent shift away from multinational corporate control. That explanation has to do with the loss of technological advantage by large, globally integrated industrial firms—the multinational corporations (MNCs).* If, as many claim, the rate at which significantly new technology is being commercialized has slowed down, an increasing share of the world's technology is relatively "mature." On average, mature technology tends to be more labor intensive than the new technology. If so, advantage in production shifts slowly to those countries in which labor is relatively cheap compared to capital. In fact, we are seeing a rather rapid shift in the production and export of manufactured goods to the more advanced of the developing countries, the so-called newly industrializing countries (NICs). If, in fact, the MNCs are losing both relative financial and technological advantage, their continued control via ownership (equity)—which is the control characteristic of the MNCs—becomes intolerable. For this reason, both host government intervention and the rise of the international trading and service companies are not surprising. One should also note the increasing cost of central control implicit in the quotation from the Das article. Cultural distance may indeed be widening between parent corporation and foreign affiliate.

The question this study attempts to answer is what is the impact on corporate decision making in the United States of government-imposed performance requirements and incentives relevant to international business, whether introduced by host governments or by the United States. The performance requirements considered are those relating to export, ownership, employment of foreign nationals, local content, local employment, investment level, production level, local research and development, training, product, level of technology, and plant location. The incentives consist essentially of outright subsidies, tax reduction, market protection, import rights, various types of guarantees, and the promise of government procurement. In the case of the United States, corporate response to a variety of programs is reported, specifically, the Overseas Private Investment Corporation, export credit financing, the Foreign Corrupt Practices Act,

---

*The technical definition of the multinational, as differentiated from the export-oriented and international corporation, is discussed in greater detail in Chapter 1.

antitrust law, export controls, tax law, domestic regulations, and a variety of other U.S. laws, regulations, and policies. However, before proceeding to the analysis itself, it is necessary to acquaint the reader with the methodology and some aggregate measures of the companies included in the survey. It then becomes possible for the reader to judge the validity and reliability of the conclusions that are drawn.

PERFORMANCE REQUIREMENTS
FOR
FOREIGN
BUSINESS

1

Methodology and Aggregate Measures

The 51 corporations included in this sample of corporate experience and executive attitudes were not selected scientifically but rather for the sake of research convenience. However, there was an effort to secure a wide range of company size, a regional spread, and a diversity of industries, but all with some involvement overseas. The extent to which it succeeded can be deduced from the following tabulations. Also, similar interviews had been conducted in 33 of the 51 firms some 24 years earlier.* Other companies were selected from the four regions in which the interviewers worked—West Coast, Midwest, New England, and Mid-Atlantic (New York, New Jersey, Pennsylvania)—from those known to be active internationally and in which knowledgeable people would be available during August 1981, when the interviews were scheduled. All but five corporations were on _Fortune_'s list of the 500 largest industrial firms in the United States.

The timing of the field work may have been important. It should be borne in mind that August 1981 was just prior to the assassination of President Anwar Sadat of Egypt. The partial sanctions imposed against the Soviet Union following its move into Afghanistan were still being observed by the United States and many of its allies. Iran remained in turmoil as did much of Central America. The People's Republic of China had demonstrably slowed its pace of development. There was still considerable doubt

---

*Reported in summary form in Richard D. Robinson, _International Business Policy_ (New York: Holt, Rinehart and Winston, 1964), chaps. 4, 5.

in the United States as to the effectiveness of President Reagan's economic program, and interest rates were at a high level. Several changes in national legislation had either been made or, it was assumed, soon would be. These changes included a significant increase in the level of foreign-source personal income excluded from U.S. taxation, a more narrow definition of what constituted "illegal" payments under the Corrupt Foreign Practices Act, and the enactment of laws permitting the establishment of something resembling the general trading company within the United States.

During the interviews, each respondent was assured of complete confidentiality with respect to the experiences and attitudes revealed. Therefore, the participating corporations are not named in the following pages and, on occasion, details have been altered to preserve the anonymity of the participants. Nonetheless, care has been exercised so that these changes in details do not lead to erroneous conclusions.

The interviews conducted on the West Coast (7) and those in the Midwest (20) were undertaken by the author and his wife. In the New England area (8 firms) and the Mid-Atlantic (16 firms) areas, the interviews were conducted by David Sharp, a research associate. In all cases, the researchers took notes during the interviews, following an outline (see Appendix B), and on the basis of those notes, the interviews were reconstructed on tape as soon as possible. Subsequently, these tapes were transcribed and analyzed. For the 50 publicly owned corporations, published financial data were likewise used. In addition to one privately owned corporation, two others had extensive family interest but were nonetheless publicly quoted.

It was felt that firm size in terms of sales and employment, its product line, sales and earning trend, capital and labor intensity of production, level of research and development, and extent of foreign operations were all possibly relevant to management response to government-initiated performance requirements or incentives. Two corporate strategy variables, control and ownership, were likewise considered.

SIZE OF CORPORATIONS

The 51 corporations ranged in size from 6 with net annual sales of over $10 billion to 7 under $1 billion (before U.S. corporate tax), with the range being roughly from $30 billion down to $50 million. Over half of the firms (26) fell into the $1-4 billion annual sales group, with another 12 reporting sales of $5-9 billion. In terms of employment, the range was from 4,300 to over 600,000.

Just under half of the firms (25) reported worldwide employment of under 50,000. All were continental, multiplant firms based in the United States.

In the subsequent discussions, firms with annual net sales in 1980 of over $10 billion are designated "large," those with $1-9 billion "medium-sized," and those with under $1 billion "small."

PRODUCT LINE

Of the 51 entities in which interviews were conducted, 5 were true conglomerates in that no single product line clearly dominated the "business." In 2 of these cases, the degree of autonomy of the divisions in which the interviews were conducted was such that data were available for that one division. Inasmuch as both of these divisions had been independent companies when the 1957 interviews were conducted, the decision was made to use the data only from those divisions.

Forty-eight of the 49 corporations and the two semiautonomous divisions of conglomerates were essentially manufacturers or processors. The other three were largely purveyors of services. Table 1.1 classifies the 49 nonconglomerates and two conglomerate divisions by principal product line.

TABLE 1.1

Classification of the Sample by Principal Product Line

Product	Number
Chemicals, plastics, fibers	7
Food processing	7
Heavy industrial, construction, and mining equipment	5
Pulp, paper, and wood products	4
Processing of basic materials (metals, cement)	4
Automotive	4
Electronics	3
Machine tools and industrial instruments	3
Rubber products	2
Pharmaceuticals and drugs	2
Light consumer goods	2
Services	3
	46
Conglomerates, unclassifiable	5
	51

SALES AND EARNINGS TREND

The recent sales and earnings record of these firms varied widely. Eight had experienced a decline in sales from 1979 to 1980 and one, no change. The range was from minus 25 percent to a positive 31 percent. Twenty reported an increase of between 10 and 19 percent in net sales. The variation in annual earnings (before taxes and from continuing operations) was equally great: from a decline between 1979 and 1980 of -338 percent to a gain of +302 percent, with 22 falling between -20 percent and +20 percent. There were 20 losers, 29 gainers, 1 unchanged, and 1 for which financial data were not available. These figures represented relative gain or loss with respect to 1980. In fact, only 2 firms reported losses in absolute terms, but for 12 others their net earnings came to less than 5 percent of net sales.

CAPITAL AND LABOR INTENSITY

Several measures of capital and labor intensity demonstrate the wide variation within the sample. For example, depreciation per employee ranged from $750 to just under $13,000. Another measure was net property and equipment per employee, for which the range was something between $1,800 and just under $100,000. A third relevant measure developed was depreciation as a percent of net annual sales. Here, the range was from under 1 percent to just under 9 percent. One suspects that this ratio is probably the best available single measure of capital intensity in terms of capital used per unit of output. Wages as a percent of net sales were likewise calculated, the range being 11 to 40 percent but with 32 firms not reporting wages. Finally, research and development as a percentage of net sales ranged between near zero to close to 12 percent.

EXTENT OF OVERSEAS INVESTMENT

The degree to which companies were active overseas varied enormously, from 60.5 percent down to 5.6 percent of total sales. When the companies are arrayed by the percent of identifiable assets at cost located outside the United States as compared to their total assets, the range is 70.6 to 6.1 percent. Five claimed that over half of their total assets were located outside the United States; 15 over 35 percent.

Further measures of the extent of the international investment of the 51 corporations are shown in Table 1.2. Overall, 23 corporations reported 20 or more foreign affiliates. Table 1.3 reveals that 20 corporations reported affiliates in more than 15 countries.

CONTROL AND OWNERSHIP STRATEGY

In our study, we distinguished between export-oriented, international, multinational, and transnational corporations, although in the vernacular the terms are often used interchangeably. Technically, an export-oriented firm is one well organized to develop export, not overseas production. Decision making is heavily biased in favor of exports and against foreign investment. Its expertise is in exporting. An international corporation is one in which decision making between domestic and foreign operations is separate. A characteristic is the existence of one or more domestic divisions plus an international division, sometimes legally constituted as a separate corporation. In the pure form, such a division or subsidiary has responsibility for all international operations, whether they are exports, manufacturing via overseas subsidiaries or affiliates, or various forms of contracts (license, technical assistance, management, contract manufacturing). The significant factor here is that decision making between domestic and foreign markets is split. There is no single corporate strategy. A multinational corporation, on the other hand, is one in which there is conscious effort to optimize the allocation of corporate resources on a global basis. A characteristic of such an organization is the absence of an international division with operational responsibilities and the presence of either a number of regionally oriented headquarters and/or global product divisions. A less common type is the functionally organized, for example, by manufacturing, marketing, and engineering. A company may have a mixture of all three, thereby taking on a matrix kind of organization. The transnational corporation is simply a multinational that is multinationally managed and owned at the center. At some point, a true transnational loses the national bias inherent in decision making so long as its headquarters is dominated by parent country nationals and the parent corporation is owned preeminently by the same, which are characteristics of the multinational corporation.

The organization of the foreign operations of the 51 firms indicated that possibly only 28 were true multinationals, as the term is used here. These structural forms are taken as proxies for control strategies, as indicated in Table 1.4.

TABLE 1.2

Number of Foreign Affiliates per Corporation

Foreign Affiliates for Firm	Number of Firms	
0	1	
1- 9	13	
10-19	14	
20-29	9	
30-39	4	
40-49	4	
50-59	2	23 firms
60-69	1	
70-99	1	
100+	2	
	51	

Notes: Range is from zero to 150+. An affiliate implies some degree of equity ownership by the U.S. firm.

TABLE 1.3

Number of Countries in Which Each Corporation's
Foreign Affiliates Were Located

Number of Countries	Number of Firms
0	2
1- 5	7
6-10	12
11-15	10
16-20	11
21-25	1
26-30	6
31-35	0
36-40	1
41-45	0
46-50	1
	51

Note: Range is from zero to 49.

TABLE 1.4

Organizational Forms

Organizational Form	Number
Export-oriented, i.e., those with an export department only with little interest in foreign production	2
International, i.e., those with an international division or subsidiary with operational responsibility for foreign affiliates, with little interest in building a globally integrated system	18
Multinational, i.e., those organized to facilitate global, equity-based integration of production	28
Organized by global product line	(15)
Organized regionally	(8)
Organized by function, e.g., marketing, manufacturing, etc.	(2)
Matrix	(3)
Mixed, i.e., those differing by product line between international and multinational	5
	51

TABLE 1.5

Preferred Relationships

Relationship	Number
100 percent ownership	10
Joint venture with majority ownership specified	5*
Joint ventures	8†
Contractual only	1
Flexible	25‡
Not specified	2
Total	51

*One, however, was beginning to license.

†One specified a joint venture plus a management contract; another, preference for a minority position.

‡One of these preferred a license or some form of contractual relationship; another would reject all contractual arrangements if possible.

All together, the 51 corporations reported 899 foreign affiliates in which they had an equity position, although this tabulation undoubtedly fails to count a significant number, in that those listed by informants often failed to agree with published totals. By far the most common was the 100 percent-owned subsidiary, 477 of the 899, or 53.1 percent. The number of majority-owned (those in which the U.S. parent owned over 50 percent but less than 95 percent) was 63, or 7.0 percent. The 50-50 pattern was reported for 84, or 9.3 percent; minority ownership for 155, or 17.2 percent; and those of unknown ownership, 120, or 13.3 percent. Against this pattern, the 51 corporations specified their preferred relationships, as shown in Table 1.5.

One purpose of this descriptive summary is to indicate the degree of foreign involvement of the corporations in the sample, as well as their characteristics concerning location, size, sector, labor and capital intensity, foreign involvement, and finally, ownership and control strategies. It would appear that the sample included a wide enough range of corporation types to make generalization possible. However, the manner in which the sample was selected and its relatively small size did not warrant sophisticated statistical analysis. Further, the data were aggregated by firm, many of which were involved in a number of quite different product lines, were vertically and horizontally integrated to differing degrees, and had recorded very different earnings records (which was undoubtedly in part due to differing managerial capabilities).

The second purpose of this summary is to set up the basis for a corporate typology against which to consider management responses to performance guarantees and incentives. This typology is developed in the next chapter.

2

Pressures, Corporate Responses, and Typology

Without delving into underlying international trade and investment theory, one can usefully classify the pressures on management to become involved in foreign production into seven general categories and perhaps 22 subcategories.

MANAGEMENT PRESSURES

1. Increasing cost of domestic natural resources, which translates into a need for:
    A. Foreign minerals, that is, nonrenewable resources, or
    B. Specific soil and climatic conditions found abroad, that is, specialized forest, marine, or agricultural products producing renewable resources, or
    C. Foreign energy, and/or
    D. Foreign water supply.
2. Increasing competition in the domestic market, which translates into:
    A. A need to source abroad for domestic sale (a "foreign-sourcing" or importing strategy),
    B. A need to sell into foreign markets (a "one-way exporting" or "local production for local market" strategy), or
    C. A need to gain access to a third country and/or regional markets (a "cross-haul" or "regional integration" strategy), or
    D. A need for all three of the above (a "global integration" strategy).

3. Availability of cheaper production factors abroad, which translates into the need to employ:
   A. Foreign labor, or
   B. Foreign capital, or
   C. Foreign technology, or
   D. Foreign management, or
   E. All of the above, a "cost-minimizing" strategy.
4. Increasing competition abroad translates into:
   A. A need to produce inside trade barriers (a "tariff-jumping" strategy), or
   B. A need to preempt a market (a "keep the competition out" strategy), or
   C. A need to respond to competitors (a "follow the leader" or defensive strategy).
5. Increasing cost of domestic regulation leads to:
   A. A need to escape consumer, employee, or environmental protection regulations (a "regulation-escaping" strategy), and/or
   B. A need to avoid politically motivated regulation (a "political-neutralizing" strategy).
6. Increasing cost of foreign regulation of alien ownership, which leads to:
   A. A need to reduce equity-based control ("spinoff" strategy), and
   B. A need to concentrate on international scale economics ("service" or "trading company" strategy, that is, "market-integrating" strategy).
7. Heightened risk and uncertainty, which translates into a need for:
   A. Geographical diversification (horizontal integration) and/or
   B. Resource capture (vertical integration).

   A few examples of the less obvious pressures to produce outside the United States might be useful. The executives of an aluminum producer observed that there were now some parts of the United States in which the power shortage is so acute after a dry winter that the company has to shut down plants during the summer months because of power deficiency. Such shutdowns place the supply of metal in jeopardy and were cited as an important reason for moving abroad.

   A spokesman for a chemical manufacturer observed that if export controls relative to environmental impact were applied, the corporation would be pushed into a number of minority ventures offshore, that is, into manufacturing ventures that the corporation did not unambiguously control and, hence, would not be legally held responsible. In the agricultural area—and he cited specifically pesticides—there had been a few abortive attempts by the United States to control export of those products felt to be environmentally harmful. The company had to "be quick on its feet to prevent enforcement." He agreed that in some cases there might be good reason for such export control but observed that things were beginning to be banned "on the basis of emotion rather than scientific evidence." He then mentioned how the company had taken up the manufacture of a pesticide, in a Southeast Asian country, which had been banned in the United States, although "there is no scientific evidence for doing so." It was due to a fallout of the Vietnam War, he believed. In any event, the banning of production in the United States had pushed the firm into overseas production in an area where the "government was sufficiently rational to realize that there was no scientific basis for proving environmental damage and encouraged [the firm] to manufacture locally."

Another form of escaping regulation is the manufacture of pharmaceuticals overseas prior to completion of the lengthy United States licensing process, which cannot begin until a patent has been issued. Rather than sit idly by for five years or so before getting any return on its investment and watching the period of its patent protection being whittled down, a pharmaceutical firm may secure a license from a foreign government and start production overseas. Possibly two firms in our sample had done this. No corporate executive admitted manufacturing abroad to escape U.S. political controls, such as those imposed on certain exports to the Soviet Union and its neighbors or to avoid U.S. sanctions against the Soviets. There were two cases in which this might well have led to overseas involvement in a <u>minority</u> capacity, but the evidence was unclear.

CORPORATE RESPONSES

To return to the classification of corporate motives, it is obvious that many of our categories overlap. Furthermore, the degree of a corporation's "multinationality" has a strong impact on which motives become preeminent. We refer here to the extent that a corporate headquarters possesses the expertise and internal motivation (incentives) to allocate corporate resources <u>globally</u> with a minimum of national bias. By globally, we mean the weighing of domestic and foreign projects on the same scale, whether that be return on investment, discounted cash flow, payback period, or whatever. A proxy for classifying corporations on this dimension is their organizational structure. Table 1.4 suggested that

28 of the 51 were "multinational" in their control structure, which
implies that the foremost strategy mix of all of these is category
2.D and category 3.E. That is, they can be expected to follow
"integrative" and "cost minimization" strategies. Of course, at
the same time, they may seek foreign resources, foreign protection, and an escape from domestic regulation. The true multinational would pursue all of these strategies simultaneously as part
of its general "cost-minimizing" strategy and, in addition, try to
reduce risk via both geographical diversification and resource
capture.

The point is, of course, that only a multinational has the
globally integrated decision-making system that renders such
strategies feasible. It can pursue such a global strategy because
both risk and uncertainty have been reduced to tolerable levels by
the breadth of its international operations and by the depth of personal experience (and interest) of its decision makers. A proxy for
breadth is the number of foreign affiliates and the percent of their
sales as measured against domestic sales. Certainly, any company that sells 35 percent or more overseas—which implies that
foreign sales are over 50 percent of the domestic—qualifies. Of
the 51 firms, 23 were in this category. Fifteen reported 35 percent or more of their total assets to be located outside the United
States. That is, their foreign assets equalled at least 50 percent
of their U.S. assets. Twenty-three companies reported at least
20 foreign affiliates each (see Table 1.2), and 20 firms listed
affiliates in more than 15 countries outside the United States (see
Table 1.3). It turns out that 12 of the 51 corporations reported
either that 35 percent or more of their sales and/or assets were
abroad or that they had at least 20 foreign affiliates and/or operations in at least 15 countries. Of these 12, 8 were multinationals
and 4 were internationals. Five had made foreign direct investments prior to World War II. All had taken their initial plunge
prior to 1960. These relative early dates imply the accumulation
of international expertise.

The experience span generally with respect to direct foreign
investment varied in our sample from over 80 years to zero. The
most popular site for a firm's first foreign venture was, as one
might expect, Canada, with the United Kingdom a close second.
In fact, the English-speaking countries (Canada, United Kingdom,
the Philippines, and Australia) accounted for 25 first foreign ventures (50 percent), even with 9 unknown. Geographical proximity
(Mexico) accounted for another 4.5; Western Europe, for still

another 3.5.* As the executive in 1 of the 51 companies observed, "In the early days, American companies liked to invest in English-speaking countries because they thought that without a language barrier, it would be easier. In fact, it was not true, and other countries would have been better, such as Japan and Germany, a fact that they learned much later. My company did the same thing in Canada, the United Kingdom, Australia, and South Africa because of the English language. The only reason we were successful in Australia was because of border protection."

I would suggest that for incentives offered by foreign governments to be more than marginally effective—or for performance guarantees to be significant and not act as a complete deterrent to U.S. investment—a United States-based company must have already invested in those countries in closest cultural and/or geographical proximity to the United States, namely the English-speaking countries, Western Europe, and Mexico. Otherwise, cultural and geographical proximity will tend to swamp all other factors.

It was clear that a number of factors were considered by management before the investment programs of governments became relevant to decisions. A major producer of rubber products opined, "Our biggest concern is financing those things we have to do. . . . Our group has adopted a North American strategy. It would have to be a hell of an attractive deal for us to invest capital resources overseas in today's economic climate. We are liquidating some of our non-strategic businesses." Indeed, during the course of our inquiry, we identified some 17 cases of recent disinvestment. However, not all executives agreed. One commented, "We do not want to pull out of a country. We feel we have a commitment to both an organization and to people, and a reputation to support. Hence, we do not willingly leave a country." A spokesman for another firm observed that he was concerned about the image of a company that invested in a country and then pulled out after a few years. "This would look bad if it wished to invest in other countries." Secondly, a pull out would not impress top management very favorably and could create a precedent against further overseas investments. Nonetheless, one should be aware of the fact that from the point of view of the host governments, the problem is not only how to attract foreign direct investment—if that is desired—but also how to keep it.

---

*When two investments were made, apparently during the same year, so that precedence could not be established, one-half was assigned to each country.

In a few companies, one heard comments about the global overcapacity in their respective industries and, hence, their disinclination to add more capacity regardless of how attractive a particular situation might look. At least one executive mentioned the high interest rates in the United States as an inhibiting factor to foreign investment.

The point is that the general posture of a corporation with respect to increasing its overseas investment—or reducing it—is an important variable. So likewise is the nature of its response. Perhaps a third of the sample are essentially reactive. That is, corporate interest must be aroused by some external pressure—customers, governments, and brokers. One had been approached initially by a representative of the Indian government and, after 17 years of sporadic negotiation, had in fact entered the Indian market—via license. Another corporation, we were told, never took the initiative with regard to foreign projects. A customer or possible partner had to make the first move.

Repeatedly emphasized was the importance of personal experience in corporate decision making. In at least 14 of the 51 companies, specific mention was made of this factor. In one, which was characterized by an executive as not being "internationally minded," Philippine, Colombian, and Mexican projects had developed specifically by reason of personal friendships. Another corporation had become seriously interested in the Egyptian market because its president had met and been impressed by President Sadat. Another, the policy of which was not to invest overseas, entered a manufacturing venture in Brazil after a visit by the chairman of the board to Brazil. Still another entered Brazil, in part because Henry Ford and the corporate president were good friends and Ford wanted to buy locally from its U.S. supplier. For another firm (a medium-sized producer of consumer products), much of its European investment, and specifically that in Spain, was attributed to the empire-building tendencies of its European manager and the president's disposition to travel. A high-technology firm's attention was drawn to Singapore because the chief executive had lived in Shanghai and was attracted to the area. The upshot was that someone was sent to investigate the area and it was decided that there was enough in Southeast Asia to justify manufacturing in Singapore, which was chosen from a list including South Korea, Hong Kong, and the Philippines. In another case, an investment in Thailand was traced directly to the fact that a number of people in the firm had been exposed to Thailand when, by reason of a personal friendship, the firm had been asked by the Agency for International Development to make a study in the country. Another had gotten involved in Spain when the Spanish government dispatched an envoy to visit the chairman of the board. The envoy had worked with the chairman years before in another corporation. A major investment emerged.

The reverse can likewise happen. Negative personal experience can be reflected in corporate decisions. Quite clearly, an unfortunate experience of an executive in a taxi between Mexico City and the airport had been important in his discouragement of a Mexican project. Another executive admitted that his personal dislike of Indians had perhaps contributed to keeping his company out of India. Governments interested in attracting investment should be aware of the importance of such factors in corporate decision making.

We unearthed only five investment projects attributed to host government initiative. The governments were Spain, Ghana, Taiwan, and South Korea. The U.S. government seemed to have had a role in stimulating only three projects; major customers influenced perhaps half a dozen cases.

The bulk of the firms in our sample seemed to rely very heavily upon internally generated initiative. One executive could not think of any specific example in which his company had proceeded on the basis of external initiation, be it customer, broker, or government. Such external pressures became effective only when the firm already had a prior interest in the region, in the European community or in Southeast Asia, for example. Perhaps the source of initiating pressure was one of the greatest differences from what had been found 25 years before. At that time, the firms relied much more heavily on external pressures. Many more were in the reactive mode when it came to overseas investment. However, the process by which a firm reached a decision to commit resources to overseas projects remained generally unchanged (see Figure 2.1).

What Figure 2.1 illustrates is the five-step decision-making process by which a firm commits resources to an overseas project. The first stage is concerned with the generation of initial pressure, which may or may not attract serious management attention. Whether it does or not depends upon company organization and policy, internally felt needs, and personal interest at the appropriate place and level. Stage 2 is concerned with the preliminary evaluation. Does the project merit further consideration? Response is very much a function of the type of preliminary evaluation to which the project is subjected and the availability of personal time. The firm then encounters Stage 3, which is the actual decision to launch a serious investigation of the project. What is the nature of the investigation to be, and at what level is it to be undertaken? Stage 4 is the actual investigation, which almost invariably involves on-the-spot management assessment. Finally, at Stage 5,

FIGURE 2.1

Process by Which a Firm Reaches a Decision to Commit Resources to Overseas Projects

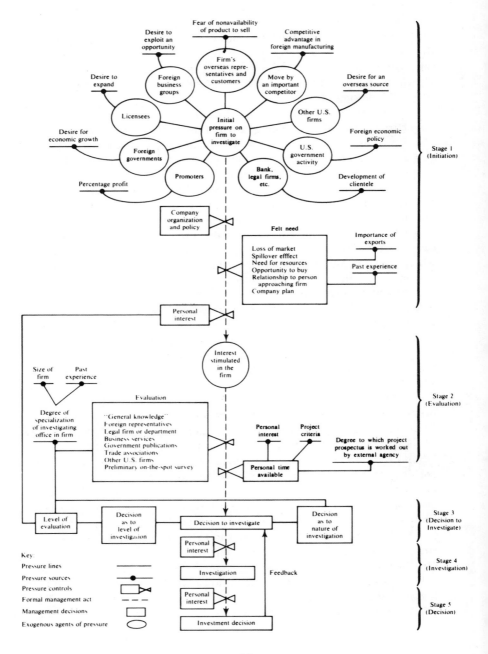

16

the investment decision itself takes place. It will be noted that personal interest—or disinterest—is relevant at every stage. The more professionalized the process becomes, the less likely the personal element is to be controlling. By professional, we mean the existence of a specialized evaluative function within the corporation that is the responsibility of people with appropriate experience and training. It became quite clear during this inquiry that the general level of professionalism in this sense had improved remarkably since the 1957-58 study.

Executives repeatedly made the point that the basic consideration from their points of view was whether a proposed investment made good economic and business sense. Several spoke of fit with the particular country. In one case, that fit was defined as a comparative advantage with respect to the industry involved. Another spoke of its Italian acquisitions as a "very nice fit." Those reporting a feeling of comfort were perhaps saying the same thing. One executive commented that his firm knew the Brazilian market well and "felt comfortable" there.

The decision-making process, and its underlying motivation in one corporation, merits description. We were told that initial recommendations for foreign involvement came from the operating units concerned, most frequently product groups, to corporate headquarters. If the project involved entering a country in which the firm had no previous operation, or involved setting up a new company, or involved an investment in excess of $2 million, the project would go to the board. However, our informant could not recall any project being rejected at the board level. The point was that once the corporate policy committee on which the board was represented had signed off on a project, it was rarely questioned by the board. Although projects could be initiated by both internal and external pressures, the global products groups were supposed to be scanning markets worldwide on a continuing basis. No overall responsibility has been assigned for this activity, although for the past five years the corporation has been conducting an economic and political survey. The effort was designed to bring out an objective measure of risk, but in fact, the real objective was to get more people to think about matters other than those directly concerned with their jobs. Countries were rated in terms of risk, and individuals were asked for their comments. In 1980 some 140 people participated in the exercise, which analyzed the political and economic situation in 63 countries. A report was then put together and distributed to others who had need to see it. The executive who was responsible for this process emphasized that what was important was to get people thinking, not the substance of the report itself "which rarely produces any surprises." He then added that the whole business of political risk analysis that had developed recently "is a bunch of bull." The firm comes up with the same results via this internal process. Political risk analysis, he felt, was sort of a fad that would pass. In the past it was exchange rate forecasting, which really had come to nothing.

This brings us to the subject of political risk analysis as viewed from executive offices. The general response seemed to be represented by this comment by an executive in a large chemical corporation, "The way we perceive risk here is different from the way in which professors of finance think companies make decisions." By that he meant that risk was represented not by a number but by qualitative judgment, also that risk varied depending on corporate policy. "What we try to do," he observed, "is to bring risk down." Whenever the subject of political risk came up in our discussions, we tried to determine whether it was ever represented numerically. Insofar as we could determine, none of the 51 corporations approached political risk in this fashion. For example, one executive noted that his company employed "no sophisticated system of political risk analysis such as outlined in such publications as the Harvard Business Review." The firm did subscribe to a number of information services, but its own people were used in developing political analysis. Another firm, a large chemical manufacturer, plugged a political risk factor in after a decision had been made on purely economic merits, but it did so on a qualitative, not quantitative, basis. The firm had never used specific figures to represent political risk factors for either countries or projects. A political analyst in another large corporation observed that the main responsibility for political analysis lay with the area management. He added, "It is my philosophy not to dismiss any country as being too risky; risk is a relevant thing, that is, relevant to corporate policy. I do not make political analyses which can be interpreted as suggesting a go-no-go situation. These analyses are simply made to alert management to the situations in particular countries and what sorts of contingencies may arise." We found no exceptions to this approach.

Although the external information sources used by business had improved vastly over the 25 years since our earlier study and the training and experience of those analyzing foreign economic and political environments was obviously better, the analysis of political risk was no more quantitative than it ever had been.

The bulk of the 51 corporations, if the views of the executives interviewed is an adequate measure, have certain target or high-priority countries in mind. In one corporation, executives had looked at more than 140 national markets and zeroed in on 17 that seemed to look especially promising. These were Mexico,

Venezuela, Brazil, Saudi Arabia, Yugoslavia, Spain, Ireland, Malaysia, South Korea, Taiwan, Singapore, Hong Kong, China, Japan, West Germany, France, and Australia. This list, with some minor modifications, was reiterated several times during the course of the study. An executive in the same firm, a medium-sized manufacturer of electrical products, observed that his company classified national environments as essentially hostile or attractive. France was given as an example of a "nationalistic" and, therefore, "hostile" environment. To some extent, Canada was seen in the same category.

One internationally experienced executive expressed his bemusement at the more congenial reception given foreign business by certain socialist countries—specifically, Yugoslavia and the People's Republic of China—than that accorded by certain market economies. He cited the suspicion and distrust encountered in Mexico and elsewhere in Latin America where he felt a very strong anti-foreign business ideology to be operating. Would knowledge of the greater pragmatism of at least some of the Marxist societies in time cause a moderation in Latin attitudes? This was possible but not for a long while, he opined.

We observed a definite tendency of executives to think in terms of regions, in part, possibly because that was how many of the firms in which we were interviewing were organized—at least 8 of the 51, many more if one included the corporations whose international divisions were organized regionally (see Table 1.4). The company reported above with a list of 17 widely dispersed countries was a notable exception. More commonly, we learned that in selecting sites for foreign operations, companies had considered countries within a particular region—Southeast Asia (or East Asia), Western Europe, Eastern Europe, sub-Sahara Africa, or Latin America. Only one executive spoke of countries linked to the European Economic Community (EEC) via the Lomé Convention when listing the options available for establishing a beachhead within the EEC tariff system. The point is that only a few corporations, possibly 7 of the 51, appeared to be actively trying to make globally optimal site selections, rather than selecting regionally optimal sites. Singapore was seen as an alternative to Malaysia, Thailand, Indonesia, and Singapore, possibly to Taiwan, the Philippines, and South Korea, but rarely as an alternative to sites further removed. Yugoslavia was the entry into Eastern Europe, not the Middle East. The relevant markets seemed almost invariably to be defined in terms of geographical (and perhaps political) proximity, unless the purpose of the project was to supply the U.S. market. Very few spoke of supplying the European, Latin American, or African markets from, say, Singapore or Taiwan.

Given the pressure to export from Brazil, some reference was made to supplying certain African markets out of Brazil, but only in two instances.

Although many firms, as one food processor, went overseas to develop strong markets in individual countries, executives in seven firms spoke specifically of worldwide sourcing. Their favorite choices were Brazil, Japan, Spain, Singapore, and Ireland. Twenty-five years before, no firm was reported to have been explicitly setting up a globally integrated production system, very few even on a regional basis. Times had changed.

TYPOLOGY OF CORPORATE STRATEGIES, PRESSURES, AND RESPONSES

The following typology was developed to provide a framework for the analysis of data generated by corporate interviews and reports related to managerial response within the 51 corporations to government-initiated performance requirements and incentives. This typology, which is based on the preceding discussion and is summarized below, classifies corporations by control strategy, ownership strategy, corporate motives for involvement in foreign production, corporate involvement in foreign production, and degree of international professionalization.

1. By control strategy
   A. Export-orientation: centralized control over exports, and/or little foreign production.
   B. International: weak central control over increasing foreign production.
   C. Multinational: centralized control over geographically dispersed production facilities.
   D. Mature multinational: tendency to relinquish control over some functions.
2. By ownership strategy
   A. Majority or 100-percent ownership preferred.
   B. Joint ventures preferred.
   C. Minority ownership preferred.
   D. Contractual relationships preferred.
   E. Flexible.
3. By corporate motive for involvement in foreign production
   A. Resource seeking.
   B. Market seeking.
   C. Protection seeking.
   D. Cost cutting.

Cost minimizing

E. Regulation escaping.
F. Technology seeking.
G. Market integration.
H. Risk reduction.

Cost minimizing

4. By corporate involvement in foreign production.
   A. Relative importance: as measured by percent of sales and assets abroad.
   B. Geographical spread: as measured by the number of foreign affiliates and number of countries in which they are located.
   C. Experience: as measured by time elapsed since first foreign direct investment made.
5. By degree of international professionalization.
   A. Degree of formalization of relevant decision-making process, that is, impersonalization.
   B. Employment of differentiated international specialists.
   C. Employment of foreign nationals in parent corporation.

These five classification categories are obviously not mutually exclusive but represent five different dimensions of any given corporation. Hence, theoretically, there are a very large number of possible permutations and combinations. In reality, there are far fewer because certain characteristics tend to be linked. For example, a corporation with a multinational control strategy (1. C) and a flexible ownership policy (2. E) tends to pursue cost-minimizing and risk-reducing strategies (3. A-H), have 30 percent or more of its sales and assets abroad, enjoy a broad geographical spread of investment, have made its first foreign direct investment 30 or more years ago, have a formalized decision-making process in respect to Foreign Direct Investment (FDI) and employ international specialists. Therefore, to bring this analysis to a practical level, we compress this classification into the seven general types described below. In each case, they are defined in terms of the 23 variables listed above.

It is necessary to enter a few words of caution about this typology. In fitting corporations into one of the types, several problems arose, and proxies had to be used in certain cases rather than a direct measure of the variable itself. For example, we assumed that the formal structure of a corporation reflected its control strategy. Ownership strategy in some cases was explicit; in others, it had to be inferred from the actual pattern of ownership reported. When in conflict, the reality was assumed to reflect policy more accurately. Corporate motive for involvement in foreign production was often made explicit by informants; in other cases it had to be inferred from the nature of the business. The technology-seeking motive (3.F) was assumed if the firm demonstrated, or had actively taken, an interest in a license for foreign-source technology. Active interest in the People's Republic of China automatically pushed a firm into the Type 4 category unless there were compelling reasons for assigning it elsewhere.

In specifying percentage of total sales made outside the United States, there was the problem of U.S. exports, which some corporations reported while others did not. In most cases, it is believed that the figure represents sales of overseas affiliates plus U.S. exports. There was also the problem of unallocated assets when tabulating the percent of total assets abroad. In some corporations, this figure was significant, while in others, it was not. Where significant, we assumed that the unallocated assets could be distributed in the same percentage as those that were allocated between U.S. and non-U.S. assets. We also had to deal with the problem of conglomerates where we were interested primarily in only one part of the conglomerate. In our sample, there were seven conglomerates.

If a company did no world-sourcing outside the United States and if it had a distinctly separate international division or subsidiary, it could not be a Type 4 or 5. It was held to have a formalized decision-making system if respondents could describe it without referring to the personal intervention of key individuals. The employment of differentiated international specialists was assumed if the interviews revealed detailed knowledge of foreign situations, and the employment of foreign nationals was assumed if there were foreign nationals on the board of directors or specific reference was made to foreign nationals at the operating level in the United States.

Type 1: The novice is an exploratory mode and is characterized by:

Either an export or newly initiated international control strategy, in which control over domestic and foreign operations is separate but weak.

Preference for contractual or minority joint ventures.

Resource-seeking and/or market-seeking motives predominate.

Very limited involvement, typically less than 10 percent of sales and assets are linked to foreign markets, with foreign assets located in English-speaking countries and/or Mexico, and with less than five years of involvement in overseas production.

Highly personalized, unsystematic decision making regarding foreign involvement.

Type 2: The _learner_ is committed to some expansion of production abroad and is characterized by:

An international control strategy.

Preference for contractual or joint venture relationships, 50-50 or majority, primarily from profit point of view, not control.

Resource-seeking, market-seeking, and protection-seeking motives, with the latter perceived as increasingly important.

Somewhat more involvement in overseas markets, possibly 15 percent or more of sales and assets linked to foreign markets, some of the assets being in continental Europe, and ten years or more of experience in foreign production.

The beginning of a somewhat less personal, more systematic decision-making system and the employment of some specialized international personnel.

Type 3: The _builder_ is committed to global expansion and is characterized by:

A well-established international or emerging multinational control strategy.

Growing preference for majority or 100 percent ownership.

Resource-seeking, market-seeking, cost-cutting, and protection-seeking motivations.

Even greater involvement abroad, 25 percent or more of sales and assets abroad, some involvement in larger Latin American and Southeast Asian countries, and over 15 years experience.

An explicit, formal decision-making system with some international specialists employed.

Type 4: The _integrator_ sees the advantage, and has the capability, of integrating operations globally and is characterized by:

Relatively new multinational control strategy.

Preference for majority or 100 percent ownership but willing to accept less when pressed.

All motives.

Unlimited involvement abroad, typically 30 percent or more of both sales and assets linked to foreign markets, worldwide spread, and over 20 years experience.

An explicit, formal decision-making system with significant inputs from international specialists.

Type 5: The opportunist is explicitly trying to maximize the comparative advantage of its global system and is characterized by:

Well-established multinational control strategy, with weakening of centralized control over some functions, particularly production.

Flexible ownership policies.

All motives.

Unlimited involvement abroad, typically 40 percent or more of both sales and assets linked to foreign markets, worldwide spread, and over 20 years experience.

High level of professionalization, including movement of significant number of foreign nationals into headquarters.

Type 6: The retrencher is explicitly trying to sell off some foreign operations and build up U.S. operations, or operations in one particular business area, and is characterized by:

Well-established multinational control strategy.

Flexible ownership policies.

All motives.

Global involvement, but decreasing percent of sales and assets abroad, reduced spread, and over 20 years experience.

High level of professionalization but with few if any foreign personnel in parent corporation.

Type 7: The maverick does not really fit into any of the foregoing types.

Compressing the 51 corporations of our sample into these seven types, we derive the following distribution: 3 of Type 1, 4 of Type 2, 8 of Type 3, 12 of Type 4, 16 of Type 5, 2 of Type 6, and 6 of Type 7.

Given these seven corporate types, the varying responses of management to performance requirements imposed by host governments and to the incentives they offer to stimulate and direct flows of foreign inputs as desired take on further meaning. How and why their responses typically differ is the substance of the next chapter. The working hypothesis is that many of these differences can be explained by relating them to the characteristics associated with the seven corporate types described above.

3

Management
Responses to
Country Programs

Do corporate responses to country-specific performance requirements and incentives tend to differentiate according to the typology developed in the last chapter? In the earlier study of country
investment programs, we classified countries into seven basic types
according to their general policies vis-à-vis business:*

Type I   Those with virtually unrestricted foreign business en-
            try and with little attempt to influence flows of either
            direct foreign investment or technology.
Type II   Those with practically unrestricted entry but with sig-
            nificant incentives rewarding flows deemed to be es-
            pecially supportive of national policies.
Type III   Those with an entry-screening process barring flows
            considered incompatible with national objectives.
Type IV   Those with selected, negotiated entry, with foreign
            ownership or contract limited in time.
Type V   Those with the socialist model, in which foreign direct
            investment is limited to minority participation in joint
            ventures.
Type VI   Those with the more restrictive socialist model, which
            bars all foreign direct investment but permits tech-
            nology contracts.
Type VII   Those enforcing almost total prohibition of all direct
            foreign investment and technology contracts.

Management responses to performance requirements and investment incentives are discussed below, country by country, under

*Robinson, International Business Policy, p. xi.

the five national policy types. (We did not address business activity in Type VI and VII countries since they lay outside the scope of this study, no investment being permitted in either group.) Under each national policy type, the discussion in this chapter is limited to those developing countries of greatest interest to management as measured by the number of reported affiliates. Reactions vis-à-vis other countries in which affiliates were reported are given in Appendix A, again organized by the five country types. However, the summary tables inserted in this chapter for each country type include all of the countries discussed, both in this chapter and in Appendix A. A tabulation summarizing experience in all five country types is presented in the concluding chapter. In each of these tables, we relate the type of national investment policy, the type of corporate parent, and the number of affiliates. For those who wish a more detailed statement of the investment policies of 25 of the 70 countries discussed in either this chapter or Appendix A, our earlier studies may be useful.*

TYPE I COUNTRIES

Those countries of Type I characteristically offer few incentives and impose virtually no restrictions. In this category we placed Austria, Belgium, Hong Kong, Lebanon, Liberia, Luxembourg, Netherlands, Singapore, South Africa, and Switzerland.

Of the developing countries in this group, Singapore was the site of the largest number of affiliates.

Singapore

Of the 51 corporations in the sample, 11 reported 12 investments in Singapore (10 100 percent owned and 2 unspecified). Executives in two corporations cited Singapore as the model of a good

---

*Ibid. Countries treated in the 1980 study were:
  Type I—Hong Kong, Liberia, Singapore
  Type II—Brazil, Ireland, Taiwan, Thailand
  Type III—Egypt, Kenya, South Korea, Malaysia, Mexico,
    Nigeria, Venezuela, Zaire
  Type IV—Indonesia, Peru, Philippines, Sri Lanka
  Type V—Yugoslavia
In the 1976 study the entry controls of the following countries were discussed in detail: Indonesia, Malaysia, Thailand, Burma, Philippines, Mexico, Brazil, the then Andean Common Market countries (Bolivia, Chile, Colombia, Ecuador, Peru, and Venezuela).

investment climate and listed the following factors: accessible, responsive, and honest government; economic and political stability; good infrastructure; skilled and efficient labor force; raw material availability; unlimited foreign ownership; reasonable taxation; and good communications.

One firm had chosen Singapore as a manufacturing site over Malaysia, Thailand, and Indonesia. Another had picked it out of a list that included Hong Kong, South Korea, Taiwan, and the Philippines. A third firm had selected Singapore in part because "they wanted us." The Singapore government had made buildings available and was prepared to provide the necessary infrastructure. Also mentioned was a specific tailoring of incentives to match the requirements of individual companies. In addition, an executive in a third firm mentioned low personal income tax, low housing costs (particularly compared to Hong Kong), and the awarding of "pioneer status" provided that the company export. The latter, he observed, was not a problem in that the Singapore market was insufficient in any event. The plant, which manufactures machine tools, now serves the whole Far Eastern market. The pioneer status meant a seven-year tax holiday, described as the period in which "we get to know the place." He quickly added, however, that the tax holiday was by no means the whole or even principal justification for locating in Singapore. More important was the long-run stability of the government. He noted that Singapore had a concept of what it wanted to be and observed that the Singapore government had helped the firm overcome customs and tax problems without the need of talking with five or six different government departments. It also provided a low-interest loan and a ready-built factory, which the firm turned down as unsatisfactory to its needs. Finally, 100 percent ownership was permitted. According to the executive, "Any less than that would represent a significant barrier because of access to trademarks and know-how." Two executives spoke specifically of the special training schools in Singapore. We heard no negative comment. It was quite clear that no one was worried about any performance guarantees imposed by countries in this category.

Although 11 firms reported investments in Singapore, 2 others were actively interested. And, of the initial 11, 2 were only modestly involved via marketing, not manufacturing. Of the 10 with active or pending operations in Singapore, 3 corporations were Type 5 (opportunists); 4 were of Type 4 (integrators); 2 were Type 3 (builders); and 1 was a Type 7 (maverick). The general motives were mixed: for Type 3 firms, the obvious objective was to reduce the cost of components essentially for assembly in the United States. For Types 4 and 5, the lure was the sourcing of cheaper products for third-country markets. The point is that in the case of Singapore (and Hong Kong, Lebanon, and Liberia as well), we are talking of a relatively small local market for most products, the availability of relatively cheap labor, and a strategic position from which to enter other markets in the region. If political risk were perceived as minimal, one would expect considerable inbound investment without benefit of incentives, and the firms would normally be interested in maximizing local value added and exports even in the absence of any performance requirements.

Table 3.1 combines the investments reported from all 11 Type I countries.

TABLE 3.1

Reported Affiliates in Type I Countries by
Type of Corporate Parent
(number of parents/number of affiliates)

Country	Corporate Types							Total
	1	2	3	4	5	6	7	
Austria	0	0	0	1/1	1/1	0	0	2/2
Belgium	0	1/1	0	4/4	12/13	0	0	17/18
Hong Kong*†	0	0	1/1	3/3	4/5	0	0	8/9
Lebanon*	0	0	0	1/1	0	0	0	1/1
Liberia*	0	0	0	0	0	0	1/1	1/1
Luxembourg	0	0	0	1/4	1/1	0	0	2/5
Netherlands	1/1	0	4/5	5/5	7/9	0	0	17/20
Singapore*	0	1/1	3/3	3/3	3/4	1/1	0	11/12
South Africa	0	1/1	3/7	2/2	8/12	1/1	2/5	17/28
Switzerland	0	0	0	0	7/8	0	1/1	8/9
West Germany	0	3/5	4/5	9/10	15/22	1/1	1/2	33/45
Total (affiliates)	1	8	21	33	75	3	9	150
Developing countries	0	1	3	7	7	1	1	20
Developed countries	1	7	18	26	68	2	8	130

*Developing countries.
†Firms with nonmanufacturing affiliates eliminated.

When these raw numbers are calculated as percentages of affiliates in each country by type of corporate parent (Table 3.2), we note that in the developing countries Type 4 and 5 parents each report 32 percent of the total affiliates located in these 11 countries. This finding is expected because the lack of entry barriers and performance requirements should tend to attract the Type 4s (the integrators) as well as the Type 5s (the opportunists). Why the latter should be more active in the Type I developed countries, however, is not clear.

TABLE 3.2

Reported Affiliates in Type I Countries by
Type of Corporate Parent
(in percentages within each country)

Country	Corporate Types						
	1	2	3	4	5	6	7
Austria	0	0	0	50	50	0	0
Belgium	0	5	5	21	68	0	0
Hong Kong*	0	0	1	33	56	0	0
Lebanon*	0	0	0	100	0	0	0
Liberia*	0	0	0	0	0	0	100
Luxembourg	0	0	0	80	20	0	0
Netherlands	5	0	25	25	45	0	0
Singapore*	0	8	25	25	33	8	0
South Africa	0	4	25	7	43	4	18
Switzerland	0	0	0	0	89	0	11
West Germany	0	11	11	22	51	2	4
Total	1	5	15	22	50	2	6
Developing countries	5	5	18	32	32	5	5
Developed countries	0	5	14	21	53	2	6

*Developing countries.
Note: Rows may not total 100 because of rounding.

Of the combined total of 150 affiliates reported, 104 were 100 percent owned by the U.S. parent, 6 were majority owned, 11 owned 50-50, 12 were minority owned, and 17 were of unknown ownership (see Table 3.3).

TABLE 3.3

Ownership of Reported Affiliates in Type I
Countries by Parent Type

Parent Type	Ownership					
	100 Percent	Majority	50-50	Minority	Unknown	Total
Type 1	0	0	0	0	1	1
Type 2	7	1	0	0	0	8
Type 3	11	0	1	0	9	21
Type 4	26	0	2	1	4	33
Type 5	54	4	8	6	3	75
Type 6	2	1	0	0	0	3
Type 7	4	0	0	5	0	9
Total	104	6	11	12	17	150

It should be noted that these countries in which 100 percent foreign ownership was not discouraged (and assuming that affiliates of unspecified ownership were distributed in the same proportions as the others), 88 percent of Type 2 parents chose the 100 percent mode; 90 percent of the Type 3s; 87 percent of the Type 4s; but only 73 percent of the Type 5s. And of the 23 affiliates reported as owned 50-50 or on a minority basis, 61 percent (14 of 23) were off-spring of Type 5 parents. All of this is as expected; Type 5 firms (the opportunists) show great flexibility in ownership even in the absence of official pressure.

TYPE II COUNTRIES

In the Type II category, we placed Australia, Bahrein, Brazil, Chile, Costa Rica, Ecuador, France, Ireland, Italy, Ivory Coast, New Zealand, Panama, Portugal, Taiwan, Thailand, and United Kingdom. Of these, Brazil, Taiwan, and Thailand were the developing countries of greatest interest in our study, and all generated significant reactions on the part of management.

Brazil

Thirty-four of the 51 sample firms reported 52 affiliates in
Brazil (34 wholly owned, 6 majority owned, 1 50-50, 7 minority
owned, and 4 unspecified). The 34 investing firms were distributed
by type as follows: 1 of Type 1, 2 of Type 2, 5 of Type 3, 7 of Type
4, 15 of Type 5, 1 of Type 6, and 3 of Type 7.

Companies gave diverse reasons for committing resources to
Brazil. The main reason for one (a Type 3) was the availability of
bauxite and electrical energy, plus a desire to reduce risk by di-
versifying its raw material sources. For another (Type 2), it was
the availability of a fast growing tree for pulping and a large domestic market. A third (Type 5) was pulled in by a promise from a
principal U.S. customer that it would buy from the company in
Brazil. The imposition of import restrictions attracted the attention of another firm (Type 1), which entered Brazil with the hope of
preempting the market. The fact that it found "a friend of a friend"
knowledgeable in the business to hire as the Brazilian general manager was mentioned as a strong positive factor. An executive in
still another firm (Type 4) admitted that pressure brought to bear
by important U.S. customers, who were producing in Brazil and
being pressed by the Brazilian government to increase local content,
had been important. Agreement was reached to source in Brazil
even though the product would cost more. Another firm, a manufacturer of mining equipment (Type 2), had been attracted by the
importance of Brazilian mining. An opportunity to participate in
Brazil's growth attracted an electronic firm (Type 3). The general
manager of the international division of a large chemical company
(Type 5) became enthusiastic about the growth potential of the Brazilian market. The firm already had a large sales presence via
exports from the United States. It seemed to him that it made sense
to manufacture locally. This was also seen as a defensive move.
In surveying the world chemical market, Brazil had been singled
out as the country with the highest incremental growth apart from
the European Community (EC), Eastern Europe, and Japan. Also,
it was felt that the export potential from Brazil was significant.
That was in the early 1970s. The company continues to expand its
operations there. Still another firm (Type 5) looked at a Brazilian
project in order not to lose the market. In general, it was the local
market that attracted attention. The president of one firm (Type 2)
who had personally investigated the Brazilian market observed,
"Brazil clamped down on imports and that was the lure that attracted
us." But another company (Type 3) had invested nothing in Brazil
because it could not figure how to get any money out of the country.

A few U.S. companies had been able to mount significant export flows out of Brazil, but most complained of noncompetitive

costs. However, one (Type 4) had recently filled a very large African order for construction equipment. This firm was given what was called "attractive export financing." The primary motive for another in sourcing out of Brazil was to gain "negotiating leverage" with the government. This company was shipping some product to the rest of Latin America, although not in large amounts. Obviously, other firms had expected to use Brazil as a source for the rest of Latin America but had been generally frustrated. Within the past six months, one company (Type 5) had exported some output due to the reduction of business activity in the country. We were left with the impression that the exports had been priced on a marginal basis. Another (Type 5), considering its Brazilian investment to be a "sunk" cost, was exporting on a variable cost basis.

The experience in Brazil reported to us was a mixed one. One executive reported that his firm's (Type 4) Brazilian plant had never been profitable, despite the incentives given by the government. Another firm (Type 4) had sold its Brazilian operations. Two food processors (Type 4 and Type 1) had likewise sold out. An executive in one (Type 4) observed that his firm would like to invest in Brazil again, but that it was very difficult. He did not feel that the present government was particularly sympathetic to foreign firms. He felt that "exchanging debt for equity was a real trap. . . . Our marketing people want the company to go in, but finance resists." An executive in the other (Type 1) commented on the "lack of Brazilian desire for foreign companies." An electronics firm (Type 3) would like to do business in Brazil but had been unable to do so because of the protection of the local computer industry. Twice it had tried to form partnerships with local companies, but in both cases plans had not been approved by the Brazilian government.

Company response to Brazilian incentives and performance requirements was very mixed, as shown in the following samples:

Firm 2 (Type 3) "incidentally" happened to receive incentives relating to duty-free import of assets, but this had not been central to the decision.

For Firm 3 (Type 3), incentives had played an important role. A company spokesman noted that the Brazilians had required exports to obtain various tax and low interest loans and that without incentives the investment would probably not have passed the company's return-on-investment criterion.

Firm 5 (Type 1), a food processor, had negotiated for one and a half years for the incentives offered for new plants in Brazil. It then looked at the restrictions imposed and gave up its plans. Specific reference was made to the export requirements that would, it was felt, take exports away from other facilities. An executive also mentioned the rather onerous reporting requirements that would have been imposed as well as a 62 percent charge for working capital loans (which he saw as discriminatory in that local competitors were paying only 28 percent). Exports had proved impossible; so it could qualify for no export incentives. The company's purpose had been to produce only for local consumption, whereas the Brazilian government wanted to export. He added, "The Brazilians simply did not like the idea of a foreign country producing food for local consumption." The upshot was that the firm sold out. Management felt that the market was definitely closed to it.

Firm 7 (Type 4), which had a minority interest in a local operation, reported a competitive company that had accepted incentives to locate a plant some 1,200 miles from the market. The plant had never been profitable.

Firm 9 (Type 4) had accepted three kinds of performance requirements: the level of exports in dollars, the level of investment, and employment. It was felt that these commitments had given the company import and financing privileges. However, a company executive mentioned two serious problems: the difficulty of subcontracting in Brazil because of close tolerance levels required; and the imposition of price controls.

Firm 10 (Type 5) had located its plant near Sao Paulo, thereby forgoing any incentives for locating in the northeast. Incentives generally had not been considered important. The most important incentive had been the cooperation given the company by local authorities with respect to finding appropriate property and recruiting.

Firm 11 (Type 2), a pulp and paper company, had been attracted originally to Brazil by a 30 percent tax allowance for tree planting. An executive observed that the company would not have entered the country without this incentive. (Subsequently, it had been reduced to 17 percent, which allegedly would have been inadequate to induce investment in this case.) Now that the firm was well established in the country, it did not see that the incentives made any difference to decisions.

Firm 13 (Type 2) had been seriously interested in 1975 in building a facility in Brazil. Everything appeared alright except the inflation rate. Another problem was that the local suppliers were deemed "terrible." (In the United States, the company bought about 35 percent out of plant.) Also, there was a perceived lack of trained, competent labor, which in fact was relatively high priced. In order to set up a viable enterprise, one would have had to become involved in a long training process, and that meant that one had to count on the loyalty of Brazilian employees. Two European competitors had gone into Brazil, but what they were supplying, a firm's executive claimed, was not satisfying local customers who "fight with government to permit imports."

In Firm 14 (Type 5), an executive reported the firm had accepted specific requirements with respect to local content, level of exports, level of investment, and the source of capital equipment. He reported that about 90 percent of the product represented local content and that about 80 percent was actually produced in-house. A company executive expressed the belief that the company had, in fact, lived up to its commitments with respect to local content and exports. The firm was required to export three times the value of its imported components. Exports went to the United States, Europe, and Asia, though the real cost of the Brazilian-produced machines was not competitive. After one plugged in the incentives for exporting, the situation became one of indifference, but it did allow the firm to make a small profit. If it were not operating an underutilized plant and producing at relatively low volume, these tax incentives might be important. Asked how critical these incentives had been in a recent decision to expand its investment in Brazil, an executive responded, "insignificant. They were excluded from all of our financial projections."

Firm 17 (Type 5) had been reluctant to enter into a commitment to export. Also the company had "stuck by its guns for 100-percent ownership." The Brazilian restriction on profit remittances was seen as only a short-term restraint. The company was, in fact, exporting from Brazil at relatively low cost because the firm considered its capital investment in Brazil as sunk cost. That is, it was pricing exports on a variable cost basis.

Firm 18 (Type 4) was aware that incentives were available in Brazil, but it had never taken advantage of them. The firm has deliberately not located in development zones, thereby forgoing certain incentives. It had also avoided taking on Brazilian partners. Recently, it had been told that it would have to meet an export quota because the Brazilian enterprise was importing essential raw materials. The quota was being met by sending some products out of Brazil for further processing in the United States.

Firm 21 (Type 4) had what was known as a "BFX" agreement, which was a special export agreement into which the government enters with a number of firms, but primarily in the automotive field. As a rule, the formula was that a firm could import $1 of goods duty-free for every $3 worth exported. The company claimed to be able to deliver products in Europe fully competitive with other sources. The company manufactured in the northeast, which meant that it could reinvest funds that would otherwise be paid out of taxes. The main problem, one executive observed, was in maintaining adequate volume to realize economies of scale. The three-for-one export-import agreement was due to expire in 1982, and the firm was trying to negotiate this down to two to one. The executive expressed the view that the Brazilian government would be obliged to set up a new set of incentives, given objections by some General Agreement on Trade and Tariffs (GATT) members that present incentives were contrary to the agreement. This company had been under no pressure to accept a greater degree of local ownership (the Brazilian public owned a small percentage), but pressures were mounting with respect to employment. Thus far, however, there had been no overall Brazilian policy in this regard. The firm had multiple product divisions, several of which were producing in Brazil. The government's export program treated all of these operations, whether organized as separate subsidiaries or not, as a single unit.

Firm 27 (Type 4) was under continuing pressure to increase local content, likewise several of its principal customers, which was one of the reasons for its entry into Brazil. Also, prior to its entry, the government had been giving financial support to the construction industry, an important sector of sales. Very shortly after the firm's plant had become operational, this financial support was removed, thereby leaving the company with excess capacity in its Brazilian plant, the market having been cut almost in half. An executive observed that it became virtually impossible to export competitively out of Brazil. In discussing its project initially with the government, various incentives had been explored, but management made a decision "not to maximize incentives." For example, it decided not to locate in the northeast. The firm had been requested not to declare dividends on its Brazilian operation until it had exported long enough to cover the imported part of its capital equipment. Also, long-term export commitments were requested. The company refused to acquiesce. A company executive commented that the commitments were not realistic and, in fact, he felt that the government officials really agreed with him on this. "They were quite open," he commented. The firm had liquidated one operation but continued a second.

Firm 28 (Type 5) had been looking at several schemes with respect to reinvesting tax money that would be generated if it were to operate in the Amazon region. The company already had one investment in the production of raw material in Brazil; that had been the price for remaining in Brazil imposed some years before.

In Firm 30 (Type 2), an executive commented, "Thank God, the CDI [a Brazilian government agency responsible for negotiating certain incentives] did not approve our project." For four years, the company had worked on developing a manufacturing project for which, in the final analysis, approval was not forthcoming with respect to import rights. The firm had been informed that a Brazilian partner would be required, without which it would be unable to get

duty relief in imported capital equipment. The project had not materialized.

Firm 31 (Type 3) was manufacturing in Brazil but faced restrictions with respect to expanding production. It did export some
product to the rest of Latin America and to South Africa out of
Brazil. The real problem was the Brazilian intent to have its own
computer industry, hence, the restraint on expansion. The firm
had been told that taking on a local partner would not make any difference. The policy was to reserve the market for 100 percent
locally owned firms, although the Brazilian government had not
really enforced that policy. An executive confided that if the company were informed that a joint venture would make a difference, it
would consider it.

Firm 35 (Type 7) had been willing to comply with local content
requirements and had made some engineering modifications to the
design of its plant in order to do so. The resulting plant had been
less efficient, technically speaking, but resulted in a lower overall
cost.

Firm 37 (Type 5), which was manufacturing a number of
product lines in Brazil, had not been able to get an import permit
to expand production of certain lines in the electronic field. The
operation was 100 percent United States owned. An executive reported that the company had surplus equipment in the United States,
which fit well with production requirements in Brazil and which was
technically perfectly alright. The company has been trying to find a
way to import the equipment and sell it to the Brazilian company.
However, it would apparently be compelled to import it as capital.
A problem was that both the United States and Brazilian governments
wanted a high valuation placed on the equipment for tax purposes.
If the machinery were evaluated above its book value, it would have
to be written up, thereby creating taxable income in the United States.
Brazil wanted a high evaluation to maximize the import duty, and to
get duty relief the firm would have to reduce ownership of its Brazilian subsidiary to a minority. In fact, the Brazilian government
had been talking about 25 percent, although an executive admitted
that the company had not been under direct pressure to reduce ownership. Also, the firm was apparently at a disadvantage in competing for local credit so long as it was majority foreign owned, in that
60 to 70 percent of available domestic credit was being directed to
national firms. The firm could gain export credits by selling to
neighboring countries, which it did in a modest way.

Firm 38 (Type 5) had taken into consideration government attitudes when developing a major project in Brazil. An in-depth negotiation had followed. In the process, the chief executive officer of
the firm had talked with the president of Brazil several times.

Subsequently, there had been conversations with regard to import quotas because so much of the raw material was being imported from the United States. In order to secure permission to continue importing, the company had been obliged to make specific export commitments, although not necessarily the export of its own products. Preceding the project, the firm had received specific Brazilian commitments with respect to property protection, remittance of profits, and the availability of some major local inputs at subsidized prices. The project involved the development of several manufacturing enterprises and was still ongoing; the final phase had not yet been committed by the company.

For most firms, the primary motive in entering Brazil was clearly access to the domestic market. In order to continue to sell in it, some firms had been willing to undertake export requirements. There were no absolute barriers to 100 percent ownership reported, except in the computer and food processing sectors. However, a jointly owned enterprise appeared to have advantages in respect to local credit facilities. In analyzing the above responses, it should be noted that the incentives offered were clearly critical to investment in only three cases (Firms 3, 11, and 28). They were seen to be of dubious value by at least five companies (Firms 2, 10, 14, 18, and 27). Four companies had refused to undertake the performance requirements requested (Firms 5, 17, 27, and 30), whereas nine had accepted them (Firms 3, 9, 11, 14, 18, 21, 28, 35, and 38). Table 3.4 illustrates these responses by firm type.

One would normally expect that firms with less involvement and experience in respect to overseas production would be most positively influenced by incentives associated with access to or protection of a large, rapidly growing domestic market, such as the Brazilian. One would also expect such firms to be most concerned about undertaking performance requirements. Likewise, the more experienced firms could be expected to be more dubious about the value of incentives in such a situation but find it easier to accept performance requirements. Such would seem to be borne out by the data given above, although admittedly the numbers are small. Perhaps of even greater interest was that spokesmen for 22 companies reporting operations in Brazil did not see fit to mention Brazilian incentives or performance guarantees, pro or con. The aggregate experience associated with these firms was relatively high. The presumption is that the political and economic environment of Brazil for most of these firms was perceived to be far more important than government-imposed incentives or performance guarantees, to which the novice or learners (Type 1 or 2) and some builders (Type 3) as well would be inclined to attribute greater

TABLE 3.4

Reaction to Brazilian Incentives by Firm Type

Firm Type	Incentives Seen as Important	Incentives Seen as of Dubious Value	Performance Requirements Accepted	Performance Requirements Refused	Investors Not Mentioning Either
Type 1	0	0	0	1	2
Type 2	1	0	1	1	0
Type 3	1	1	1	0	4
Type 4	0	2	3	1	5
Type 5	1	2	3	1	8
Type 6	0	0	0	0	1
Type 7	0	0	1	0	2
Total	3	5	9	4	22
Mean	3.3	4.2	4.0*	3.0	3.9

*Type 6 and 7 firms excluded.
Note: Totals do not add up to 34 because of double counting (6) and inclusion of noninvestors (2).

weight. Obviously, there were—not surprisingly—many exceptions,
but the tendency seemed to run in the direction suggested by these
data.

Taiwan

Although like Brazil, Taiwan is classified as Type II with respect to its policies vis-à-vis foreign business, corporate response
was quite different. Only 9 of the 51 corporations reported subsidiaries or affiliates (11 in all) there, 6 of which were wholly owned,
2 50-50, 3 minority owned. Of these investing companies, 1 was of
Type 3 (builders); 2 of Type 4 (integrators); 5 of Type 5 (opportunists);
and 1 of Type 7 (maverick). Executives in only four investing firms
commented at any length about Taiwan, which suggested that corporate interest in new or expanded investment on the island had slack-
ened. In addition, one Type 2 firm reported a recent licensing relationship. It had not, nor did it intend to, make any investment.
It developed that this latter firm (Firm 13, a Type 2) had become aware of opportunities in Taiwan when the local company had
approached it in the United States. Apparently, the Taiwanese firm,
a manufacturer of automobile engines, had been under governmental
pressure to increase local content. The upshot was that the U.S.
company had given the Taiwanese a license, which included a prohibition against exporting. Although the license had not yet been approved finally by the Taiwanese government, management did not
anticipate difficulty. Queried about the nonexporting provision, a
spokesman for the U.S. firm indicated that it would not be easy for
the Taiwanese enterprise to export in any event because, he pointed
out, "our customers would not buy from them." Getting the license
approved by the Taiwanese government was entirely the responsibility of the licensee.
Another noninvestor was Firm 19, a relatively small Type 1
enterprise. Some four years before, it had sent a task force to the
Far East to visit Taiwan, Singapore, and certain other countries.
The decision was that the high-volume products manufactured by
the company, trucks, did not have sufficient labor content to justify
manufacturing in low labor-cost countries* and that its other products were too difficult to build offshore. An executive noted that
Firm 24 (see below) had already won the right to manufacture trucks

---

*Relatively speaking, this was not correct. The firm's annual
depreciation as a percent of sales revenue was only 2.56.

in Taiwan, and that was all that would be needed in that area for some time. It would appear that the protection sought by Firm 24 had been effective, not only in Taiwan, but in the region as well.

Executives in four of the nine investing firms spoke of their respective firm's operations in Taiwan:

Firm 16 (Type 4), in electronics, had a wholly owned venture in Taiwan. An executive observed that it had taken out an Overseas Private Investment Corporation (OPIC) investment guarantee, but that it would have gone into Taiwan in any event. No other incentives or performance requirements were mentioned. Production was targeted not only at the local market but also as a source for certain of the more labor-intensive components for assembly in final products elsewhere. Local production had also opened up the local market for the import of certain products not manufactured locally.

Firm 18 (Type 4) executives considered that its investment in Taiwan was part of the natural evolution of marketing chemicals in that country. It already had a sales presence, and several of its multinational customers had plants there. Incentives had been a minor consideration. An executive noted that there were export requirements attached to import duty concessions. That is, there were zero tariffs on those components that were subsequently exported, whether directly or indirectly. An important reason for moving into Taiwan initially had been competitive; if the firm had not done so, one or more of its major competitors would have. He felt that a U.S. company servicing other U.S.-based firms had an advantage in Taiwan over non-U.S. firms. Management had not negotiated any contracts with its potential customers prior to investment and, indeed, such would have been "very rare" in the opinion of one executive. After investment, the firm realized that its Taiwanese employees were much more highly skilled than originally thought, and since there was space on the site it would be possible for the company to manufacture a widely used component (as the firm had done in Singapore). This production had been initiated and was successful to such a degree that raw materials were imported from the United States and the finished product shipped back. Shortly, however, management expected to use all of the output of its Taiwanese plant to supply Asian markets. The Taiwanese government provided some tax incentives, but they had been considered unimportant.

Firm 24, a large Type 5 company in the automotive field, had been visited several years before by the Taiwanese vice-premier for economic affairs. At the time, the Taiwanese government had been planning its entry into the engine and truck business and had asked the company to make a proposal, which it had proceeded to do. Subsequently, it had been selected to enter a joint venture with a local firm. The only incentive here was the promise of limited entry and, hence, market protection.

Firm 44 (a Type 5 in the wood, pulp, and paper sector) normally did not go into a country in order to be an exporter, although it had done so in a number of cases and was operating in 19 countries. An executive noted, however, that in the case of its Taiwanese venture an export commitment had been necessary. He added that the firm would have gone into Taiwan without any incentives, but that in retrospect, this would have been a wrong decision. The firm had been motivated really by the anticipated growth in the market as well as the availability of raw material (which constituted 50 to 60 percent of the manufacturing cost).

In the case of Taiwan, the differing responses of different types of corporations became very clear. The two noninvestors, which reported some interest in Taiwan, were of the Type 1 and 2 variety. In both cases, management action was primarily reactive and highly personal. With respect to Firm 19, the obvious question was: Why send a task force into the area if the firm's products were perceived as not benefiting from the relatively low labor costs prevailing in Southeast Asia? This act seemed to be an indication both of inadequate planning and commercial intelligence. All of the investing firms had looked at Taiwan as both a potential market and a production platform from which to supply other markets—either the United States or regional. Given the lack of comment to the contrary, it was apparent that no company had really been troubled with the insistence of the Taiwanese government on export commitments. The inquiry revealed no other performance requirements imposed on incoming firms. It should be noted that the 1978 Benchmark Study reported neither incentives nor performance requirements relative to investment in Taiwan (See Table I. 1). It would appear that responding firms did not even perceive the export commitments given in return for market access as being in the nature of performance requirements.

Thailand

Only six companies reported enterprises in Thailand, nine in all. Five of these were wholly owned; one, majority owned; two, minority owned; one, of uncertain ownership. Of the six, two were Type 4 and four were Type 5. In addition, two firms had withdrawn from investments there (one Type 4, one Type 5), and one (Type 4) had considered investment but had not proceeded.

One of the two withdrawing (a Type 5 animal feed producer, Firm 42) had been in Thailand until 1978. The venture had been 77 percent owned by the U.S. firm, the balance being owned by the local public. It had been sold in 1978, after six years of operation. Why had the company opted to invest in Thailand in the first place? An executive explained that the country was a producer and exporter of agricultural commodities and that it had a reasonable history of animal raising. There was a perceived need to improve the production of Thai meat, poultry, and eggs. Also, there had been a large and very sound Thai firm in the expansion mode at the time, which reinforced management's judgment that the Thai development provided a good opportunity. Finally, Thailand had a reasonably large population that liked to eat well. As mentioned before in another context, the company's original involvement in the country had occurred some 15 years previously when a U.S. government agency, which was working with the Thai Ministry of Agriculture at the time, became involved in a project for the improvement of the storage and shipping of grains from interior Thailand. There had been a search to find someone to look at it, and a high-level U.S. government official, a friend of a number of executives in the U.S. firm, had asked the latter to look at the situation. The result was that the corporation headed a fact-finding mission to Thailand. Although at the time nothing came of this activity, it did expose a number of executives to Thailand. In about 1967, for undisclosed reasons, the company started looking at South Korea. Once a South Korean operation had been started, someone suggested looking at Thailand. A couple of years later, the decision was made to build a plant there, which started producing in 1971. In so doing, the company formed a local corporation with the approval of the Thai Board of Investment and, as a condition of entry, agreed to sell 40 percent of its ownership in public offerings. By the time the firm retired from Thailand, some 23 percent had, in fact, been sold locally. The firm had received tax incentives, including a ten-year partial exemption. However, an executive declared that this tax relief had nothing to do with the firm's decision to enter Thailand. The reasons cited by executives for the company's withdrawal were: the slow growth of the market as compared to the growth of the competition; the amount of investment required for the firm to remain competitive; the increasing risk the firm perceived in the area; plus opportunities management perceived elsewhere for investment that looked more attractive. An executive made references to the fact that Kissinger had referred to Thailand about this time as "the last domino." In any event, the U.S. firm had sold its interest to a large Thai firm and licensed it to use U.S. trademarks, name, and some formulas. It had also entered into a two-year technical assistance agreement with the Thais.

A second case involved a large chemical manufacturer, Type 5. Agricultural chemicals were the focus of its Thai investment. The U.S. firm already had a presence in the market, but its competition had gone local and was doing some manufacturing in Thailand. This competitive pressure was the main reason for investing. A second reason was the expectation by the U.S. management that the Thai government would shortly require that some processing of the product be performed locally, even though it was cheaper to import the product. An executive noted that the firm had good local contacts and an excellent sales organization in the country. He also pointed out that the particular division of the company involved was already very world oriented. According to the executive, "They didn't have to be led. They were out there looking already." He went on to observe that sometimes a division would rely heavily on the international division for overseas expertise, but not so in this case. He remarked that of great relevance were the key personalities in each division. In any event, in the Thai case, incentives offered by the government had not been important. They were accepted, but the firm would have invested in any event. Incidentally, the investment was directed to the Thai market only, although management believed that there would be a later possibility of exporting into Burma.

It was quite clear that Thailand, despite its relatively attractive domestic market, was the exclusive domain of the more experienced, sophisticated firms. The involvement of only Types 4 and 5 surfaced in our study. It should be observed that possibly one of the distinguishing features of a Type 5 firm is its willingness to withdraw from a country when it is perceived that it has lost advantage over domestic competition and to do so without serious loss of either money or reputation. It will be noted that in the case of Firm 42, it withdrew with apparent ease to a purely contractual relationship with its local successor. In such a case, government incentives would normally not be seen as sufficient to overcome longer-term loss of competitive advantage. To avoid serious financial loss, a Type 5 firm would opt to withdraw before it is faced with a forced sale situation, which is precisely what this firm did.

In the many hours spent in discussing Brazil, Taiwan, and Thailand with U.S. executives, very few performance requirements were mentioned. Of course, whenever incentives were given, there was always an implicit requirement that the firm would indeed proceed with the investment plans as revealed to the government and on which basis the incentives were given. Note the admission by the one firm having second thoughts about the wisdom of its Irish venture (see Appendix A).

One of the deterrents to withdrawal was the perceived need to pay back the subsidies given to the company by the Irish government. Yet in Thailand, this was not mentioned as a problem. In none of these countries had entry been blocked because the U.S. firm would not undertake a specific performance requirement, although a variety of incentives might be withheld, including the right to foreign exchange permits to cover imports. The nonbestowal of an incentive on a certain enterprise might make that enterprise noncompetitive, but a performance requirement was rarely the price of entry, although Brazil was possibly moving close to doing so in certain situations. When executives observed that their firms had not entered because of certain requirements they would have to satisfy, they were referring primarily to the fact that the proposed projects were not likely to be competitive without the incentives, and the firms were not willing to pay the price in terms of making the commitments to become eligible for the incentives.

If one looks at the total group of 16 countries with Type II investment policies (see Table 3.5), it becomes clear that the opportunists (Type 5) were dominant, accounting for 54 percent of the affiliates reported (170 out of 315). Similar dominance (54 percent) emerged when the number was plotted as a percentage of affiliates reported in Type II developing countries (see Table 3.6).

In this group of countries, characterized by relatively open access, but liberal incentives for investment seen as desirable, 60 percent of all affiliates were wholly owned (Table 3.7). The flexibility of Type 5 firms in this regard should be noted. Sixty-eight of Type 5 affiliates, or 41 percent of those in which ownership was specified (68 of 166), were less than wholly owned by the U.S. parent, but only 17 percent (3 of 18) of Type 4 affiliates.

TYPE III COUNTRIES

Type III countries were characterized by the imposition of a screening process with respect to incoming foreign investment. Incentives for that investment deemed to be particularly attractive by the host government might be rewarded by incentives, in return for which performance requirements were frequently imposed, most commonly with respect to exports, ownership, local content, employment, and/or plant location. For example, if an enterprise were located within a designated development zone, special incentives might be given. This would also be true if it were to introduce technology of a pioneering nature.

TABLE 3.5

Reported Affiliates in Type II Countries
by Type of Corporate Parent
(number of parents/number of affiliates)

Country	Corporate Type							Total
	1	2	3	4	5	6	7	
Australia	0	1/1	4/7	7/10	11/39	1/1	0	24/58
Bahrein	0	0	0	0	1/1	0	0	1/1
Brazil*	1/1	2/2	5/6	7/8	15/29	1/1	3/5	34/53
Chile*	0	0	0	0	3/5	0	0	3/5
Costa Rica*	0	0	0	1/1	2/2	0	2/7	5/10
Ecuador*	0	0	0	1/1	2/3	0	0	3/4
France	0	0	5/8	6/11	8/17	0	1/1	20/37
Ireland	0	0	2/2	5/7	3/3	0	0	10/12
Italy	0	0	3/4	4/5	8/12	0	2/2	17/23
Ivory Coast*	0	0	0	0	1/1	0	0	1/1
New Zealand	0	0	0	3/3	6/8	0	0	9/11
Panama*	0	0	0	1/1	0	0	1/4	2/5
Portugal	0	0	0	1/1	3/3	0	0	4/4
Taiwan*	0	0	1/1	2/2	5/7	0	1/1	9/11
Thailand*	0	0	0	2/3	4/6	0	0	6/9
United Kingdom	2/3	2/2	7/9	10/18	15/34	0	2/5	38/71
Total (affiliates)	4	5	37	71	170	2	26	315
Developing countries	1	2	7	16	54	1	18	99
Developed countries	3	3	30	55	116	1	8	216

*Developing countries.

TABLE 3.6

Reported Affiliates in Type II Countries by Type of Corporate Parent
(in percentages within each country)

Country	Corporate Type						
	1	2	3	4	5	6	7
Australia	0	2	12	17	67	2	0
Bahrein*	0	0	0	0	100	0	0
Brazil*	2	4	11	15	55	2	11
Chile*	0	0	0	0	100	0	0
Costa Rica*	0	0	0	10	20	0	70
Ecuador*	0	0	0	25	75	0	0
France	0	0	22	30	46	0	0
Ireland	0	0	17	58	25	0	0
Italy	0	0	17	22	52	0	9
Ivory Coast*	0	0	0	0	100	0	0
New Zealand	0	0	0	27	73	0	0
Panama*	0	0	20	0	0	0	80
Portugal	0	0	0	25	75	0	0
Taiwan*	0	0	10	20	60	0	10
Thailand*	0	0	0	33	67	0	0
United Kingdom	4	3	13	25	48	0	7
Total	2	2	11	25	44	7	9
Developing countries	1	2	7	16	54	1	18
Developed countries	1	1	14	26	54	0+	4

*Developing countries.
Note: Rows may not total 100 because of rounding.

TABLE 3.7

Ownership of Reported Affiliates by Parent Type in Type II Countries

Parent Type	Ownership					Total
	100 Percent	Majority	50-50	Minority	Unknown	
Type 1	2	0	1	0	1	4
Type 2	5	0	0	0	0	5
Type 3	15	3	0	0	23	41
Type 4	47	0	1	7	13	68
Type 5	98	24	21	23	2	168
Type 6	1	1	0	0	1	3
Type 7	18	1	1	2	4	26
Total	186	29	24	32	44	315

Countries of greatest management interest in this category were, among the developing countries, South Korea, Malaysia, Mexico, and Venezuela. All told, 381 affiliates were reported in the 35 Type III countries. Of these, Type 2 parents claimed 15; Type 3, 37; Type 4, 7; Type 5, 228; Type 6, 7; and Type 7, 21. One hundred sixty-five were 100 percent owned; 24 majority owned; 45 50-50, 93 with minority U.S. ownership; and 54 of unspecified ownership.

South Korea

Of the 51 corporations, 10 reported 14 ventures in South Korea— 2 100 percent owned, 1 majority owned, 3 50-50, 7 minority owned, and 1 unspecified. Of the 10 investing companies, 3 were of Type 4 and 7 of Type 5. In addition, 2 others had tried to negotiate licenses. Two more had made an effort to invest, but had pulled back. Another was responding to the South Korean engine and truck program, but no details were reported.

Firm 17, a Type 5 chemical producer, had become involved in South Korea in a major way, the company having put one plant on stream within the past year. Negotiations for this enterprise had started in the late 1960s, shortly after the company had shifted its organizational structure from that of an international corporation to a regionally organized multinational. This move had put a group of people into the Pacific area. Shortly thereafter, they had organized themselves into a regional headquarters and had begun exploring the region. At that time, South Korea was beginning to look promising as a growth area. Park's regime had opted to specialize in the chemical industry, among other things, and government representatives had been sent to the United States to seek out possible investors. "It knew what it wanted to do and where it wanted to do it, and it picked those companies with good technology, probably two or three in the United States and one in Europe," one executive observed. The upshot was that things had come together, and the firm had begun a series of conversations with the South Korean government. At the time, the company had been trying to avoid 50-50 joint ventures, but it had learned that such might not be possible in South Korea. A long negotiation started. By this time—two or three years later—the South Koreans were talking only with Firm 17. The result had been the definition of a project to which the company agreed: a 50-50 deal with a government-owned company but with the understanding that, after the enterprise was operating, the government equity would be put into a holding company and eventually spun off to private

South Koreans, which in fact had been done. Recognizing that the
U.S. company had done a good job in this project, the South Koreans
had asked it to become involved in a major chemical complex, which
represented a security-driven industrial dispersion plan. The government wanted the U.S. firm to plan the entire project and then
undertake one part of it itself. The balance would be operated by a
government enterprise. The U.S. company had been able to negotiate 100 percent ownership for its part of the complex. Simultaneously, the 50–50 venture had been expanded. The incentive used
here by the South Korean government had been permission for 100
percent foreign ownership of the one plant. This ownership was
believed to have been unique in the heavy industry field in South
Korea; in all other cases, a joint ownership had been a condition
for entry. The South Koreans finally agreed to 100 percent foreign
ownership, the U.S. management believed, in part because they
were pleased with what the firm had done up to that time. As it
turned out, the entire complex worked well, but one executive observed, "The timing was bad from an economic point of view." He
went on to add, "Part of our problem, initially, was concern about
our exposure due to the possibility of the North-South conflict becoming heated up." At that time, the firm's board of directors had
put some very stringent restraints on its planners. Hence, Overseas Private Investment Corporation (OPIC) insurance and the way
the project was financed were very important. It turned out that
the company's exposure was in fact quite modest, roughly one-sixth
of the total value of the project. However, due to the subsequent
economic slowdown, the firm had failed to get its money out as fast
as expected and consequently, its equity—and exposure—built up
well beyond the one-sixth level. Other than the ownership deal,
plus market protection, no further incentives had been given nor
requirements imposed. The primary South Korean motive had been
a desire to secure modern technology and assistance in designing a
world-scale industrial complex.

Firm 21 (Type 5) considered its South Korean enterprise to
be an example of an unsatisfactory investment. Thus far, the firm
had invested well over $1 million in a 49 percent-owned manufac-
turing facility, for which it had OPIC coverage. The main problem, an executive observed, was that the factory was in the wrong
place; it was currently being moved to a site near Seoul. The reason for investing in South Korea had been purely market motivated,
but the market had proven somewhat less than expected, both in
terms of domestic sales and exports. Management had viewed the
investment as the price the firm had to pay to get into the market.
It had done little previous marketing in South Korea because a Japanese company, a licensee of the U.S. firm's technology, had sold in

South Korea. When this licensing agreement had terminated, the U.S. firm had set about finding a local sales representative but found that selling against the Japanese was difficult. In talking with people in the government, in industry, and in the Economic Development Commission, company representatives had met a potential joint venture partner, and negotiations started. The government had been willing to offer incentives, such as preference with respect to government contracts and some initial tariff protection (which would be removed when the industry was deemed strong enough to compete on its own). The principal negotiator for the firm observed that he had to argue vigorously for these incentives, none of which, however, had been put into writing. He noted, "The Minister himself was unwilling to do so because of the Government's declared willingness to maintain free trade." The result was that subsequent political upheavals had rendered the verbal promises worthless. An executive contrasted these negotiations unfavorably with those in Japan conducted with the Japanese Ministry of International Trade and Industry (MITI). He observed that MITI was reliable, but the Korean Development Board was not. A further problem in the negotiations had been the South Korean perception of added value. From the firm's point of view, added value consisted of hardware, software, and labor. The firm had decided that it would manufacture components in the United States, where it could be done most efficiently, and then assemble and test them in South Korea. To the government, however, this did not constitute manufacturing. In any event, the market had "gone to pieces." Manufacturing on a modest scale apparently continued.

Firm 37 (Type 4) had a man in South Korea for two years trying to negotiate a joint venture. When asked why South Korea was being considered, an executive responded that South Koreans were very hard working and well educated. Further, the company had wanted a facility in Asia to sell to the East Asian market, that part of the world "being a long way from the United States." The South Korean project had involved a product not produced elsewhere in the Far East. Part of the problem, we were told, was that the company had wanted merely to negotiate a technical assistance agreement with a local firm but that it had been compelled to negotiate a joint venture instead. The U.S. firm had held out for a majority position and, in fact, received permission to go ahead on a 60-40 basis, with the 60 percent being held by the U.S. firm. As part of the deal, the firm had been required to make an export commitment for a certain percentage of the output. The firm seemed to be relatively well pleased with the outcome.

For Firm 44 (Type 5), the attractions of South Korea had been threefold: (1) its phenomenal growth rate in terms of both

GNP and population; (2) the relatively low utilization of the firm's product as measured by kilograms per capita (which had suggested a good growth market); and (3) the existence of a small existing market (that is, the product was known). In addition, the firm had found an ideal partner, described as financially sound, with a demonstrated capacity to grow and an ability to run a manufacturing business. He also had good relations with the government, possessed "political entries," and had contacts with the appropriate financial institutions. It was pointed out to us that personal contact had been made between top government officials in South Korea and the top executives of the firm. South Korea was chosen as an investment site in 1979 without comparison with other countries in the region. An executive noted that the firm had not made the investment to export but rather to supply the domestic market. In the South Korean case, no export requirement had been imposed, possibly because the U.S. company ended up with a minority interest, 49 percent. No incentives or other commitments were reported.

The reasons four firms had rejected involvement in South Korea are of interest. Firm 5, a Type 1 producer of processed foods, had seen a very large market in South Korea for a given product. There was one producer already there with limited capacity; its existence, according to one executive, prevented the U.S. firm from getting permission to produce. Although the large-scale marketing of this product would have involved changing South Korean eating habits, management felt that this was possible. The firm had gone so far as to find a potential licensee in South Korea, which had sent several people to the United States to become familiar with the product. The South Korean management had felt certain that it could get official permission to enter the market, but it had failed to do so. Apparently the South Korean firm already in the field was "too tightly tied in politically."

Firm 13, a Type 2 manufacturer of industrial machinery, had been approached by a South Korean government representative some ten years before to help establish an industrial park. The president of the U.S. firm had felt it premature for South Korea to get into the manufacture of products of the type manufactured by his firm. He observed, however, that much of the special machinery imported into South Korea was being sourced from his firm and that "even if we had token manufacturing there, the market would be locked up." The government was currently negotiating with the automotive industry, a major customer for Firm 13's product,

to determine who was going to manufacture what, * and management
was waiting on the government decision before proceeding to negotiate a license. There was no thought of an equity investment. By
way of contrast, Firm 16, a Type 4 producer of electronics, had a
policy of owning all overseas manufacturing facilities 100 percent.
According to a company spokesman, the firm would not consider
any other relationship. Although South Korea had a general requirement for joint ventures, it had nonetheless been willing to
waive this ownership requirement in this instance. Even so, management had refused a South Korean undertaking due to excessive
government corruption. An executive stated that the firm was scru-
pulously honest and refused to pay bribes anyplace. And finally,
Firm 41, a Type 3 producer of photographic equipment, had investigated South Korea but chose not to enter. The reason given by one
executive was that the lack of economies of scale were not adequate-
ly compensated for by tariffs and the South Korean government was
not prepared to place tariffs on competing products. It had not proceeded far enough to negotiate ownership or control.

It would appear that the mixed signals, length of time required
to negotiate entry, and corruption were partially defeating the effectiveness of the South Korean investment policies. Of the four companies reporting interest but no investment, one was Type 1, one
Type 2, one Type 3, and one Type 4. But the reasons for noninvestment differed. For the first two, there had been no intention to invest, only to license. For the second two, both of which looked at
South Korea from the point of view of investment, one had been re-
pulsed by corruption; the other, by government unwillingness to
offer protection.

It may be significant that of the 51 corporations reporting investment in South Korea, Type 5s outnumbered Type 4s by 7 to 3,
which was not surprising, given the South Korean reluctance to permit foreign controlled enterprises. The Type 5 corporations, the
opportunists, are, by definition, generally more flexible in their
ownership policies than the Type 4s, the integraters, many of which
insist on 100 percent ownership, as shown by Firm 16.

---

*A spokesman for Firm 14 (Type 5) reported that his firm
had recently responded to a South Korean government tender an-
nouncement with respect to an engine and truck program. He was
unable or unwilling to specify the performance requirements and
incentives involved.

Malaysia

Of the 51 firms, 9 reported 13 ventures in Malaysia. Three of these were 100 percent owned; 3 majority owned; 2 50-50; 3 minority owned; and 2 unspecified as to ownership. One Type 3 firm, one Type 4, and 7 Type 5 were involved. In addition, one firm (24, a Type 5) had withdrawn from a minority-owned venture to a licensing position, and one other (Firm 42, a Type 5) had given consideration to Malaysian projects but had not moved into any actual negotiation. Spokesmen for four companies detailed their respective firm's involvement:

Firm 7 (Type 4) had been looking at Southeast Asia for many years; likely candidates had been Malaysia, Thailand, and Indonesia. Management had realized that the relevant market, which was regional, was large enough to support one economically sized plant, but not more. Therefore, an agreement had been entered into with the firm's single competitor in that part of the world to set up a joint venture. A promise of duty-free import of the capital equipment by the Malaysian government had made the project more attractive; so had a commitment to permit the import of raw materials and the promise of a prohibition against the import of low-cost materials then coming from Eastern Europe. Sometime after startup, duties had been imposed on the imports of raw materials, but management had not considered this to be serious. Tax incentives had also been granted, although these had not been given much weight, according to one executive. In fact, he reported, they had helped the local investor more than the U.S. company, because of U.S. tax treatment of foreign-source income (which gave no credit against U.S. tax liability for foreign taxes not paid). The reason for choosing Malaysia had been the fact that it was the largest market in the region and was growing rapidly. Also, it had been seen as the most politically stable country in Southeast Asia. In general, the following factors had been considered important, in descending order: market size, market growth potential, capital cost, and return on investment. The Malaysian venture was owned 49 percent by the U.S. firm and 51 percent by a local Malaysian corporation.

Firm 28 (Type 5) had held a 50 percent ownership in its Malaysian manufacturing affiliate since its startup in 1971. Prior to that time, another foreign company had manufactured the firm's product under contract, but the latter had distributed the product via its own local marketing company. In entering a manufacturing venture, Firm 28 had committed itself to export 10 percent of the production. Later, when it received a license to expand production, it had committed itself to export 20 percent. This commitment had been embedded in an exchange of letters that included the phrase, "when surplus conditions exist in the Malaysian market." An executive felt that although the company was not then exporting at that level, the Malaysians would not make an issue out of the matter unless conditions were to change radically. The firm did receive a number of incentives and was given "pioneer status" under the Malaysian investment law, including a tax holiday for five years (which had been extended subsequently to six), plus accelerated depreciation. The first year during which the company would be required to pay any Malaysian tax was 1981. Under the newly announced economic policy in Malaysia, at least 30 percent of all enterprises were required to be in the hands of indigenous Malays (that is, Bumiputra), no more than 40 percent foreign, and the balance (not more than 30 percent), other Malaysian (that is, Indian or Chinese-Malay). It had been clear from the start that the government did not want the firm to have a majority interest, although there had been some dispute between the ministers of finance and of industry on this score. Originally, the firm's local partner had been Pernas, a government organization whose equity had been transferred recently to the National Bumiputra Trust, another government organization. The firm considered the Malaysian government to have been an excellent partner. An executive did say that every time the firm approached the government for a license to expand production it was "needled" with respect to equity. In its most recent expansion, we were told, the firm had felt compelled to agree to negotiate a different equity position, which meant that the chairman of the board would meet with the Malaysian prime minister to discuss the matter. In fact, the prime minister had very recently issued a statement questioning the 30-40-30 policy by observing that the policy was of a general nature and did not necessarily apply to specific companies.

Firm 37 (Type 5), which already had one operation in Malaysia, had decided to develop a second activity. In so doing, it had opted for setting up a completely separate organization because of the Bumiputra requirement (see above). It had been permitted to retain 60 percent ownership because it had come up with 40 percent Bumiputra ownership. Another requirement had been that the product be locally produced in order to qualify as a supplier to the government-owned telephone company. The U.S. management seemed satisfied even though its overall policy had given heavy preference to 100 percent ownership. Apparently, the firm's 100 percent ownership of the first venture had been protected by a "grandfather clause," although pressure to spin off some ownership to local nationals was anticipated.

Firm 44 (Type 5) had set up two ventures simultaneously, one in Singapore, another in Malaysia. The former was perceived as the marketing arm for the manufacturing operation located in Malaysia. The factory had been located there for reasons of tariff and incentives. The latter consisted of a six-year tax holiday, plus some grants. To qualify, the plant had been located in a development area where most of the labor was unskilled. Another factor had been the greater ease of exporting out of Malaysia into Singapore, which constituted about a third of the market, rather than the other way around because of a 40 percent tariff differential. Currently, some raw material was being imported to Malaysia, but the firm hoped to develop local sources of supply in time. A final factor had been the difficulty of finding adequate space in Singapore for a large plant of the type planned.

Firm 24, a Type 5, had withdrawn recently from both Malaysia and Thailand. The withdrawal from Malaysia had led to no bitterness on either side and according to one executive who had been involved, the firm could easily get permission to reenter if it so chose. The firm had retained 100 percent ownership up to the time of withdrawal, at which time it had given a license to assemble a particular product (a consumer durable) to a local firm. But neither the licensee nor the distributor had been able to find the necessary resources to set up an assembly operation or a Bumiputra partner. Consequently, production had never started. The U.S. firm had withdrawn essentially because of low volume and high cost, in part due to the fact that the design of the product really did not meet market requirements. Another (Firm 29, Type 6) had examined and turned down a possible project in the country for the processing of a locally produced agricultural product. Initially, it had been interested in the project, which had been recommended by a consultant as a result of a study commissioned by top management to examine ways of developing new products. The firm was already buying the relevant raw material out of Malaysia (a plantation product), had local expertise, and had been training people in the prospective industry. In the final analysis, however, it boiled down to a tradeoff between a secure supply, at a slightly higher cost from the firm's own facility in Malaysia, against greater flexibility and more variability in cost by buying on the world market. It had opted for the latter. Also, certain inputs to production would have had to be shipped from considerable distance, which introduced a logistical problem. Further, the EEC regulations defining food products were vague, and it was uncertain whether they permitted substitution of the new product for the more traditional one. In any event, as one executive observed, the incentives offered by the

Malaysian government would have had only a very small impact on the decision.

It was clear from this experience that there was real doubt about the effectiveness of the Malaysian investment incentives. They were taken, but companies tended to be drawn to Malaysia for quite different reasons, including the relative honesty of government, the size and growth of the local market, and apparent political stability. The commitments were not seen as onerous, nor the incentives of great significance. However, it should again be noted that of the firms investing in Malaysia, those of Type 5 outnumbered those of Type 4 by 8 to 1. Only two Type 3 firms reported Malaysian ventures. These results are entirely consistent with the pattern.

Mexico

Management experience and attitudes with respect to the Mexican foreign investment regime ranged from enthusiasm to frustration. All together, 25 firms (nearly 60 percent of the total sample) reported 51 equity investments, plus 3 with licenses only. The former included 18 that were wholly owned, 3 majority owned, 28 minority owned, and 2 unspecified. In addition, Firm 5 (Type 1) reported having negotiated with the Mexicans but without success. Two Type 4 firms were still in negotiation, and another was considering making a move.

Spokesmen for 12 of the 25 firms with active operations in Mexico gave some of the reasons for their involvement:

Firm 2 (Type 3) had two small (wholly owned) processing plants in Mexico dating from the mid-1950s, and management had frequently investigated the possibility of further investment. According to one executive, management saw a rising market, and "we would love to be there in a more substantial way." However, the firm had an overriding preference for majority ownership of its foreign ventures, the reason being that its industry was very capital intensive and required substantial know-how. Perhaps 50 percent of the profit would be adequate, the executive said, but without the firm's control this might well be 50 percent of nothing. Therefore, the company had refused to risk its capital for less than 50 percent ownership. Frequent internal studies of the investment climate in Mexico had always "come up against a blind alley" because of the Mexicanization laws requiring minority foreign ownership. Also mentioned was the lack of adequate electric power. The executive concluded that because of these ownership restraints and the power

inadequacy the firm would not invest any further in either Mexico
or Venezuela. It had obviously been comparing the two.

Firm 6 (Type 5) had three affiliates in Mexico (two wholly
owned, one minority owned). Currently, it was wrestling with two
added projects. One of them would be a joint venture with a Mexican company in the chemical sector. Although labor costs were low,
an executive observed, one needed to look at total cost. Would
Mexican workers be more productive than their counterparts in the
United States? Would the U.S. government intervene in the industry (automotive) more than the Mexican government? When the
executive was asked why the firm considered producing in Mexico,
he responded that the real question had to do with whether his firm
would be shut out of the market and someone else get in and "knock
us out of the box." The proximity of Mexico was a positive factor,
but the wage rate differential "gets eaten up when one considers
efficiency and transportation costs." The same firm was already
producing a line of industrial products in Mexico, which it was selling to Pemex, the government-owned oil company, from a 100 percent owned Mexican manufacturing subsidiary. The firm had heard
nothing about any Mexican ownership being demanded by the government. The executive felt that the firm had considerable leverage
because it had been selling to such a critical industry as Pemex
and, consequently, the Mexicans had said nothing about ownership.
In fact, the firm planned to initiate some Mexican ownership in this
facility, but on the terms and at the time chosen by the U.S. firm.
The executive opined that the right time had not yet arrived.

Firm 8 (Type 3) was negotiating currently with the government
in order to avoid price control. It operated one wholly owned food
processing plant and insisted on retaining that level of ownership.
An executive actively involved in the situation felt that the firm could
maintain its ownership if it increased production. In any event, he
doubted that there was a local buyer for any of the equity. He then
observed that the government had a basic product program, the object of which was to increase capacity for the production of certain
specified products and to bring those products to the market at low
prices relative to the minimum wage. The current problem facing
the firm had to do with what sort of price increases would be permitted. In the face of inflation in Latin America generally and given
the fact that the firm was in the production of foodstuffs, the executive perceived that the overwhelming risk his firm faced in the area,
including Mexico, was price control.

Firm 10 (Type 5), a chemical producer, had been in Mexico
for many years in diverse products via a minority-owned affiliate.
An executive commented that it had a number of operations in
Mexico's development zones due to the 25 percent discount available

on energy and raw material inputs for the initial ten years arising
out of such location, if the firm committed itself to export 25 percent of its output for three years. The U.S. firm had been drawn
into this posture because on the raw materials list were a number
of products for which it had been the sole supplier in Mexico. The
U.S. firm's investments, therefore, had been of a defensive nature.
The executive claimed that the scale of investment would have been
less and the timing of the investment longer had these incentives
not been offered. In order to stay in the market and supply its Mexican customers, the firm was even prepared to take a loss on exports
if necessary.

Firm 14 (Type 5) was in Mexico because of an "act of government." The state had had a monopoly in manufacturing a product
for which the firm had been invited to supply an important component.
It had started to produce locally via a licensee with the state-owned
enterprise but had been asked subsequently by the government to
participate more directly in the manufacturing. The outcome had
been that the U.S. firm had taken a 40 percent equity position in return for a cash investment and some small value for the technology.
The firm's name had been licensed to the venture, and the license
was coterminous with the ability of the firm to exercise quality control over the product. It also had a management contact but, in fact,
a Mexican national appointed by the government headed the operation.
The contract was in perpetuity but was subject to periodic renegotiation. An executive observed, "We might have been thrown out had
we not accepted part of the Mexican company." He went on to point
out that his firm had been the preferred supplier, that a good relationship had developed over the years, and that the Mexican government had felt that it needed more direct help in the manufacturing
operation. The firm really had not wanted a minority interest but
had felt compelled to accept. To get the management contract, the
firm had felt obliged to make commitments with respect to export,
local content, and production level. It was not asked to commit itself to spin off management to local nationals, inasmuch as the government very much wanted the firm's continuing involvement. Nor
was the firm required to make an employment commitment. The
Mexican enterprise was not then selling anything into the United
States, but the executive speculated that if the Mexican venture got
into a real financial bind, the parent U.S. firm would probably buy
from it and cut off some U.S. suppliers. Some tax incentives had
been given by the Mexicans "to sweeten the deal," specifically due
to the plant's location in a priority-incentive zone, which generated
a 30 percent tax credit on future profits for a given number of years,
a per-head credit for hiring people in the zone (which the executive
believed would be credited against the value-added tax), plus a tax

credit that arose because the automotive industry was classified as a strategic industry. He also spoke of export incentives in the form of extended, long-term export financing (8 percent over ten years). Overall, management seemed well pleased with its operation, although it was still too new for a definitive judgment; the arrangement had only gone into operation during the past year.

Firm 15 (Type 7) had one plant of unspecified ownership operating in Mexico for over four years, which produced entirely for the local market. The firm had become interested in an additional enterprise to process a local agricultural product for worldwide distribution. An executive observed that if a foreign firm committed itself to export virtually its entire output, which this firm did, the government would permit up to 60 percent foreign ownership. No tax incentives had been offered in this case. Because the facility was located in a "restricted area" close to the coast, the government made it possible for the site to be acquired and placed in trust with a long-term lease to the firm. The project had been initiated by a Mexican entrepreneur who offered to help get permission for the 60 percent interest for the firm and to put up the remaining 40 percent himself. The plant had started up two or three years before. The market had been reasonably well assured, inasmuch as other affiliates of the firm would use the product. It had been anticipated that the U.S. cost of production would rise more rapidly than in Mexico but, in fact, the reverse had proved to be the case.

Firm 17 (Type 5), a chemical producer, was reluctant to invest further in Mexico by reason of the ownership requirements; it had one wholly owned plant in Mexico, which it had purchased in the 1940s, its first foreign venture. An executive felt that the firm could do more for itself and for Mexico if it were more active in the country. Asked about the possibility of management control with a minority interest, he replied that the important factor was how much the local interest had contributed to the project. He commented, "In some areas, all you want is control. In other situations, the rewards are not great enough as measured against our contribution. It simply does not produce an adequate return." He then went on to express the view that the Mexicans tended to be "socialistic" and to consider an adequate profit to be unacceptable. A technical assistance agreement, he argued, would not generate adequate return if the firm's contribution in the technical area were high. Mexico, he observed, insisted on controlling both streams of income: that from an equity investment and that from a technical assistance or licensing agreement. This control indicated a high degree of suspicion on the part of the Mexican authorities. He then observed that it was indeed curious that avowedly Marxist countries, such as Yugoslavia and the People's Republic of China, were more flexible. Apparently, the political authorities in Mexico needed to protect an image and had to sell their people on the notion that they had been winners in any negotiation with a foreign firm. They also had to sell the unions. He agreed that the fact the firm had negotiated deals with both Yugoslavia and the People's Republic of China might ultimately change the attitude in some countries, Mexico included, but he opined that this would take a long time. It did not seem that the Mexicans knew what the firm was doing elsewhere.

Firm 26 (Type 4), a producer in the automotive sector, had been stimulated to invest in Mexico by reason of the Mexican policy of accelerating development of local manufacturing capability. A decree had been announced two years before that by 1982 any company selling products in Mexico that were either partially or totally imported was obliged to balance its imports with exports in terms of foreign exchange, enterprise by enterprise. In the automotive industry, Mexico had already laid down the requirements that 50 percent by value be of local content and that the 50 percent include certain parts. In the case of this firm, it had moved to virtually 100 percent local content, some of which was achieved by buying components from locally owned firms. The export-import balance rule, however, also required that 50 percent of the exports be produced by these local suppliers. For example, a Mexican-owned company, which was supplying the U.S. firm's Mexican subsidiary with a given part, was required to export half of its output directly, which meant that the U.S. subsidiary's parent firm would have to buy its output, thereby forcing the U.S. parent to source to some extent in Mexico. The executive explained further that the U.S. subsidiary in Mexico had to buy from these other companies in order to get their export credits. But if the products were not, in fact, exported to its own parent in the United States or other affiliated firms elsewhere, the subsidiary had to have an equity interest in the supplying company or an active role in developing the export. In the latter event, it was obliged to explain what the subsidiary did to develop the export. Just how this was to be done was not clear since there had not been a clear set of guidelines issued. Although this rule technically applied in all sectors, the automotive sector was "more advanced" in this respect. The rule was just being implemented, and only in 1982 would it be fully effective. To resolve the local content-export credit dilemma, the U.S. firm had entered into several joint ventures with Mexican corporations. In all cases, the U.S. equity had been limited to 49 percent and without management control. The export rule, it was explained, had caused great difficulty within the U.S. parent because, as one executive pointed out, how did one in the Latin American regional organization tell the North American organization to purchase components out of Mexico when it might not be to its advantage to do so? Each region was a profit center. The problem had been resolved only "with great difficulty." The suboptimization implicit in some of these deals had created "squabbles in headquarters," which were only settled by the intervention of top management. Management did encourage other U.S. firms that were corporate suppliers in the United States to start up in Mexico. A company spokesman felt that the Mexican position in all of this was reasonable; all that it wanted to do was balance its trade in and out. Further, economics were beginning to justify Mexican sourcing although, admittedly, it was still a marginal situation. He did point out that the firm had profited from the sale of products in Mexico, which would not have been made in the absence of local manufacture, and the import credits earned by reason of exports. For example, by exporting $1 million of products, it could import a similar amount and thereby make possible the manufacture and sale of $10 million of products in Mexico. The firm made money on the sale of these additional products, which had to be taken into consideration in the decision to manufacture in Mexico. Would the firm have sourced to the extent that it had in Mexico without the official pressure? An executive admitted that it would have been more reluctant and probably the Mexican operations would have developed more slowly. He pointed out that in addition to limiting exports to the dollar value of exports Mexico had also given tax credits on exports, which tended to reduce the cost of manufacturing and improve the competitive position of Mexican exports. These incentives were admittedly not large, and the executive felt that they probably would not continue for long. He reported that there was pressure via the GATT to modify these kinds of export incentives and, although Mexico was not a member, it was sensitive to the issue. The firm had laid out an export plan for the next year and had been compelled to negotiate an anticipated import-export imbalance for the year. The plan had to show how the firm would improve the balance in the future. In effect, it called for a pooling of export credits that would have to be repaid later, with interest. One final point must be made: Mexico had imposed no limit on the employment of expatriates by the firm.

Firm 21 (Type 5), a relatively small firm in the industrial equipment business, was operating a small plant in Mexico that was 100 percent owned by the U.S. firm. From time to time, threats with respect to ownership had been made, which the firm had not taken very seriously. An executive felt that it had been in Mexico long enough to be tolerated. The size of the Mexican operation had been increased very slowly. Were there a major expansion, the executive admitted that the Mexican government might be expected to take action, possibly even expropriate its assets.

Firm 27 (Type 4) had recently been involved in a major expansion of a plant providing important components to the Mexican automotive industry. Factors contributing to the decision to undertake the expansion had been the lifting of price controls on relevant products, the growth of the automotive industry, and pressure brought to bear by members of the automotive industry. An executive added, however, "We really look to our own interest. Management believed that Mexico wanted to become competitive on a worldwide basis." It also was convinced that the government would not license expansion in a way that would produce a proliferation of small plants, although there were one or two local entrepreneurs that the government would find politically difficult to block. An executive reported that the firm had used the example of Venezuela in its negotiations with the Mexican government, in that it could be demonstrated that the large number of relatively small plants in Venezuela had driven costs and prices to an unnecessarily high level there. The Venezuelans had then introduced price controls, which had reduced profitability and discouraged further expansion of capacity. The result was that excess demand had built up, and Venezuela had become subject to politically compelling pressure to permit imports. In securing license to expand production in Mexico, the firm had given no commitment to export.

Firm 32 (Type 3), an automotive parts manufacturer, had just entered into a joint venture with a Mexican government-owned enterprise. An executive expressed optimism that his firm might, as a result, capture 100 percent of the Mexican market for certain products. The company had undertaken an ongoing search program in Mexico by reason of the local content law although, he added, the government writes the local content law differently for its own companies: "the law becomes what anyone can negotiate, and a lot depends on whether the Government wants the company or not. If not, the rules are written in a way which a foreign company can't live by." He felt that so long as Mexico needed his firm, it would be in a strong position. For that reason, it retained the manufacture of a few key parts in the United States that the Mexicans would find difficult to manufacture.

Firm 39 (Type 2) had developed its Mexican enterprise in part to take advantage of Mexico's export credit facilities. It had tried to secure competitive export financing via the Export-Import Bank of the United States but had failed. As a result, management felt almost compelled to manufacture elsewhere. It had rejected a number of countries because of either political and/or financial problems, such as Greece, Argentina, and the Philippines. It had rejected Nigeria because of local content requirements. In Mexico, the firm had accepted local content and export commitments but seemed happy with the arrangement.

Three other firms reported continuing interest in entering Mexico. For example, Firm 1 (Type 4) was currently negotiating in Mexico. An executive described it as a country in which everything required approval: the amount of capital, the location, the extent of national participation, the level of exports, and employment. The way that this is done, he went on, was for the company to make a detailed proposal to the government, which then either approved it or not. The only incentive that had been offered was a promise of protection against competing exports. In fact, in this case very little was being imported in any event. The government insisted that the firm export 60 percent of its product which, the executive observed, would have an impact on U.S. exports. He felt that this was "an extremely selfish policy, exceeded possibly only by France and Japan."

Firm 9 (Type 4) was likewise actively interested. A company team was studying several alternatives for entering Mexico. An executive pointed out that one of the major problems the team faced was trying to figure out what Mexican government policy really meant. He observed that the government did not allow a foreign firm to have majority ownership and then speculated on how a firm might maintain control in the absence of majority ownership. He cited Sears Roebuck in Venezuela as an example of a firm operating on the basis of a management contract with little or no equity position. In any event, the investigation in Mexico was going forward, and there was an awareness that the firm should be manufacturing in Mexico in order to stay in the market.

A third firm (30, Type 2), a manufacturer of mining equipment, had been looking since 1972 at the possibility of doing something in Mexico. It had opted not to license because management felt that it would be too much of a "hassle." Subsequently, it had turned to the joint venture option. For a time, an executive explained, management attention had been diverted to developments elsewhere. But in 1975 the firm did ask a Mexican firm about becoming a joint venture partner. By 1978 there had been agreement on both sides to study the idea, and in mid-1981 the deal had been about to materialize. At that point, negotiations were suspended because of financial difficulties on the Mexican side. By that time, the firm had negotiated for 18 months and had indicated willingness to accept a 49 percent share, but everything remained in abeyance. When asked why the firm wanted to invest in Mexico, a company spokesman replied, "Where else would you invest? The company is already in the other important mining countries with relatively stable regimes. Zambia has no money; Nigeria is not attractive. Would you invest in Brazil?" Obviously, he saw high risk in Brazil.

Executives in five other firms implied past interest on the part of their respective corporations, an interest that had lapsed due to perceived deficiencies in the Mexican investment climate.

An executive in a food processing firm (5, Type 1) sounded bitter. His company had what he called "a headache" in Mexico in that the patents on food products, including a product of central interest to the firm, had been wiped out by action of the Mexican government. (He noted that the Brazilians had done the same.) The Mexican government had itself built a plant that turned out "lousy products, but it keeps us out," he observed. Subsequently, the firm had attempted to sell its technology to the government but without success. "We have spent a lot of time and money looking at Mexico," he concluded.

Firm 13 (Type 2) had been under pressure from U.S. auto manufacturers to manufacture in Mexico, the government having exerted pressure on the latter to buy locally, although that would invariably result in an inferior product, according to the firm's president. One of the company's competitors was reported to be going into Mexico and that "worries us," the executive commented. "It will capture the market without making any money, and everyone will lose." This firm had only four foreign operations, all in Europe.

Firm 19 (Type 1) was not investing in a Mexican operation, although management realized that the market had grown over 100 percent in the last year for the firm's products. A spokesman for the firm had gone to a seminar quite recently in which it had been predicted that Mexico would soon have a local content law. In any event, Mexico seemed corrupt to the management, and he cited a recent personal experience in Mexico in which he had been witness to petty corruption. Rather, the firm is setting up in Brazil and plans to export to the rest of Latin America from that base. He hopes that the "made in Brazil" label will enhance sales elsewhere in Latin America. Firm 23 (Type 4), a medium-sized food producer, considers Mexico marginal as a site of investment because one can get only 49 percent ownership. An executive did admit that a minority position could be the basis for control, but obviously the firm was not giving Mexico serious attention.

Finally, Firm 33 (Type 6) had not to date taken up an investment opportunity that had arisen in Mexico three years before. If made, the investment would consist of the purchase of several factories in the same industry, which constituted a very significant part of Mexico's total production in that sector. The plants had been taken over by their bank creditors. Despite the fact that operation of these plants would involve it in a business not considered its "core" business and despite Mexican ownership restraints, the firm had negotiated. An attraction had been that the U.S. firm could have had full ownership for five years. A serious problem, according to one executive, had been the slow pace of negotiations; another, the price to be paid for the firm's investment after the initial five-year period. In addition, some of the factories were overmanned and of high cost. Management felt that there was nothing that it could have done with the plants other than sell them. These considerations, plus the Mexican labor laws, had resulted in a negative decision by the firm. It had, it was claimed, considered the proposal very seriously and had spent nearly $100,000 on the investigation. Still, one got the impression that management was looking for reasons not to invest.

It was quite clear that the management of different firms had reacted to Mexican performance requirements and incentives quite differently. It seemed that Type 5 firms had been the least put off by the various requirements imposed by the Mexicans (see Table 3.8). As can be noted, only 22 percent of Type 5 affiliates were wholly or majority owned, whereas almost twice as many (40 percent) of Type 4 affiliates were of that type. The single Type 2 firm investing in Mexico had been forced into foreign manufacture by the inadequacy of U.S. export credit facilities but had been pleased with the results. Only three Type 3 firms had invested, all in wholly owned subsidiaries (plus two of unspecified ownership). Of the five firms that had been unable to consummate a relationship in Mexico, three were of Types 1 and 2. A third was a Type 6 firm, which was in the retrenchment mode in any event.

Venezuela

Of the 51 firms in the sample, 16 reported some 19 manufacturing subsidiaries or affiliates in the country (13 were 100 percent owned, 1 majority owned, 4 minority owned, and 1 unspecified). Firm 50 (Type 7) would still be in Venezuela had it not been for government policy; it had been expropriated. An executive in Firm 8 (Type 3) observed that his priorities in Latin America were Chile and Venezuela, Venezuela being his firm's largest market on the continent. Still, it had not invested there. An executive in Firm 10 (Type 4), which had a majority-owned facility producing in Venezuela, aired the criticism that Venezuela had a 2 percent interest penalty for foreign borrowers. Curiously, one of this company's major competitors, Firm 38 (Type 5), which had no facility in Venezuela, saw the Venezuelan market in a very negative light. According to a company executive, it was not large enough to warrant production and, consequently, the firm would have to produce for export

TABLE 3.8

Mexican Affiliates by Parent Type and Parent Ownership of Affiliate

| Parent Type | Number of Parents | Number of Affiliates | | | | | | |
		100 Percent Owned	Majority Owned	50–50	Minority Owned	Unknown Ownership	Total
Type 1	0	0	0	0	0	0	0
Type 2	1	0	1	0	0	0	1
Type 3	3	4	0	0	0	2	6
Type 4	8	6	1	0	8	0	15
Type 5	12	6	0	0	20	1	27
Type 6	0	0	0	0	0	0	0
Type 7	1	0	1	0	0	1	2
Total	25	16	3	0	28	4	51

were it to manufacture in Venezuela. The question then arose about whether the regional arrangements, that is, the Andean Pact agreements, would give a Venezuelan product an advantage over exports from the United States or Mexico. The executive doubted it.

Executives in only two firms with investments in Venezuela spoke in detail of their firm's experience there:

Firm 25 (Type 5) had made an investment in a manufacturing enterprise in Venezuela in the mid-1950s, which was currently subject to strict control with respect to expansion. No expansion was permitted without a company commitment with respect to both exports and employment. The export requirement, an executive stated, was considered serious, for in order to export it would be necessary to find a country into which the product could be imported. As one executive observed, the firm was suffering the results of its own success in that it was represented in most countries (a producer of consumer goods for mass consumption, the firm was operating in 27 countries and distributing in some 100). Exports, therefore, could be made only at the expense of another country's output, and this led to consideration of reduced margins in other countries, that is, the allocation of markets and profit. As a result, the imposition of the export requirement by Venezuela was sufficiently onerous to prevent the investment in expansion taking place. (It is useful to note that the company had a similar experience in Argentina, where as it turned out the firm had been more fortunate. It had agreed as a condition for investment to export a certain percentage of production for seven years. Shortly thereafter, the firm had found that the product in question had a much shorter life than that. There was no way it would be able to export this particular product. Fortunately, local demand was sufficient to absorb all of the production, and the firm went back to the government to renegotiate the deal. The firm had been released from its export pledge.)

Firm 42 (Type 5), a producer of animal feeds that was producing locally in Venezuela, had been concerned primarily about price controls. An executive observed that the raising of animals was a very cyclical business and that it would be difficult for a public corporation such as his to maintain credibility in that business since earnings would vary too greatly. It only participated in animal raising in situations where the market demanded that it do so. He cited the example of Venezuelan government policy that almost required the firm to remain in both sectors, feed production and animal raising. The government exerted this pressure via price controls, which it imposed either on meat or on feed but rarely on both. Normally, it rotated the rigor of price controls from one sector to another. That is, if price control were imposed rigorously on feed, the control on animal products was relaxed. The control tended to go back and forth. The government treated both foreign and domestic business the same in this regard. A company spokesman felt that this rotation was simply the response by government to varying consumer pressures—on the one hand, to control the price of meat at the expense of the animal industry; on the other, to control the price of feed at the expense of that industry. Eventually, one or the other hurt badly enough that it countered via political means, and the government relaxed control and imposed price control on the other industry. Where the government came out depended upon the political pressures that either industry could bring at any given moment. The executive was not complaining; he was only describing a situation.

Overall, one heard very little displeasure with Venezuelan policies vis-à-vis foreign investment and, curiously, virtually no discussion of the much publicized Andean Common Market (ANCOM) rules regarding foreign investment and access to ANCOM. Firms simply were not reacting. Thirteen of the 20 affiliates reported were 100 percent foreign owned. Nonetheless, no Type 1 and 2 firms invested and only 2 Type 3s. Sixteen of the 19 foreign affiliates reported were offspring of Type 4 (6), Type 5 (9), and Type 6 (1).

When data for all 34 countries with Type 3 investment policies were aggregated, we found that the opportunists (Type 5) in an even more dominant position in that they reported 60 percent of all affiliates listed for this category of country, 228 out of 381 (see Table 3.9).

When these data are distributed by percentage across these countries (Table 3.10), differentiating between developing and developed countries, the Type 5 parents account for 62 percent of all affiliates in the former, that is, in the Type III developing countries. Type 4 parents (the integrators) report only 19 percent of the total. Again, this is what one would expect in that the screening process imposed by these countries and requirements imposed were less of a barrier to the opportunists than to the integrators.

If one distributes ownership of affiliates across parent types, we discover that both Type 3 and Type 4 parents report wholly owned affiliates in Type III countries in roughly the same proportion, 40 and 41 percent, respectively (see Table 3.11).

TABLE 3.9

Reported Affiliates in Type III Countries by Type of Corporate Parent
(number of parents/number of affiliates)

Country	Corporate Type							Total
	1	2	3	4	5	6	7	
Argentina*	0	1/1	0	1/1	8/15	0	1/2	11/19
Canada	0	3/10	5/11	7/12	13/57	2/4	3/3	33/97
Colombia*	0	0	0	3/3	6/11	1/1	0	10/15
Dominican Republic*	0	0	2/2	0	1/1	0	0	3/3
Egypt*	0	0	0	0	1/1	0	0	1/1
Gabon*	0	0	0	0	0	0	1/1	1/1
Ghana*	0	0	0	0	1/1	0	0	1/1
Greece*	0	0	0	0	2/2	0	1/1	3/3
Guatemala*	0	0	0	1/1	2/2	0	2/2	5/5
Guinea*	0	0	1/1	0	0	0	0	1/1
Honduras*	0	0	0	1/1	0	0	1/6	2/7
Iran*	0	0	0	1/1	1/1	0	0	2/2
Jamaica	0	0	2/2	0	3/4	0	0	5/6
Japan	0	1/1	5/7	6/15	10/35	1/1	1/1	24/60
Kenya*	0	0	0	0	3/3	0	1/1	4/4
Kuwait	0	0	0	1/1	0	0	0	1/1
Malaysia*	0	0	1/1	1/1	7/11	0	0	9/13
Mexico*	0	1/1	3/4	8/15	12/30	0	1/1	25/51
Morocco*	0	0	0	0	3/3	0	0	3/3
Nicaragua*	0	0	0	1/1	1/1	0	0	2/2
Nigeria*	0	0	0	2/2	1/1	0	0	3/3
Norway	0	0	1/1	1/1	0	0	0	2/2
Pakistan*	0	0	0	1/1	1/1	0	0	2/2
South Korea*	0	0	0	3/3	7/11	0	0	10/14
Spain	0	0	3/4	6/7	10/15	0	0	19/26
Sudan*	0	0	0	0	1/1	0	0	1/1
Surinam*	0	0	1/2	0	0	0	0	1/2
Sweden	0	1/2	0	1/1	3/3	0	0	5/6
Turkey*	0	0	0	0	2/2	0	0	2/2
United Arab Emirates	0	0	0	0	2/2	0	0	2/2
Uruguay*	0	0	0	0	2/2	0	1/2	3/4
Venezuela*	0	0	2/2	5/6	7/9	1/1	1/1	16/19
Zaire*	0	0	0	0	1/1	0	0	1/1
Zimbabwe*	0	0	0	0	2/2	0	0	2/2
Total (affiliates)	0	15	37	73	228	7	21	381
Developing countries	0	3	14	36	116	2	17	188
Developed countries	0	12	23	37	112	5	4	193

*Developing countries.

TABLE 3.10

Reported Affiliates in Type III Countries by Type of Corporate Parent
(in percentages within each country)

Country	Corporate Type						
	1	2	3	4	5	6	7
Argentina*	0	5	0	5	79	0	11
Canada	0	10	11	12	59	4	3
Colombia*	0	0	0	20	73	7	0
Dominican Republic*	0	0	67	0	33	0	0
Egypt*	0	0	0	0	100	0	0
Gabon*	0	0	0	0	0	0	100
Ghana*	0	0	0	0	100	0	0
Greece*	0	0	0	0	67	0	33
Guatemala*	0	0	0	20	40	0	40
Guinea*	0	0	100	0	0	0	0
Honduras*	0	0	0	14	0	0	86
Iran*	0	0	0	50	50	0	0
Jamaica*	0	0	33	0	67	0	0
Japan	0	2	12	25	58	2	2
Kenya*	0	0	0	0	75	0	25
Kuwait	0	0	0	100	0	0	0
Malaysia*	0	0	15	0	85	0	0
Mexico*	0	2	8	29	59	0	2
Morocco*	0	0	0	0	100	0	0
Nicaragua*	0	0	0	50	50	0	0
Nigeria*	0	0	0	67	33	0	0
Norway	0	0	50	50	0	0	0
Pakistan*	0	0	0	50	50	0	0
South Korea*	0	0	0	21	79	0	0
Spain	0	0	15	27	58	0	0
Sudan*	0	0	0	0	100	0	0
Surinam*	0	0	100	0	0	0	0
Sweden	0	33	0	17	50	0	0
Turkey*	0	0	0	0	100	0	0
United Arab Emirates	0	0	0	0	100	0	0
Uruguay*	0	0	0	0	50	0	50
Venezuela*	0	0	11	32	47	5	5
Zaire*	0	0	0	0	100	0	0
Zimbabwe*	0	0	0	0	100	40	0
Total (affiliates)	0	4	10	20	60	2	6
Developing countries	0	1	8	19	62	1	9
Developed countries	0	7	12	19	57	3	2

*Developing countries.
Note: Rows may not total 100 because of rounding.

TABLE 3.11

Ownership of Reported Affiliates by Parent Type in Type III Countries
(percentages in parentheses)

Parent Type	Ownership					Total
	100 Percent	Majority	50–50	Minority	Unknown	
Type 1	0	0	0	0	0	0
Type 2	10 (67)	3 (20)	1 (7)	1 (7)	0	15 (100)
Type 3	12 (32)	0	0	6 (16)	20 (53)	38 (100)
Type 4	29 (40)	3 (4)	99 (13)	21 (29)	10 (14)	72 (100)
Type 5	94 (41)	15 (7)	34 (15)	62 (27)	23 (10)	228 (100)
Type 6	3 (43)	1 (14)	0	2 (29)	1 (14)	7 (100)
Type 7	17 (81)	2 (10)	1 (5)	1 (5)	0	21 (100)
Total	165 (43)	24 (6)	45 (12)	93 (24)	54 (14)	381 (100)

Note: Rows may not total 100 because of rounding.

TYPE IV COUNTRIES

Type IV countries, those ostensibly enforcing a policy of selected, negotiated entry with foreign ownership or contract limited in time, included India, Indonesia, Peru, the Philippines, Saudi Arabia, and Sri Lanka. Of greatest interest to investors were India, Indonesia, Peru, and the Philippines.

India

Nine of our 51 sample corporations reported 12 affiliates in India: 4 wholly owned, 2 majority owned, 2 50-50, 4 minority owned. Included were 2 Type 4 parents, 5 Type 5s, 1 Type 6, and 1 Type 7. In addition, 3 had withdrawn, 1 Type 4 and 2 Type 5s.

One company, a Type 5 in the consumer goods industry, had been forced out of India, we were told. Domestic sources had become available and the government did not wish to expand more foreign exchange for the import of materials. An executive in another firm, a Type 3, observed that the blockage of earnings in India from imports had forced his company to become involved in local production, but only temporarily, one judged. In still another, likewise a Type 5, a spokesman reported that it had become almost impossible to secure work permits from the government for expatriots, particularly in the marketing and personnel management areas. If one did not have a formal degree, an expatriate employee—however technically skilled—found it exceedingly difficult to obtain permission to work. An executive in a Type 4 firm mentioned the 40 percent limit on foreign ownership imposed by the Indian government as a reason for caution in entering India. Management in a food processing firm, a Type 4, had been looking at a joint venture proposal in India as part of a continuing search for local sourcing in India in order to qualify the company for participation in large projects there. Thus far, it had only been involved in some subcontracting. Already cited in another context was the case reported by an executive in a large Type 5 company who complained that the Indian government had permitted parent government support in the competition for entry into one sector, which the U.S. firm simply could not match.

Only one firm reported in any detail on its experience in India, a Type 1 food processor. The company held a patent, valid in India, on certain production equipment. Subsequently, it had become known that an Indian company had been infringing the patent, an organization that turned out to have an intimate link with a branch of a U.S. church organization. The upshot was that management had decided that it was poor policy to try to prosecute and so gave the Indian firm a license to manufacture. Meanwhile the U.S. Agency for International Development (AID) had supplied the same equipment to an Indian university, likewise unsanctioned by the firm. When management found out about this transaction, it asked AID for the payment of royalties. The result was that the university donated the equipment to the company's Indian licensee. This had led to a situation, a company executive observed, in which the firm might get paid in other products and, hence, undertake barter for the first time. It had had no initial intention, apparently, of getting involved in India to this extent.

The lack of comment in the interviews with respect to the Indian market led us to conclude that the level of management interest in India generally was low. No one spoke of India with any enthusiasm. Government bureaucracy and regulatory inconsistency were seen as the major problems. The incentives offered were inadequate to offset the risks and uncertainties perceived by management.

Indonesia

Of those countries classified as having a Type IV entry control regime, Indonesia was perhaps of greatest interest, although only seven corporations reported eight operating affiliates in the country (four 100 percent owned, one majority owned, one 50-50, and two unspecified), plus two leased properties. Two others (one Type 5) reported negotiations either in progress or under serious consideration. Two others (one Type 4 and one Type 5) had withdrawn from serious consideration. Executives in only two detailed their respective firms' Indonesian experienced:

Firm 17, a Type 4 producer of chemicals, was not uncharacteristic. An executive contrasted the approach of the Indonesian government with that of Malaysia by noting that each investment in Indonesia required a presidential decree that included "all the packet of goodies" (that is, incentives), which had nevertheless not been a decisive factor for this firm in the investment decision. He noted that the process for obtaining such a decree had been exceedingly slow and frustrating. The prime reason for entering Indonesia had been the existence of a large and growing market. For planning purposes, management looked at a ten-year time span, and it had been hoped that Indonesia would "stay together" that long. An executive noted that government had been unable to guarantee that other companies would not enter the market. Also noted was the requirement that a certain percentage of employees should be

Indonesian (prigumi, or indigenous Indonesian, as opposed to those of Chinese extraction). This had not constituted a problem but had been a factor considered. Initially, a company could start out with 80 percent foreign ownership, we were told, but by the tenth year it was expected to be only 49 percent foreign owned. In this firm's case, the local affiliate had started out as a 50-50 joint venture, although a spokesman for the firm observed that management generally preferred 100 percent ownership. The reason for this policy, he explained, was "he who travels alone travels fastest." Management did agree, however, that spreading ownership had reduced risk. Specifically, in reference to Indonesia, we were informed that the "infrastructure" (read, the administration) had been very slow. The top people were easy to deal with, but the next level of administration was much inferior, and anything below that was "quite hopeless." Management had a complete lack of confidence in the Indonesian bureaucracy. It was fine while the "top guy was there and working with us," but in his absence nothing could be done.

Firm 28, a Type 5 processor of a basic material, had been faced with a rapidly expanding market for its products in Indonesia and had been constantly expanding its local plant, which had been returned to its ownership in 1967 (the plant was expropriated by the Sukarno government several years prior to that time). Under an agreement made with the government in 1968, the Indonesians had insisted that a specific amount of new investment be brought in over a given number of years. Also, the company had been obliged to "agree to consider" the sale of equity at an appropriate time. He added that this vagueness was "typically Indonesian." The upshot was that the government had authorized a given capacity and operation by the firm for 30 years as well as the right to lease land on which the plant was located for a comparable period. The plant itself had been 100 percent owned by the firm. An executive observed that, in his judgment, so long as the firm's operations were seen as useful to the economy, there would be no problem during this period. However, no specific agreement had been entered into with respect to a spinoff of ownership. In 1974 there had been a government pronouncement that foreign companies would be required to sell off 50 percent within ten years. Later, when executives had talked with the chairman of the Indonesian Investment Board, they had been told that this limitation did not apply to the firm's operation, that it was one of the "old guard" companies, apparently meaning a company from the pre-Sukarno era. In any event, no one had pushed the firm to sell off any equity, although a couple of years ago government officials had told the firm that the time was right to begin selling some equity. As a result, the firm had put 15 percent of the company up for public sale, which was very quickly oversubscribed. An executive reported that the company had been "very pleased" with this development. The firm was just then putting in an application for a major expansion, and he felt that the government might well seek further divestiture, although the company might get away without making a commitment. He observed that a Japanese competitor had just put in an application for expansion, and "we see no offer referred to in respect to selling any equity." Also, management had just become aware of a policy statement, internal to the Indonesian government, calling attention to a significant shortfall in capacity in the relevant industry. There was an existing government policy that additional capacity should be allocated among existing producers. In granting new capacity licenses, the government directive apparently specified that such capacity licenses be valid through 1989, that licenses be given only to those companies with "good performance records" (a phrase that went undefined), and that preference be given to those firms with research and development and a technology of international standard. Executives felt that this latter provision meant that small local producers without such technology would be out of the running. One added, however, that there had been no pressure on the firm to do any research and development locally. An export requirement had been suggested for the first time in 1975, when a competitor had tried to increase capacity. An executive commented, "We fought them—that is, their entry—but they finally got in via some payments and a huge export commitment, conditions in the local market permitting." But in the final approval, no export requirement had been mentioned. In the early 1970s, the government had requested that the U.S. firm take over some "derelict plants," which it had done under management contract, which had since run out. It was of interest to note that this firm was producing for an international competitor in its Indonesian plant under a contract manufacturing relationship, apparently as a device to discourage the construction of another plant locally by the competitor. The U.S. firm had occasion recently to add a chief chemist, an expatriate U.S. citizen. To get permission to do so, it had been obliged to offer a three-year training program for a local national replacement. Given the long history of this firm in the country and the profitability of its activities, management was not critical of the pressures from the Indonesians to spin off ownership, undertake exports, and train local nationals.

The same corporation had been operating a plantation in Indonesia under a long-term lease. An executive noted that the government had been very enthusiastic about the firm's getting into a new agricultural development in an undeveloped area. It had been expected that the government would, in fact, provide subsidized financing for the undertaking. The Indonesian five-year program was very ambitious and, if implemented, it would mean that Indonesia would become the world's premier producer of a particular raw material. The government had required that Indonesian nationals hold a majority interest in the project. On its part, the firm had required that the government guarantee any loans used in the project, grant the firm a full management contract for the life of the agreement, and approve "bridge ownership" held by the International Finance Corporation (IFC) which, under Indonesian law, had been considered to be a local owner. In such event, the government's Estate Agency would have ended up owning less than 50 percent. The new ground rule for such an agreement had been 30 years, plus 25, for a total of 55. The life cycle of a planting, an executive explained, was somewhat less than this. The product derived from the project was to have been sold on the open market at international prices, subject only to a specified ad valorem percent export tax. The Indonesian government had been trying to impose the use of Indonesian flag carriers to move the exports, but this had not constituted a serious problem, an executive explained. The proposal had also carried a provision for external arbitration and the use of the International Center for the Settlement of Investment Disputes (ICSID). The firm expected to receive a tax holiday. The law provided for four years for agricultural projects, but this particular project, the executive opined, would probably receive pioneer status and, hence, be awarded a somewhat longer tax holiday. The firm had been trying to convince the government to give the tax holiday commencing from the inception of profits, which would probably be 10 or 12 years from the planting. The government position was that the tax holiday should start with commercial production. Asked how the firm could justify investment in a project that would not generate revenue for 10 to 12 years, the executive responded that it could do so only if it received subsidized loans, possibly at 6 to 8 percent. The company was talking about going in on a 30 percent ownership basis, with the balance owned by the IFC and the government-owned Estate Agency holding the other 70 percent, possibly split 30-40 between them. Hence, it would be an "off-balance sheet" project. An executive felt that such treatment made justification of the project easier than might otherwise be the case. It was pointed out that Indonesian law required that 25 percent of the capital be paid in at the start of the project. The firm would construct its own processing plant. Executives expected the arrangement to be approved by both sides.

The managements of two corporations explained the reasons their firms had desisted from entering Indonesia. Firm 18 (Type 4) had a strong preference for 100 percent ownership, although an executive admitted that it had sometimes accepted less than that, depending upon circumstances. He noted that, in a number of cases, local restrictions had forced a spinoff of ownership over time and cited Indonesia as an example. Thus far, it had rejected all Indonesian projects, in part for this reason, although the market had been attractive.

Firm 36 (Type 4) likewise saw Indonesia as a large market, but it had no operations there. This was due to corruption, an executive explained. Management felt that the political environment was unreliable and that government promises would probably not be kept. Also, the firm had faced a smuggling problem of its own product into Indonesia, which probably could not be constrained even if it were to produce there.

Another company in the electronics sector (Type 4) had picked Singapore over Indonesia (and Thailand and Malaysia as well). Two of the firms investing in Singapore had been interested in Indonesia but had rejected projects there for undisclosed reasons.

It should be noted that while the top government personnel were highly regarded, the corruption and inefficiency of the lower bureaucracy had rendered the Indonesian investment policies less effective than they might otherwise be. In actual implementation, the requirement with respect to ownership spinoff was not viewed as unduly onerous, but of the seven investing firms, four were opportunists (Type 5) and three were integrators (Type 4). Those data conform to the pattern; the opportunists become more evident as country policies become more restrictive (see Table 6.4).

Peru

Six firms reported seven enterprises in Peru, four of which were 100 percent owned, two minority owned, and one unspecified. Of the six firms, one was a Type 2, one a Type 3, four were Type 5s. Executives in only two firms spoke of Peru in any detail, one of which was a noninvestor.

The first, a rather small manufacturer of mining machinery (Type 1), had considered a Latin American investment and had singled out Peru. An executive commented that the objective had been to serve both the Latin American market and the Andean Common Market, and also the Peruvian market. He reported that management had looked at Bolivia and Chile as well but had been more favorably inclined toward Peru. Brazil, he said, had not been included because it constituted a lesser market for his firm's machines. Thus far, the company had been able to cover the South American market out of the United States, but he felt that the firm might be on the verge of losing business to foreign competition, particularly to English and Australian manufacturers. Despite the inability of the firm to meet competitors' terms, with respect to export financing, management hoped that the Peruvians and others would recognize the superior quality and durability of the firm's machines. It was not convinced, however, that this would happen because its equipment had been used for many years in Peru and that of its competitors not long enough to test durability. An executive felt that if the firm did move into Peru a joint venture would be necessary, given Peruvian restrictions, and he did not know how his board would look at the idea of a joint venture with a local majority. He did not feel that the company could maintain control through its technology because the technology was not really that sophisticated nor could it be protected via patents. Management would not feel comfortable, he felt, with a management contract and control through contract because of doubts about the enforceability of such contracts in case of conflict. The upshot was that negotiations had been initiated.

A food processor, a Type 5, had made an investment in Peru over ten years before. Originally, tax exemption had been given, which had been scaled. That is, it had consisted of a 100 percent holiday for the first five years, 50 percent for the next five, and 25 for the next five. In any event, by the end of the sixth or seventh year of operation, the direction of development had become very evident. The firm's local business was still profitable, but it had made sense, according to the executive, to forgo the balance of the tax holiday because it was becoming "a subject of conversation, not ours, but in general." He felt that the writing had been on the wall to disallow such tax incentives for foreign business. The corporation was, however, still in business in Peru.

The only general observation that could be made about reactions to Peru was a lack of interest. The market was seen as small and the regime unstable, in terms of its track record in changing the relevant rules. No one seemed to know what to expect next.

The Philippines

Twelve of the 51 companies (2 Type 3, 1 Type 4, 1 Type 5, 2 Type 6, and 1 Type 7) had 14 operating facilities in the Philippines. Of these, 9 were 100 percent owned, 2 minority owned, and 3 unspecified. Another (a Type 5) was seriously considering a Philippine undertaking; a second (a Type 2) had done so but withdrawn; a third (a Type 1) had liquidated a minority position; a fourth

(Type 4) had liquidated its interest in some land holdings and with-drawn a technical assistance contractual relationship. Spokesmen for 4 of the 13 investing companies described these experiences:

Firm 24 (Type 5) was in a Philippine joint venture with an-other foreign company, which meant that the Philippine enterprise was 100 percent foreign owned, although the U.S. firm had only a minority interest. This ownership had been permitted inasmuch as the venture had been established before the regulations forcing the spinoff of foreign ownership to 60 percent had been decreed. How-ever, a newer venture by its foreign partner had obliged it to enter into an agreement to spin off some ownership over time.

Firm 25 (Type 5) had invested in a manufacturing facility in the Philippines over ten years before. The firm had built what an executive called a "mini plant" on the understanding that the govern-ment was going to "lock us out" with high tariffs. The tariffs were never imposed; so the company had been facing serious competition from imports.

Firm 33 (Type 6) had what an executive called "virtually a portfolio investment with a technical service contract." At the time, the company had taken a small minority interest in the largest Phil-ippine corporation in its industry. Subsequently, that share had been reduced even further. The company had not and would not put any more money into the Philippine investment, an executive ex-plained, due to the corrupt nature of the country. "We are very conservative in our investments," he added.

Firm 44 (Type 5), which was in an industry closely related to that of Firm 33, had a somewhat similar experience. It had moved into a 100 percent ownership position of its Philippine operation be-cause "the way decisions were being made there were inappropriate," as one executive explained. He called a joint venture in that atmo-sphere "impossible."

In short, we unearthed no serious objections to the Philippine foreign investment policy, including the ownership spinoff provi-sions, but did find a great deal of concern with the politicization of business and the corruption encountered both at a public and private level. From the vantage point of the executives interviewed, the Philippine investment policies were not being implemented fairly and honestly. One firm, not included above, had withdrawn because of the Philippine law barring foreign ownership of land. Others, however, had found ways of circumventing the law. Executives in Firm 5 (Type 1) described what seemed to have been a relatively typical situation. Their company had been in a minority position in a Philippines venture but had decided to get out by reason of "political implication. " It had an engineer on the site for a little over a year, as well as a manager. The Philippine company was still acting as its agent for sales in the Philippines. The upshot was that the plant had been constructed entirely by the firm's ex-Philippine partner. The U.S. firm had perceived, part way through the project, that the operation of the plant had changed from a normal business venture to one that was heavily politicized in that the government would supply the raw material, the plant would process it at a negotiated price, and sell the product back to the government. Management knew, according to one executive, that the project would be a big money maker, but it also realized that it would be unwise to continue its involvement because of the political implications and the unfavorable publicity that it might eventually receive. The firm was able to negotiate a withdrawal without financial loss.

All told, 46 affiliates were reported from the 6 countries classified as having Type IV investment policies. We would have expected to see an even higher percentage of opportunist parents (Type 5), but such was not the case (see Tables 3.12 and 3.13). The percentage was 58 (26 of 46) and 21 percent (9 of 46) for the integrators (Type 4). Comparable figures for those countries with Type III policies were almost the same: 60 and 20 percent, respectively. That is, despite the greater restrictiveness of the investment policies in this group of countries, the percentage of affiliates with Type 4 parents was not lower than that in the Type III countries with somewhat less restrictive environment. Possibly the explanation lay in the fact that a curiously large percentage of the affiliates were wholly owned (22 of 46, or 48 percent) plus another 9 percent that were majority owned (see Table 3.14). Well over half (65 percent) were at least 50 percent owned by the foreign parent, despite the allegedly restrictive policies of these countries. The explanation may lie in the fact that policies of these countries were peculiarly vulnerable to evasion through extralegal payments. That is, for any corporation that desired "to play the game, " the official policy could be effectively waived. Even so, at least 3 (2 in India, 1 in Saudi Arabia) of the 8 Type 4 offspring reported 25 minority-owned affiliates, that is, 50 percent of Type 4 affiliates for which ownership was specified.

TYPE V COUNTRIES

At the time of the preparation of our 1980 study, Yugoslavia was the only interesting example of the more moderate socialist model, Type V in our typology, which was defined by an active posture in attracting direct foreign investment into those activities

TABLE 3.12

Reported Affiliates in Type IV Countries
by Type of Corporate Parent
(number of parents/number of affiliates)

Country	Corporate Type 1	2	3	4	5	6	7	Total
India	0	0	0	2/2	5/7	1/2	1/1	9/12
Indonesia	0	0	0/0	3/3	4/5	0	0	7/8
Peru	0	1/1	1/2	0	4/4	0	0	6/7
Philippines	0	0	1/2	2/2	7/7	1/1	2/2	12/14
Saudi Arabia*	0	0	0	2/2	2/2	0	0	4/4
Sri Lanka	0	0	0	0	1/1	0	0	1/1
Total	0	1	4	9	26	3	3	46
Developing countries	0	1	4	7	24	3	3	42
Developed countries	0	0	0	2	2	0	0	4

*Developing country.

TABLE 3.13

Reported Affiliates in Type IV Countries
by Type of Corporate Parent
(in percentages within each country)

Country	Corporate Type 1	2	3	4	5	6	7
India	0	0	0	17	58	17	8
Indonesia	0	0	0	38	63	0	0
Peru	0	14	29	0	57	0	0
Philippines	0	0	14	14	50	7	14
Saudi Arabia*	0	0	0	50	50	0	0
Sri Lanka	0	0	0	0	100	0	0
Total	0	2	10	21	58	2	6
Developing countries	0	2	10	17	57	7	7
Developed countries	0	0	0	50	50	0	0

*Developing country.
Note: Rows may not total 100 because of rounding.

TABLE 3.14

Affiliates in Type IV Countries by Parent Type and Ownership of Affiliate

Corporate Type	100 Percent	Majority	Ownership 50-50	Minority	Unknown	Total
Type 1	0	0	0	0	0	0
Type 2	1	0	0	1	0	2
Type 3	0	0	0	2	2	4
Type 4	2	1	0	3	2	8
Type 5	13	3	4	4	1	25
Type 6	4	0	0	0	0	4
Type 7	2	0	0	1	0	3
Total	22	4	4	11	5	46

deemed to be desirable but with a 49 percent foreign ownership limit. Subsequent to the writing of that analysis, the People's Republic of China came out with its foreign investment law designed to encourage foreign participation in joint ventures in which the foreign equity was to be not less than 25 percent. As previously noted, several of the executives in our present survey indicated their surprise at the greater flexibility and lesser suspicion and hostility exhibited by these avowedly Marxist governments than by some of the more capitalistically inclined governments of the Third World. Many Latin American and African governments, both rightist and leftist, were seen by executives as basically against foreign business. Their investment programs were seen at best as permissive rather than supportive. Attitudes toward government policies in East Asia were somewhat more receptive. There, executives saw support at the top echelons of government but often hostility and corruption at the lower. In Yugoslavia and China, executives saw problems but not flowing from government policy or the underlying ideological posture of these regimes. No corruption was reported in either case.

Yugoslavia

Five firms (four Type 5, one Type 4) reported six operations in Yugoslavia, all minority owned, as required by law. One had been there since 1973, a company that had adopted a general policy of joint venturing; all of its foreign ventures during the past ten years had been jointly owned. Another company (Firm 25, a Type 5) had gone into a 45 percent venture with a Yugoslav enterprise, essentially an operation to support its West German subsidiary. Three others spoke of their experience in Yugoslavia in some detail:

Firm 6 (Type 5) had entered into a joint venture agreement in Yugoslavia to manufacture a particular industrial chemical. What was proposed was a multimillion dollar plant soon to be operational. The purpose was to capture more of the Yugoslav market. If the firm did not do it, a competitor would, an executive observed. He added, "We in the treasurer's office were very negative." The problem, as he saw it, was that the firm would not have adequate control. Even though it might have a veto power over certain decisions, there was no way it could really "run" an East European operation, in the opinion of this executive. Apparently, company representatives had spoken to those in another U.S. firm that had moved into a Yugoslav joint venture some time before, but he had not been persuaded by the good reports from this other firm. For it, the risk might have been acceptable. He also pointed out that a number of top people had spent a couple of years on the Yugoslav project when they should have been doing something else of more immediate value to the firm. The project had been approved, he felt, because the company was putting in an obsolete technology. "When you are coming out of the dark ages," he observed, "what else?" Consequently, the firm was committing very little cash investment and, at least at the start, it could sell its product to the joint venture. He predicted that it would prove difficult to capture profits since there were inherent conflicts between the two partners. The Yugoslavs obviously wanted to export the product to Western Europe, whereas it would be against the U.S. firm's interest to add competition in already developed markets. One of the problems, as he saw it, was that the Yugoslavs could have gone elsewhere for newer technology. The company's real edge was in its marketing expertise, plus the use of its well-established brand name, which was number one in the industry worldwide. Asked about incentives in the form of government guarantees, he observed that protection had been offered with respect to the division of income, which we gathered to mean a guarantee of the convertibility of profits. But the problem remained, in his view. The Yugoslav partner could control whether there was any profit or not. There was the additional problem in that the Yugoslavs were much interested in maximizing employment and dispersing industry into rural areas, in one of which this plant was being constructed. The Yugoslav border was to be closed to competing imports so long as local manufacture was taking place, but he did not feel confident that this would prove to be the case. He observed that one is better off if involved with a product essential to national interest, which he did not feel this to be. The most important criterion for the success of a joint venture, he observed, was compatibility with national interest. "But," he added, "despite the misgivings of the treasurer's department, marketing carried the day." They felt that there would be a market in Eastern Europe, and that Yugoslavia could become a principal source. He added, "It is naive to think of owning 100 percent of a foreign company any more. In the long run, national interest will prevail, and the days of exporting obsolete stuff to a new market are over." Obviously, this executive did not object to the joint venture notion, but rather to the possible conflict of interest that might arise specifically in the Yugoslav venture.

Firm 17 (Type 5) had been sought out by a Yugoslav enterprise. The firm had been selling certain chemical products into the country, and it so happened that the Yugoslavs had approached the firm at the very time that it was considering producing within the country. Negotiations started, in which the provincial government had been very much involved in that a variety of permits would be required at that level. It, in turn, had proved to be supportive later when various permits were needed from the federal government. Finance was made available for the project through a foreign bank consortium in the form of a loan to the partnership that emerged. The firm's involvement in this relatively small project led the Yugoslavs to ask the firm to put together a much larger industrial complex, in which one of Yugoslavia's largest enterprises would be involved. A spokesman for the firm observed that the principal Yugoslav negotiator had been a very strong individual who wore two hats, one as a government representative and the other as the chief representative of the Yugoslav enterprise. After the project had been sketched out and initial agreement reached, he had become the joint venture's leading proponent in Belgrade vis-à-vis the federal government in negotiating final approval. The conditions that emerged were: (1) that the U.S. firm's ownership be limited to 49 percent; (2) that the firm agree to transfer modern technology (which was specified in a subsidiary licensing agreement); (3) that the joint venture earn enough foreign exchange via exports to cover its needs (imports, depreciation on the foreign capital, payment of interest, and dividends). No time limit on the venture was specified. The Yugoslavs did not insist on a performance guarantee with respect to the plant, possibly because they realized that the U.S. firm's resources were at risk, just as were their own. No tax holidays had been given, and no accelerated depreciation provided. There were export incentives in the form of export rebates to be paid by the federal government in order to keep the exports competitive in the international market. Insofar as transfer prices between the U.S. firm and the joint venture were concerned, both parties agreed that prices in the international market could be easily verified. In any event, pricing formulas were spelled out in the basic agreement and included import costs and the freight to Western Europe, which was assumed to be the major market for earning hard currency. There had been no insistence that the U.S. partner withdraw either managers or technicians over time. On the contrary, the Yugoslavs wanted the firm to continue supplying personnel as long as possible. Asked why the firm had become interested in Yugoslavia in the first instance, an executive responded that management had felt the risk to be low (even though the commitment had been made prior to Tito's death), that a reasonable return was expected, and that the project provided an opportunity to work within a socialist country and with a self-management system. The executive observed that worker participation in management was possibly a forerunner of what one might anticipate in Western Europe and elsewhere in years to come. He cited as an example the intense interest of the People's Republic of China in the Yugoslav notion of self-management. The Yugoslav project was an opportunity, management felt, to learn how to work with such a system effectively. In retrospect, an executive reported, the firm had found the Yugoslav system as being quite adaptable to the needs of a Western investor. For example, in the joint venture, job positions had been posted, and salaries and assignments recommended by the Joint Business Board had not been questioned by the Workers' Council. Management had had no difficulty in convincing the council that people doing more demanding work should receive more pay. "At the start," one executive said, "we got approval from the Workers' Council to give bonuses to people who, in our opinion, did outstanding jobs in getting the plant started." Another executive observed that the Joint Business Board initiated action and thus far "we have always gotten approval for what had been suggested. Of course, this sometimes requires some preselling." The main problem that had evolved had to do with Yugoslavia's balance-of-payments problems and its slowdown of economic growth, generally. Had it been a wise investment? The firm's response was that one had to look at the total package, which involved increased sales in Yugoslavia for a variety of the U.S. firm's products and a contract for increased purchase of chemical inputs by the joint venture. There had been, in one executive's opinion, very little exposure for the firm, in that 75 percent of the cash investment had been borrowed from local banks and the foreign investment had been very largely derived from the export credit agencies of various governments from which countries capital equipment had been obtained. Although the larger complex was somewhat behind schedule and would not be fully functional for another year or so, the original plant had been operating and producing profits. Incidentally, the delay in the startup of the large complex was, an executive admitted, as much the fault of the U.S. firm as of the Yugoslavs in that there had been some problems in retaining key U.S. personnel due to a number of unfortunate personnel events. There had been no problem in getting permission to replace people or in obtaining work permits for them. The Yugoslav government had put in the infrastructure necessary for the project, without charging the project but with the understanding that when the plant was on stream it would pay "nominal fees." In the long run, the U.S. firm would probably retain only four or five expatriates in Yugoslavia—possibly the head marketing employee, the head technical employee, the head financial employee, and one or two others—but the head of the enterprise was a Yugoslav. The project would export entirely via the U.S. firm's international distribution network.

Transfer prices would not be a problem, executives felt, because these would be products traded elsewhere. The firm would simply get paid a commission for handling the export on a "net-back-less-commission" basis. Asked about possible conflict of interest, if the firm had a choice between selling a product from the joint venture and a product from a wholly owned subsidiary in Western Europe (it had several), an executive said that he did not anticipate a problem in this regard. Admittedly, the Yugoslav venture, as noted, did have an export requirement to meet if it were to cover its foreign exchange requirements. But in any event, most of the production would be sold within the country at the start, and local consumption could be well over 50 percent for some years, although this might well go down over the longer run. The U.S. government had been helpful in the project via ambassadorial support. An OPIC guarantee had not been used; it was felt to be too expensive, given the risk involved. The Export-Import Bank of the United States did participate, but to a much lesser extent than the firm had hoped initially. Because of this restraint, the Yugoslavs had been stimulated to buy much more of the capital equipment elsewhere than would have been the case otherwise.

Firm 22 (Type 4) had committed itself to participate in a 49 percent-owned joint venture with a Yugoslav enterprise in the food processing industry for the manufacture of three specific products. The first was already being manufactured in Yugoslavia but not well. In this case, the U.S. firm had merely contributed know-how. The other products had not been produced in the country previously. The attractions had been (1) that the Yugoslavs permitted 49 percent ownership and equal representation on the joint board; and (2) that the firm had been allowed to import, duty-free, the two products new to the market for the purpose of a six-month test marketing operation (the results of which had been considered very promising). Most of the U.S. firm's equity had been in the form of capitalized technology, and only 22 percent had been a cash injection. One requirement imposed had been that the joint venture export $2 worth of goods for every $1 of dividends repatriated. This had been a very stringent requirement in the firm's view; so it had insisted on making some profit on the raw materials it would sell to the joint venture, which was an arrangement agreeable to the Yugoslavs. An executive observed that Yugoslav enterprise had been a high-cost manufacturing company and that his firm was already manufacturing the same products in at least 16 other countries. Additionally, there had been strict price controls on the three products within Yugoslavia. Therefore, he expected that the joint venture would never show "a bottom line profit." He did mention that there might be some possibility of export to such countries as Syria and Libya, which had "reasonably good relations with Yugoslavia," although such sales would be incidental and certainly had not been a reason for investing in the venture. The major reason, he admitted, had been the opportunity to sell more of the firm's products profitably in Yugoslavia. It had negotiated an agreement to import into Yugoslavia a one-year's supply of materials. Any further imports were likely to depend on the joint venture's ability to export. At this point, the U.S. management was not concerned, although it was watching the situation. It appeared that it might be able to buy Yugoslav meat for the Italian market, where it had an importing partner. An executive noted that the firm had asked for tax incentives for the Yugoslav venture, but had been unable to get any. It had also applied for OPIC guarantees, which, much to the firm's surprise, had not been forthcoming. At the time of the interview, the firm was still awaiting official Yugoslav government approval to operate, although construction of the facilities was well under way. Only one representative of the U.S. firm, a U.S. citizen, was in Yugoslavia. He was described as the "nominal marketing director." The original investigation of the project had been launched some three years before, and since then a number of factors had changed. An executive opined that a call for any further cash investment would probably be subject to "further evaluation of the situation." He noted the precarious economic position of Yugoslavia and the fact that the foreign debt per capita was substantially greater than that of Poland. Inflation, he pointed out, was currently running in the region of 50 percent per annum. Although clearly worried about the commercial success of the venture, the executive's comments reflected no lack of confidence in the Yugoslavs or any indication that this firm had not been treated fairly.

It would seem that these accounts relative to Yugoslavia speak for themselves. They convey quite a different feeling from most of those relating to Latin America, Africa, and East Asia. It should be noted that four of the five investing firms were opportunists (Type 5).

People's Republic of China

Although not included in the 1957-59 study, the People's Republic of China had generated sufficient management interest to warrant inclusion in the present survey. If anything, on the face of it, the Chinese entry control policy was even less restrictive than that of Yugoslavia. However, in practice it was entirely too early to pass judgment, and the lengthy negotiation preceding any investment was an important and costly barrier in itself. Although the regulations specified that direct foreign investment must constitute at least 25 percent of the equity of a Chinese enterprise, with no upper limit specified, in fact, all of the discussion we encountered had to do either with a contractual relationship or a minority foreign holding. There was some hint that 100 percent foreign ownership might be permitted in one of China's new processing or export trade zones, but no executive in this sample referred to that possibility. However, of the 51 firms in the survey, 7 were either considering an activity in China or were in the process of negotiation; 2 others had entered technical agreements; 1 had been exploring offshore for oil; and 1 had entered into a joint venture agreement in a minority position. All told, executives in 18 firms expressed some degree of interest (1 Type 1, 2 Type 2, 3 Type 3, 3 Type 4, 7 Type 5, 1 Type 6, and 1 Type 7).

Firm 3 (Type 3) had participated in a major geophysical evaluation program off the Chinese coast during the past year. The firm, along with others, was awaiting word from the PRC government on the parcels that would be put out to bid and the contract terms for exploration work.

Firm 4 (Type 4) had recently signed agreements with China involving hydropower equipment and related technologies for the development of China's hydroelectric industry.

Firm 9 (Type 4) had been interested in China for some time, and the corporation's president was currently on the board of a national U.S.-China trade organization. An executive felt that the firm would probably focus its attention on China sometime in late 1982. The problem was that the company was spending so much time at that moment trying to survive in today's market, that management had little time to give attention to moves to expand, whether in the United States or elsewhere. He felt that China really did not have anything to trade, even though its people were probably very trainable. In any event, the time commitment would have to be very long term.

Firm 5 (Type 1) had held seminars for the Chinese Ministry of Food in Beijing and was working very hard on putting together some sort of project in China. The current discussion was with an organization that wanted to produce edible proteins. One of the major obstacles had been, according to one executive, that the Chinese had placed a value on the land on which the proposed plant would be built, which management felt to be unreasonable. Conversations had been in terms of a joint venture in which the land would be part of the Chinese contribution. Also, there was an export problem. Management felt that there were already more than adequate production facilities worldwide to meet current demand, but the Chinese wanted to export. The question was: In what other facility would capacity be cut? In fact, China wanted an export commitment in terms of a given percentage of the output of the Chinese plant. This executive felt that "the lack of business people" in China had been a "big headache." Management had even discussed the possibility of taking coal in payment for its services and had talked to several Japanese trading companies about marketing the coal. However, the firm's principal business was in the agricultural and food sector. Management felt very uneasy about taking coal for sale worldwide.

Firm 13 (Type 2), a machinery manufacturer, was in the process of negotiating a license in China, a process that had been going on for about ten years, according to one executive. He suspected that it would "be tied up" very soon. Thereafter, it would require another five to ten years before significant production could be achieved.

Firm 14 (Type 5) had signed a ten-year technical assistance and license agreement with China for the sale and manufacture of a series of engines. It was reported that the signing of the agreement culminated two and a half years of intensive consultation and negotiation. It was still subject to the approval of both the PRC and U.S. governments, the latter due to the fact that the arrangement called for the export of possibly sensitive technology to a communist country.

Firm 17 (Type 5) had had a lot of contact with China, including an internship in the U.S. firm for three months for a Chinese professor, who had made "a very substantial impression" on the firm's management. It was hoped that he could be induced to spend further time in the company's Hong Kong office. According to one executive, the firm had signed a protocol with the Chinese government at the very time it had been terminating a number of contracts with the Japanese. He felt that this move had been an indication on the part of the Chinese of the high regard that China had for his company. He stated that the firm was attempting to negotiate a joint venture project with a Chinese enterprise, but no further details were revealed.

Firm 21 (Type 4) had actually negotiated a provisional joint venture agreement with a Chinese enterprise with respect to the construction of two plants, one for electronic devices and one for pneumatic equipment. The agreement was to run for 20 years, and a team of Chinese technicians had recently completed six months' training in one of the firm's U.S. plants. The main problem with investment in China, an executive observed, was related to the foreign exchange situation and the requirement that the foreign partner take payment in product. The U.S. firm had indicated that it would be willing to take goods presently purchased from other sources. Another problem related to the Chinese perception of patent laws in that many of the products the firm would buy in China would be in apparent violation of patents owned by others. Another problem had to do with scale of operations; the Chinese wished to have relatively large-scale plants, but the U.S. firm could only take products commensurate with a much smaller operation. He felt that if the Chinese really wanted a large-scale operation, they would have to find the foreign exchange. Another concern of the U.S. management was that China might slip back to its previous restrictive policies, thereby leaving the firm without a source of product. Finally, the executive observed, there were very few commercially minded people with whom the firm could negotiate. He thought that the Chinese were having some difficulty "being capitalists."

Firm 28 (Type 5) had corporate executives in China many times, but thus far nothing had materialized. Sales to China, however, had been good, according to one executive, partly because of contacts the firm had made there many years ago. Obviously, the firm was interested in working out some continuing relationship.

Firm 29 (Type 6) had made a study of possible business opportunities in China. The chairman of the board had made a trip recently to China upon the invitation of the Chinese government. An executive speculated that it was "likely" that the firm would "go into" the natural resource area in China. Thus far, no agreement had been reached. One sticking point had been the Chinese unwillingness to pay for the technology and insistence that the firm take interest in a joint venture instead.

Firm 30 (Type 2) had been interested in negotiating a joint venture or "some other arrangement" in China. But, as one executive observed, the delay on the part of the Chinese had been discouraging. On one occasion, the Chinese had promised to visit the corporate headquarters in the United States but had simply not showed up. The executive felt that perhaps the timing had been a bit premature, but management was watching the situation closely. There was considerable uncertainty, he reported, with respect to the foreign investment and foreign exchange laws in China. "No one knows the Chinese priorities," he said.

Firm 32 (Type 5) had sold a lot of machinery to China, but recently sales had slowed up substantially. Subsequently, the firm had sent a large team to China to train people for servicing the equipment. No manufacturing proposal had been made yet by either side, according to one executive. He felt that such a development was a little premature but that it would undoubtedly come.

Firm 38 (Type 5) had sent a delegation to China the year before in response to what executives perceived to be a large market.

Firm 40 (Type 5) had become the "first known Western consumer goods company to open a service center" in China—even though the firm's products had not been sold there since 1949. It reported that it had been doing a substantial volume of business since.

Firm 42 (Type 5) had been the target of a number of consultants and others trying to get the firm interested in some project in China. The executive with whom we talked had met a couple of Chinese delegations, but thus far the corporation had done nothing. He also mentioned that their specialists in protein had talked with the Chinese and that if the firm did anything in China, it would probably be in that area initially, even though it might not be for another ten years or so. He then pointed out that a U.S. grain-milling company had agreed to build a poultry and animal feed plant in China. He observed that such companies had always had a significant grain trade with China and that they were essentially trading companies; hence their expertise was more relevant to the needs of China at the moment than that of his firm.

Firm 47 (Type 3) had been looking at China as a possible site for manufacturing one of its products.

Firm 49 (Type 7) had been involved in negotiations with China, and the chairman of the board had been there very recently. Management's interest lay in the production of two food products. An executive observed that negotiations had gone very slowly, but he felt that this was the Chinese government's "way of doing things." He believed it had overcommitted itself in recent years and that, within U.S. business, it had become something of a fad to get into China. He felt personally that relations would develop slowly, but the slow pace did not discourage the firm.

Firm 51 (Type 3) had signed what was called "an historic agreement" with China for technology transfer and the supply of some heavy equipment in the electrical machinery field. This was, a company spokesman said, the first major electrical equipment and technology contract between China and a U.S. company.

The general tenor of these comments by corporate executives was that doing business in China was slow and that few Chinese negotiators were commercially minded. However, long-term agreements and joint ventures had been negotiated. There was no hint of deliberate bureaucratic obstructionism or corruption. Of the 18 firms in which interest in China had surfaced, almost half (7) were of Type 5, while the other half attracted to China were scattered with regard to type. Firm 21, the only company that had actually consummated a joint venture, was an integrator (Type 4). A decisive factor apparently had been the desire to plug a Chinese source into its production system.

It should be noted that in neither Type V country, Yugoslavia or China, did any executive suggest that concern about being under pressure to accept a minority equity position, rather than a majority role, had blocked his firm's involvement. There seemed to be no exception to the minority rule; in all seven affiliates reported from the two countries, the foreign interest was a minority one. Significantly, the opportunists (Type 5) were involved in 71 percent of the ventures (five out of seven).

4

Performance Requirements and Incentives

In our survey of corporate experience and executive opinion, we were able to separate out 12 areas in which host governments had either explicitly or implicitly imposed performance requirements on foreign business firms. In some cases, of course, these requirements had been placed on both foreign and domestic enterprises, although it was not the purpose of this study to address that issue directly. The areas in which requirements had been imposed were: export level; ownership; employment of foreign nationals; local consent; employment; investment; production level; local research and development; training; product; level of technology; and location.

It will be noted that the requirements did not always run in the same direction. In some cases, a host government tried to depress foreign ownership; in others, to increase it. In some instances, the use of foreign technicians and managers might be discouraged; in others, the reverse. In some situations, a host government might require the transfer of "modern" or "advanced" technology; in others, "appropriate" or labor-intensive. In some cases, the commitments imposed might not be entirely consistent, such as the requirement that "high" technology be used (assuming that meant capital-intensive technology) and a high level of employment be maintained at the same time, or the imposition of production limits (if that meant that economy of scale could not be achieved) and simultaneous pressure for greater export.

Also, as certain cases revealed in the last chapter, it was not always easy for a corporation to respond to these host government requirements. For a firm organized into regional profit centers—

for example, North America, Latin America, Middle East, Africa, Europe, and the Pacific—an export requirement could mean that some other region would have to import. Unless that import were fully competitive in terms of price, quality, and delivery, the other regional headquarters might well resist. Even so, those other corporate divisions undoubtedly had already developed a network of suppliers with whom they were accustomed to work and with whom they were linked by contract. An example was the automotive firm that had been obliged to export from Mexico to keep its Mexican affiliate operating. The logical buyer was the North American company, the management of which resisted vigorously. The Mexican product was not competitive with other sources, and the North American division of the corporation was a profit center. And how was the firm with approximately 60 plants scattered around the world expected to export from all of the countries in which it was producing? Nor was it only the developing countries that felt compelled to press for exports because of persistent balance-of-payments problems.

It may be true that corporations organized by product group, in which each global product group was a profit center, had a somewhat easier time in satisfying export requirements—that is, so long as the products did not move from one product division to another. The logistical decision could be made by a single decision-making body. However, it cannot be claimed that our study demonstrated this to be true. All one can say is that it would be surprising if it were not.

We came across no instance in which a firm had been obliged to post a bond or deposit funds in a blocked account as tangible guarantee that it would fulfill a specific performance requirement.

Executives in several firms expressed uneasiness about possible nonfulfillment of commitments made. An interviewee in one firm reported that his management was quite worried about promising what it could not deliver in terms of specific requirements for exporting, external financing, ownership, and employment. In another firm, an executive admitted that management was very much concerned about living up to commitments in Mexico with respect to exports. But in another, management felt that the Norwegian government had not lived up to its side of the bargain and, hence, the firm was absolved from fulfilling the employment commitment it had made.

Export Requirements

We noted at least 17 countries that had requested that firms enter into export commitments, most frequently from Brazil (11 cases) and Mexico (6 cases), Colombia (2 cases); from all others, 1 each.* In some instances, a commitment to export had led to the relaxation of ownership requirements (Mexico and India) or to a reduction of the local content requirement (Australia and Mexico). In others, such a commitment had been a precondition for the right to import. At least one country had treated all of the local affiliates of a given U.S. firm as a single unit for the purpose of calculating export credits for import rights (Brazil). The tradeoff between exports and import rights varied somewhat from country to country and apparently, even from company to company within a single country. The standard seemed to have been a one-to-one tradeoff; that is, a dollar's worth of exports would give the right to purchase a dollar's worth of foreign exchange for imports, but it might go as high as three to one (as it had in Brazil in at least one case). In Yugoslavia, a local affiliate had been required to earn all of its foreign exchange requirements, whether used for imports or remittances of earnings, fees, and depreciation allowance. In some cases, a firm had been required simply to export a given percentage of its production. Five firms had refused to enter into such commitments but no pattern emerged. The question had arisen in one country (Mexico) about whether a U.S. affiliate could capture the export credits (that is, credits arising out of exports that could be used to secure license to import) earned by a local subcontractor. The rule of thumb seemed to be that such was possible if the foreign customer of the subcontractor's export were the parent or an associated firm of the U.S. affiliate, or if it could be demonstrated that the exports had been made possible by the subcontractor's association with the affiliate. One way to be certain of capturing export credits, of course, was for the affiliate to invest significantly in its subcontractors. The Mexican affiliate of one U.S. firm had acquired minority interest in a number of its Mexican suppliers to lay claim to the latter's export credits, which had then made possible imports and greater production in Mexico—and more business for the suppliers as a result. The problem of interdivisional or interregional sales within an international corporation has already been discussed above. Specific reactions from a variety of U.S. firms are given below:

---

*Australia, Brazil, Colombia, Ireland, India, Indonesia, Yugoslavia, South Korea, Malaysia, Mexico, Morocco, New Zealand, People's Republic of China, Singapore, Taiwan, Turkey, and Venezuela.

In Firm 1 (Type 4), an executive felt that any commitments to maximize exports from a country in which the firm was doing business was dangerous to the United States in that it reduced U.S. export possibilities, U.S. employment, and so on. He commented, "If such commitments work—which I doubt—it will gum up ordinary economic decision-making." He cited several companies in Brazil that had entered into export commitments but were floundering. "One needs a cost advantage to compete in exports, and that is impossible in Brazil under present circumstances," he observed.

Firm 7 (Type 4) was not willing to undertake an export commitment. An executive stated, "We have no idea where we'll be five years down the road." The firm would not invest where such a commitment was required.

Firm 8 (Type 3), according to one executive, did not invest abroad to go into export; it looked only at the local domestic market.

Firm 16 (Type 4) had invested in Ireland and, in the process, the Irish had offered certain tax incentives if the firm would undertake to export. The tax incentives had been refused.

Firm 25 (Type 5) saw export commitments as a serious problem, for they required finding countries into which the firm could import. As one executive observed, "We are suffering from our own success in that we are already in most countries." Yet the firm's Colombian and Venezuelan enterprises would not be permitted further expansion of capacity without export commitments. This resulted in a decision not to invest further.

Firm 18 (Type 4) had been told recently by Brazilian authorities that it would have to meet an export quota because it was importing. The quota was being met by exporting some product as input to the corporation's U.S. operations. It had also established a trading company through which it exported nonrelated products.

Despite these negative comments and general misgivings, most firms, when faced with an export requirement, had nonetheless gone on with their investments. At least 29 cases were recorded during the course of this inquiry. It is impossible to estimate, of course, how much investment had not taken place because of the imposition of export requirements, but one judged not much. We heard of only the five instances, one each in Brazil. Colombia, Ireland, South Korea, and Venezuela. Whether firms were living up to the commitments was another matter, although, when linked to import rights, such commitments were relatively easy to monitor and enforce, assuming that the administration was honest.

Ownership Requirements

Both the experience and attitudes that surfaced during our inquiry varied substantially from firm to firm and from country to country. Executives in virtually all firms in which interviews were conducted addressed this issue in one way or another. Several referred to the difficulty of maintaining adequate control in the absence of a majority interest. Executives in others were not concerned; their firms had entered into management contracts with minority equity participation and seemed perfectly content. There was concern about the division of earnings with partners who had not contributed to an enterprise in a way that was commensurate to their equity and, hence, claim on earnings.

One hundred percent ownership had been permitted to one firm in Mexico on the basis of a commitment to export 100 percent. Another firm had been protected by "grandfathering" in Mexico. (The same had been true of a firm in the Philippines.) Yet many managements reported considerable pressure from the Mexican government to limit the foreign participation to 49 percent. One executive felt that his firm would be in a position to do a lot more for both Mexico and itself if it were to become more active in Mexico. It was the ownership restraint that was binding. Another firm had a wholly owned operation in Mexico and had been under no pressure to relinquish any equity. An executive felt that the operation was probably too small to merit attention. Another felt that his company could maintain its 100 percent position if it increased production. In any event, he doubted that there were any local buyers. Another corporation had been permitted to retain 100 percent ownership in its Mexican venture for five years. Still another had heard nothing about any Mexican ownership being demanded by the government.

One executive reported that his firm had been under no pressure in Brazil to relinquish any ownership. Yet another reported that his company had not been permitted to enter the country without a local partner. In this case, the industry was perhaps the important variable. The former had been in the electronics sector; the latter, in heavy industrial machinery. Another, a chemical producer, had been encouraged to buy out its local partner in Brazil, and there had been no government interference when still another, a machinery producer, had converted its Brazilian joint venture into a wholly owned subsidiary.

An engine manufacturer had been under pressure by the Indian government to reduce its equity in a local venture below 50 percent, a pressure the firm had resisted. As yet, it had not been forced to yield. Another, a supplier to the automotive industry, had been under pressure in Canada to reduce ownership from 100 to 75 percent, but it had resisted, and nothing further had been heard. Also, a farm manufacturer had been discouraged from majority ownership by the French government.

The South Korean government had used the promise of 100 percent ownership in one case, if the U.S. company, a chemical producer, would become involved on a minority-contractual basis in a much larger project. The same company had insisted on 100 percent ownership in Brazil but had readily accepted a 49 percent involvement in a large Yugoslav project. The country and the reward made a difference.

An executive in one firm, another chemical producer, stated that his corporation had a very strong preference for 100 percent ownership, but that it varied from country to country. Since 1965 the firm had attempted to obtain 100 percent ownership, but he noted local restrictions where this was not possible: in Indonesia where ownership had to be reduced over time; in India where there was a 40 percent maximum; in Mexico where the percentage varied (for petrochemicals it had been set at 40 percent); and in Brazil where there were no requirements but substantial disadvantages for non–Brazilian companies. In years prior to 1965, management had not been confident of its knowledge of foreign markets and had sought out foreign partners, for example, in Japan. But management was now "confident of its expertise" and at the very least desired a controlling interest. This policy seemed characteristic of Type 4 firms (integrators).

A food processor had indicated a preference for a controlling equity participation in overseas ventures. But recently, according to an executive, it had been looking more toward profitable licensing arrangements, especially if a clause were included giving the firm an option to take an equity share at some later date. Such policy was characteristic of Type 5 firms (opportunists). A spokesman for a rubber goods firm with important brand names observed that management, particularly the chairman of the board, did not like equity-based control on a minority basis even in a widely held company. The concern was with the precedent that this might establish. Management wanted to be able to tell governments that it never permitted its name to be put on products by companies of which it did not own a majority. A manager in a metal-processing firm observed that his company never entered into less than a 100 percent ownership agreement. "It would be difficult," he observed, "for part of an integrated system to be owned differently from the central component. It leads to inevitable conflict over transfer prices." Yet, his firm reported a number of jointly owned enterprises. Policy was obviously one thing, but practice another. This

conflict between preferred policy and practice was not uncharacteristic of relatively new type 5s (opportunists).

In total, some 33 instances of host government requirement
relative to ownership were reported from 12 countries:* 11 from
Mexico; 4 from Brazil; 3 from Indonesia; and the rest scattered,
with no more than two cases per country. There were only 7 specific instances reported in which membership requirements were
cited as a principal reason for noninvestment.

It was significant that a little over half of the 132 firms included in the 1957-59 study had indicated a firm commitment to
100 percent ownership with respect to overseas investments, although a few had been actively seeking joint ventures.† In the current study, we note that in terms of preferred policy only 10 out of
the 51 firms declared a strong preference for, if not insistence on,
100 percent ownership (see Table 1.5). But of these, only 5 had,
in fact, not entered into at least one 50-50 or minority-owned joint
venture. That is, only 5 reported no ventures abroad in which the
U.S. firm held less than a majority interest. Ownership policy had
become demonstrably more flexible over the intervening twenty-odd
years.

Our initial set of hypotheses, which was built into the classification of firms (see Chapter 2), included several having to do with
ownership policy. It was suggested there that those companies most
insistent on 100 percent ownership would be the learners (Type 2)
and integrators (Type 4); those most willing to enter joint ventures,
the builders (Type 3) and opportunists (Type 5). From Table 4.1,
it can be noted that there did indeed seem to be some tendency in
these directions. For example, of the 16 learners and integrators
(Types 2 and 4) in the sample, 8 manifested a 100 percent ownership policy, or 50 percent. However, of the 24 builders (Type 3)
and opportunists (Type 5), only 9, or 38 percent, seemed to insist
on a policy to control foreign affiliates via majority ownership.
And of those 22 firms with flexible ownership policies, the Type 2
and 4 firms (that is, those expected to be most resistant to such
policy) totaled 14 and accounted for 23 percent. In contrast, Type 3
and 5 firms (those predicted to find such policy most appealing)
totaled 13, or 40 percent of the total. Company size, as measured
by 1980 annual sales, did not seem to be related to ownership policy,

---

*Brazil, Canada, France, India, Indonesia, Yugoslavia, South
Korea, Malaysia, Mexico, Morocco, Nigeria, and the Philippines.
†Richard D. Robinson, International Business Policy (New
York: Holt, Rinehart and Winston, 1964), p. 13.

TABLE 4.1

Ownership Policies Associated with Type of Firm

Ownership Policy	Company Type							Total
	1	2	3	4	5	6	7	
Equity control (100 percent plus majority ownership)*	0	3	6	5	3	1	2	20
(Explicit equity control policy with only one exception in practice)	(0)	(0)	(4)	(2)	(0)	(1)	(1)	(8)
Unclear policy[†]	0	0	2	2	0	0	1	5
Noninvestors (i.e., in apparent policy)[‡]	2	1	0	0	0	0	0	3
Flexible policy acceptance of 50-50 or minority-owned joint ventures)**	1	0	0	5	13	1	2	22
Contractual only	0	0	0	0	0	0	1	1
Total	3	4	8	12	16	2	6	51

*Defined as a firm reporting 67 percent or more of its foreign affiliates (the ownership of which had been specified) as wholly owned or majority owned, unless the number of 50-50 or minority-owned affiliates was ten or more (whether the firm had an explicit policy favoring equity-based control or not), or firms for which practice was unclear but had an explicit policy preference for equity-based control.

†Firms neither explicitly stating an ownership policy nor specifying ownership of over 33 percent of their foreign affiliates and for which there was some scattering of ownership (of those in which ownership was specified) between wholly or majority-owned and those owned 50 percent or less.

‡Firms reporting fewer than six foreign affiliates, unless a specific ownership policy preference was explicated.

**All other firms, including those that had an explicitly flexible ownership policy, even though actual practice was unclear as defined above; also those with an unspecified policy but in practice reflecting a flexible policy.

Note: When a firm was considered to be only marginally committed to a particular ownership policy, as defined above, the explicit policy was used.

although 3 of the 5 "large" firms reported flexible policies (1 other favored an equity-based control policy; for 2 the ownership policy was unclear).

To summarize the experience we recorded, there seemed to have been only seven cases in which direct investment may not have occurred by reason of ownership requirements imposed by host governments: two each in Mexico and Brazil, one each in Morocco, Nigeria, and France. The reverse may also happen. That is, a corporation may be pressed to take on a greater share of ownership than it really prefers.

An executive in a Type 5 firm reported that the Tunisian government had put pressure on the corporation to assume at least a 20 percent equity position in its distribution-assembly operation there, which had been operating strictly on a license basis. The idea was to force the commitment of the corporation in order to identify it more closely with the success of the local operation. The executive observed that there were, in fact, some advantages for the corporation in these independent assembler-distribution contractual relationships, inasmuch as it was possible for the firm to extract itself from situations when the economics of the market so indicated, whereas it was very much more difficult if it had committed itself heavily via major capital expenditures. Hence, the logic of the Tunisian government pressure was revealed. This same objective was reflected in the PRC regulation that a foreign investor hold not less than 25 percent ownership.

Requirements to Limit Employment of Foreign Nationals

Very few executives expressed any concern over entering into commitments to reduce expatriate personnel. As one put it, "We normally hire local people in any event." Another observed that it was company practice to turn over local management to local nationals. An executive in a third firm felt that there should not be "arbitrary limits" on the number of foreign employees, and he cited Nigeria as a bad example. He opined that the country was trying to localize its work force too rapidly and in too arbitrary a manner. An executive in a second firm, likewise, felt that it was important that the number of expatriates given entry into a country should not be too restrictive. But yet another observed that his company could understand the desire of host governments to have as many local nationals employed as possible, including management. It was, in fact, in the interest of his firm to move in that direction as well. An executive in one firm explained that the training of local people was always a problem. The company had an international staff of approximately two dozen people who moved into a country as a startup team. When a new plant was running successfully, they were moved on to another development. He went on to comment that the right to bring these people in was an important considera- tion. For example, in negotiating with the Egyptian government, the firm had insisted on the free access of its personnel.

An executive in one firm reported that in some functional areas it had been almost impossible to get work permits for ex- patriates, specifically in marketing and personnel management. However, he observed, it was relatively easy to get work permits for people with technical degrees, but not so for individuals with high levels of technical expertise but who lacked the formal de- grees. A case in India was cited. He also pointed out that in Indonesia the firm had to commit itself to a training program for an Indonesian to replace, within three years, an expatriate technician who had been added recently to the local staff. Malaysia was given as a country in which it had been less of a problem to get work permits for expatriates. This matter was of particular concern to a large, service-oriented corporation with worldwide operations. It felt great need to maintain mobility of expatriate staff. In an- other firm, a manager stated that he always made sure that "we can get a limited number of expatriates into the country." Without that assurance, the firm does not invest in a country.

In our interviews, however, there was no hint of an invest- ment's having been blocked by reason of restrictions on the use of nonlocal personnel, and there were only six cases reported of ex- plicit host government pressure at this point (in Egypt, India, Indonesia, Malaysia, and Nigeria). In certain cases, the reverse had happened; a government had insisted that the U.S. firm keep expatriate managers and technicians on the job as long as possible. One firm reported such an experience in Yugoslavia.

Local Content Requirements

An executive wondered out loud how far one should allow a country to go in demanding local sourcing. It was one thing to permit a developing country, such as Mexico, to demand such, but it was quite another when a country such as Japan, which was an industrial competitor, did the same thing. "How long do we play with different decks of cards ?" he asked rhetorically. An executive in another corporation was very blunt: "In our industry, which is very volatile, there is over-capacity worldwide. And it is not an industry appropriate to development in less developed countries in any event. The local content rules make less sense from our point of view." He was speaking as a manufacturer of special purpose industrial machinery. Another firm had been willing to comply with local content rules in the case of its Brazilian venture and had made some engineering modifications to the design of its plant in order to comply. The resulting facility, however, had been less efficient, management claimed.

As can be noted in material dealing with individual countries, firms in our sample had faced local content requirements at least in Argentina, Australia, Brazil, Malaysia, Mexico, Nigeria, Spain, Thailand, and Turkey. The only countries cited more than once in this regard were Mexico (six instances) and Brazil (four instances). In one case, a U.S. firm in Australia had been able to trade off exports for a reduced local content requirement. The same firm had enjoyed a reduced local content for increased exports in Mexico on a dollar-for-dollar basis. Still another had been able to negotiate a downward reduction of a local content rule because it had taken over an ailing Spanish enterprise and had agreed to maintain employment. Another had gone into Thailand in anticipation that shortly the government would require final processing locally.

Local content rules became particularly serious when the U.S. firm was not a highly integrated manufacturer in the United States and there were not available to it competent subcontractors in the country in which it was investing. For example, a firm in Brazil reported that it had been forced to manufacture inhouse a higher percentage of a given machine than it did in the United States, by reason of the local content rule. It could not find adequate external suppliers. The result was higher cost, thereby rendering exports even more difficult, because maximum economy of scale could not be reached for certain parts that were manufactured customarily in large volume by U.S. suppliers.

Two firms, one in Mexico and one in Turkey, cited the local content rules as contributing reasons for their nonentry. Another had rejected a Nigerian project for the same reason, at least in part. (However, this firm had, in fact, faced local content requirements in another situation, Mexico, where it had nonetheless gone into a minority-owned venture.) There were no other cases of blocked investment. One other general observation: local content rules appeared particularly onerous with respect to the automotive industry, but apparently such controls had not caused any firms to desist from investing and expanding when the economics of the situation promised financial reward. We concluded that such requirements had not been generally significant in diverting or blocking investment.

Employment Level Requirements

One corporation had been required by the Canadian government to give an employment guarantee when it had acquired a local
firm, but the company had not been able to live up to this commitment. However, it was a small operation, an executive observed,
and it would probably be overlooked. Similar requirements had
been imposed by the Panamian and Nicaraguan governments, but
there the company had been able to fulfill its commitments. Another
had made an employment commitment in Brazil, but still another
had encountered no such pressure. An executive noted that no
further expansions of investment would be authorized in Colombia
and Venezuela without guarantees of exports and employment. As
part of a general agreement, one company had agreed to maintain
the employment level in a Spanish enterprise that it had taken over.
All together, we found exactly nine investment projects in relation
to which employment commitments had been given, one each in
Brazil, Canada, Egypt, Nicaragua, Nigeria, Norway, Panama,
Spain, and Venezuela. In two others, Indonesia and Malaysia, companies had undertaken to employ given percentages of certain ethnic
groups (prigumi, or indigenous Indonesians, in Indonesia, and
bumiputra, or indigenous Malays, in Malaysia). In no case did it
appear that an investment had not taken place because of the requirement that an employment commitment be given.

Investment Level Requirements

One firm reported that it had made a commitment to a certain
level of investment in Brazil, which seemed to be quite common
practice. This appeared to be more of a statement of intent, however, than an actual commitment. Another had been required, when
seeking a license to expand production in Indonesia, to make a commitment that it would invest a specific amount over a given number
of years. These were the only two instances specifically mentioned,
but one can assume that in all cases where an entry screening process, investment incentives, or negotiated entry agreements were
in place, the foreign business firm would have made some sort of
investment commitment. Problems of evaluation were mentioned
by several executives. Such problems arose when intangibles were
to be capitalized as part or all of the foreign investment in the event
used machinery were to be contributed as capital.

Production Level Requirements

Here again, many of the commitments were more in the nature of statements of intent, on which basis various permits and incentives had been given. But this was not always the case. A requirement for a certain level of production had been forced on one firm in Mexico—along with export and local content requirements—in order to get an open-ended management contract with respect to a local venture in which the U.S. firm had a 40 percent equity interest, the balance being held by the government. This was the only explicit quid pro quo in which a specific production commitment had been part of the price of a government commitment of some sort. In any event, this commitment is possibly the most difficult to monitor from the point of view of the host government, and it would appear to be of little real value. The economics of the market, plus the impact of government incentives, will determine the level of production.

Local Research and Development Requirements

Fifteen firms reported foreign research and/or development activities in 18 countries: Belgium (1), Brazil (4), Canada (2), Costa Rica (1), France (3), West Germany (3), Honduras (1), Ireland (2), Japan (4), Luxembourg (1), Mexico (1), New Zealand (1), Nicaragua (1), Peru (1), the Philippines (2), South Africa (1), Switzerland (1), and the United Kingdom (4). In addition, one firm reported 19 foreign laboratories; another, 1 marine-related research station in Latin America. One other claimed to have overseas research and development activities but did not specify where.

But only one incident was reported in which a host government had virtually required a U.S. firm to undertake local research and development, and that had been in France. An executive in a pharmaceutical company observed that the French government, in issuing product licenses, had insisted on a commitment to develop local technology. The company had been told, in one recent instance, that it might get a better price review if it were to engage in local research and development. (Pharmaceutical prices were under control.) Another firm reported that the Indonesian government had declared that it would give preference in granting licenses for expanded capacity in one industry to those firms with research and development and "a technology of international standard." However, an executive said that the firm had not been under any pressure to do research and development <u>locally</u>. Nonetheless, other companies, not included in this present survey, had reported Indonesian pressure for local research and development activity at the time of application for capacity expansion.

Training Requirements

Although training was obviously a very common activity by virtually all direct foreign investors, only two firms mentioned the imposition of specific requirements in this regard. One had undertaken the obligation to train a local Indonesian to replace an incoming foreign technician. The granting of the latter's work permit was contingent upon the commitment. Another company had agreed to a specific training program in Kenya as a condition for entry. In this case, an executive observed that the firm had been glad to enter such a commitment because it wanted to do the training anyway. A third had encountered rigid controls in France with respect to the training required for new insurance agencies. In this instance, the French subsidiary had failed because of the company's inability to hire good sales people. In no case was such a commitment referred to as a disincentive to investment. On the contrary, it was often cited as an indication of realism on the part of the host government.

Requirements for Products, Level of Technology, and Plant Location

Commitments to satisfy requirements imposed as conditions for entry and/or the granting of incentives were frequent, but only those having to do with product had given any trouble. In some situations, executives reported, it had been impossible to secure permission to produce locally because an indigenously owned firm was already manufacturing the same or comparable good. An executive in one firm, a food processor, opined that possibly 15 or 20 national markets were closed to his firm for this reason, and he gave Brazil, South Korea, and Mexico as specific examples. This view was corroborated in another food processing firm. All together, we encountered 19 specific instances in which firms had encountered difficulties by reason of the product with which they were involved: Brazil—computers, food processing, industrial instrumentation, steel; Canada—restaurants, timber; Egypt—canning; France—computers, insurance; West Germany—employment services, insurance; Japan—insurance; South Korea—food processing, vehicles; Mexico—food processing; Nigeria—vehicles; the Philippines—land ownership; Taiwan—vehicles; and Venezuela—steel.

Withdrawal or blocked investment had resulted in virtually all cases. We did not become aware, however, of any situation in which requirements imposed relative to technology or plant site had been a significant factor in an investment decision.

All together, executives in the 51 firms reported 126 instances in which host governments had imposed performance requirements of some variety (see Table 4.2), or over 2 per company. There is no claim that this constitutes anything like a complete listing of those actually encountered by the 51 corporations, but they were the ones that surfaced in conversation with knowledgeable managers. And it should also be borne in mind that one of the prime purposes of each interview was to ascertain the significance of performance requirements in the recent allocation of corporate resources overseas. The general finding was that performance requirements were not very significant. As can be seen, only 33 cases of nonentry due to these requirements were indicated, or 26 percent. If one were to eliminate those cases of investment blocked by reason of sectoral restrictions, which is more realistic, then the percentage drops to 13.

INCENTIVES

It was very difficult, we found, to discuss performance requirements divorced from incentives. A country might, on the one hand, enforce an export requirement or, on the other hand, reward a firm for exporting. The reward, however, might be such that the firm could not really remain competitive within the market without the reward. Export credits might be required for an import license, or they might be used as credits against taxes that would be otherwise levied against local profits.

During the course of the inquiry, we identified essentially six types of incentives:

1. Subsidies (for land and plant, debt, research and development, imports, exports, energy, raw material inputs, and infrastructure);
2. Tax reduction (on imports and on revenues);
3. Market protection;
4. Import rights;
5. Guarantees (on availability of foreign exchange for remittance of earnings, on right to import of essential materials, and against expropriation); and
6. Government procurement.

TABLE 4.2

Instances Reported of Performance Requirements
by Country and Nature of Requirement

Country	Requirements												
	1	2	3	4	5	6	7	8	9*	10†	11*	12*	Total
Argentina	—	—	—	1	—	—	—	—	—	—	—	—	1
Australia	1ad	—	—	1ad	—	—	—	—	—	—	—	—	2
Brazil	11	4	—	4	1	1	—	1	—	4	—	—	26
Canada	—	2	—	—	1	—	—	—	—	2	—	—	5
Colombia	2	—	—	—	—	—	—	—	—	—	—	—	2
Egypt	—	—	—	—	1	—	—	—	—	1	—	—	2
France	—	1	—	—	—	—	—	—	—	2	—	—	3
India	1b	3	1	1b	—	—	—	—	—	—	—	—	6
Indonesia	1	3	1	—	—	1	—	—	2	—	—	—	8
Ireland	1	—	—	—	—	—	—	—	—	—	—	—	1
Japan	—	—	—	—	—	—	—	—	—	1	—	—	1
Kenya	—	—	—	—	—	—	—	—	1	—	—	—	1
Malaysia	1	2	—	1	—	—	—	—	—	—	—	—	4
Mexico	6cd	11c	3	6d	—	—	1	—	—	1	—	—	28
Morocco	1	1	—	—	—	—	—	—	—	—	—	—	2
New Zealand	1	—	—	—	—	—	—	—	—	—	—	—	1
Nicaragua	—	1	—	1	1	—	—	—	—	—	—	—	3
Norway	—	1	—	—	1	—	—	—	—	1	—	—	3
Panama	—	—	—	—	1	—	—	—	—	—	—	—	1
People's Republic of China	1	—	—	—	—	—	—	—	—	—	—	—	1
Philippines	—	1	1	—	—	—	—	—	—	1	—	—	3
Singapore	1	—	—	—	—	—	—	—	—	—	—	—	1
South Korea	1	2	—	—	—	—	—	—	—	2	—	—	5
Spain	—	—	—	1e	1e	1	—	—	—	—	—	—	3
Taiwan	1	—	—	—	—	—	—	—	—	1	—	—	2
Thailand	—	—	—	1	—	—	—	—	—	—	—	—	1
Turkey	1	—	—	1	—	—	—	—	—	—	—	—	2
Venezuela	1	—	—	—	1	—	—	—	1	1	—	—	4
West Germany	—	—	—	—	—	—	—	—	—	2	—	—	2
Yugoslavia	1	1	—	—	—	—	—	—	—	—	—	—	2
Total instances	33	33	6	18	8	3	1	1	4	19	?	?	126
Rejections	4	7	0	3	0	0	0	0	0	19	0	0	33
Acceptances	29	26	6	15	8	3	1	1	4	0	0	0	93

1 = Export	5 = Employment	9 = Training
2 = Ownership	6 = Investment	10 = Product (sectoral)
3 = Employment of aliens	7 = Production	11 = Technology
4 = Local content	8 = Local R&D	12 = Plant site

aa, bb, cc, dd, ee = Indicate linkages specified in the form of tradeoffs.

*Although infrequently cited as specific entry requirements, very frequently it was understood that certain training would take place, that certain technology would be used, and that the plant would be placed on a specified site, particularly in Type III, IV, and V countries.

†Such a requirement would have to be assumed in all Type III, IV, and V countries. The only situations discussed in interviews were those in which investment had not taken place by reason of the imposition of a requirement that investment not take place in a sector.

Not all firms in the survey paid attention to the variety of incentives offered by host governments. Comments by executives were revealing.

Firm 1 (Type 4): the firm's Irish project had been motivated by the desire to produce within the EEC. Although the Irish government had offered various incentives, they had not even been reflected in the capital proposal to management, having been mentioned only in a footnote. An executive observed that tax laws could be changed easily and that launching a business venture on the basis of a special tax deal could not be justified.

Firm 2 (Type 3): incentives were described as "low on the totem pole." What management looked for were the right products in the right growth markets. Incentives were "incidental" and might influence where the company put a plant, but even then, if there were no long-term reason to stay in a particular location, the firm would close a plant down. It was important, therefore, that an incentive not be a short-term feature. Incentives were included in an investment calculation, provided there was a likelihood of their being of a continuing nature. Risky incentives were excluded. Management evaluated the rationale for an incentive to determine whether it made economic sense. If it did not, it would assume that it was unlikely to be continued. In discussing one current investment decision, the locale of which was not disclosed, an executive observed that the company would not have made a positive decision without incentives.

Firm 10 (Type 5): according to one executive, "A project has to make business sense. Incentives simply distort judgment." An example cited was a $16 million investment in Quebec, which was evaluated on the basis of $16 million, although in fact management knew that it would probably be able to negotiate $5 million worth of "up front" concessions. Nonetheless, the proposal submitted to the board had carried the $16 million price tag.

Firm 11 (Type 2): an executive felt that incentives were important, especially tax incentives, to attract industry in the first place. The tax incentive was important because of the way in which it improved cash flow, which was important in this firm's business (wood products).

Firm 12 (Type 4): the host government had very little input, according to one manager, and incentives were not important—with one exception, a guarantee of raw materials. "Otherwise, we don't give a damn."

Firm 14 (Type 5): "Where you have a good business opportunity, incentives make little difference. But where you have a marginal project, the incentives work," observed an executive. In

Mexico and Brazil, for example, incentives had made no difference, but in the United Kingdom they had. The problem is that incentives were often coupled with performance requirements. Governments were, in effect, buying commitments with respect to exports, employment, and so on. It could be a nuisance, he went on, but incentives could overcome the cost of satisfying a requirement in certain instances. Asked about the viability of government policies and the risk of relying upon them, the executive agreed that there could be certain risk. He cited Ford, which allegedly had made an investment in Nigeria on the basis of a Nigerian government commitment to close the border to competing products. Subsequently, Ford had discovered that the border was not being kept closed. When the same executive was asked how critical incentives had been in the firm's decision to take up a 40 percent interest in a Mexican venture, he responded, "insignificant." They had been excluded from all of the financial projections.

Firm 16 (Type 4): an executive explained that the firm would look first at the experience of other firms in a country offering incentives, plus the host government attitude toward foreign investment and the repatriation of profit. The point was made that the published incentives did not necessarily equate with the actual incentives. His feeling was that the country "must want us."

Firm 17 (Type 5): an executive spoke very favorably of incentives "up front," such as loans at subsidized rates, which he characterized as a direct subsidy, as well as land at a subsidized price. But, in any event, a project had to be commercially viable first and fit the firm's expansion strategy for the product or products involved. "Whether a project flies or not may depend upon the availability of incentives and insurance." However, he obviously felt that this was rarely the case. Another executive commented that tax holidays, if they occurred in the early years, when the company was not making a profit anyway, were of little value. They are a kind of "window dressing," he explained. The firm did not go into a project just because of incentives. The same executive questioned the wisdom of country competition that national incentive schemes were producing. With respect to the impact of incentives on the structure of an investment, he observed that in order to make a capital-intensive investment, one needed greater confidence because one was prepaying a lot of expenses, the benefits from which would be delayed over a substantial period of time. From that point of view, a labor-intensive type of investment was less risky, thereby implying that up-front incentives were more effective in more capital-intensive projects. He went on, "Where we are concerned about the stability of an area, we look at projects not involving a lot of capital. For example, the formulation plant in Colombia would be a good example."

Firm 18 (Type 4): incentives had been available in Brazil, but the firm had not taken advantage of them. According to one executive, the plant had been deliberately not located in a development zone, thereby forgoing incentives. It had also deliberately not sought out a Brazilian partner, thereby forgoing other incentives. In the case of Thailand as well, incentives had not been important. Although certain incentives had been taken there, the firm would have invested in the country in any event.

Firm 21 (Type 4): there had never been an instance of "moving to incentives." Fundamentally, an executive observed, the costs of doing business are such that management preferred to have one product manufactured only in one location, and this consideration overrode all incentives. When the firm made an overseas investment, it was seen in a marketing context. "We take a market position," he explained.

Firm 23 (Type 4): an executive reported that incentives were very closely calculated, and credit was given to the operation generating those incentives on an ongoing basis.

Firm 24 (Type 5): in Chile, tariff protection was about to be removed, which meant that the firm would close down its operation there, an executive reported. Singapore had done the same thing and had wiped out incentives. The same firm, however, in Spain, had fed all of the Spanish incentives offered related to a major investment into a computer analysis of the financial viability of the project. They had been so favorably treated with respect to incentives that fire had been drawn from the local press. A company spokesman insisted that the incentives offered by host governments were plugged into the financial analysis and carefully monitored to ascertain whether the company had lived up to the requirements imposed, as a quid pro quo for the incentives. After all, there were requirements for all the incentives that one was given. The commitments into which the company entered were weighed carefully on a case-by-case basis to ascertain whether they were desirable. Management calculated the present discounted value of expected return and then showed the impact of the individual incentives offered. Of course, he explained, if the incentive were contingent upon some future act of a government, the value of the incentive was reduced by a risk factor. Of special interest to the corporation were cash grants that reduced the initial investment, as well as training grants and low interest loans. The importance of a tax holiday would depend on the overall tax situation as to whether the company was in an excess foreign tax situation or not. If not, it was very difficult to use such an incentive.

Firm 25 (Type 5): two approaches had been used in going overseas. In the first, an executive explained, the company responded to an action by a foreign government. Typically, the firm had been importing into a country, and the government took some sort of blocking action. In order to maintain its presence, the firm might start up local manufacturing as one possible alternative. The second was a situation where the incentives for local manufacture were so great that they attracted management's attention. The only two examples cited in this latter category were Puerto Rico and Ireland. All other instances of investment had been the result of government intervention in the trade of the relevant products.

Firm 26 (Type 1): "I never saw a government incentive that made a bad project into a good one," an executive commented. He went on to add that "up-front incentives" were naturally of considerable interest, for example, the duty-free import of capital equipment. These up-front incentives were put into the economic analysis that went to the board of directors, and they sometimes gave the deal added attractiveness.

Firm 27 (Type 4): government incentives tended to get into two areas, an executive observed. First, there were those intended to make a deal more attractive financially. Incentives that were quantifiable up front, such as subsidized loans, duty-free import of capital equipment, and grants ("which tend to be associated with desperate circumstances") may be important. Second, there were those incentives designed to improve "the risk-reward profile." Another executive observed, "tax gimmicks do not carry a lot of weight." He then added that anything that is quantifiable and could be put into the analysis was important in selling a project to management.

Firm 28 (Type 5): according to one executive, decisions were made without being overly influenced by incentives that governments offered inasmuch as there were always reasons for those incentives, which implied additional cost. The executive then admitted that the firm's plant in Northern Ireland had been very largely sold to management—and expanded—on the basis of incentives offered by the U.K. government. The executive obviously had not agreed with the decision to build in Northern Ireland. He felt that the firm had not been able to achieve the necessary economies to make the plant a successful source of exports, even though the government had given the firm all sorts of incentives to maintain and expand employment. There was a corporate policy, we were told, not to go into any projects that required tariff protection for more than five years.

Firm 30 (Type 2): a company spokesman observed that incentives were considered usually as "a kicker in a marginal project." A tax incentive had been a consideration in a Mexican project because the vehicle had been a Mexican majority-held company. In such cases, a tax incentive was given almost routinely to new investments.

Firm 33 ("Type 6): according to an executive, one must divorce incentives from a project. Anything that a government offered but might be taken away—even though it might make the project seem more attractive—was removed from the initial evaluation. A project had to stand on its own merits. Another executive elaborated. Incentives such as capital grants and subsidized sites were included in the analysis. There had been no significant tax incentives associated with its Mexican project, the executive told us. But they would not have been important anyway.

Firm 36 (Type 4): an executive explained management attitudes. There was competition within the firm with respect to supplying overseas markets from foreign plants. It almost develops into a fight between the "hard engineers"—that is, those responsible for costing and for profit and loss—and the subsidiary managers who see the marketing side of it, including incentives. In the case of Puerto Rico and Ireland, he observed, the incentives had been so great that they had been recognized as being different. The firm would not have located plants in either place in the absence of incentives. Incentives in other countries, he felt, might make a small difference in the timing of investment. The corporation was in a regulated industry, and it was therefore important that host governments see the company as a good citizen. It would thus invest in many places with or without incentives in the long run. He added that a major reason for the firm's investing in Third World countries was trade barriers. It was the only way to continue to have a market presence.

Firm 37 (Type 5): management does not put government incentives "up front," we were told by one executive. Rather, they are put at the end. Management is interested about why a government feels it necessary to offer incentives.

Firm 38 (Type 5): an executive recalled that the firm had located in a particular Belgian community by reason of tax relief and training assistance. The site had been narrowed down for economic reasons to three countries, but the final selection had been dependent to a degree on government incentives. He noted that European countries had bid against one another in terms of incentives. Another executive stated that evaluations of projects were done strictly on economic merit. If investment incentives were committed prior to the investment, the present discounted value of the incentives was calculated very specifically. But if one had to negotiate an incentive after the commitment of the investment, that was quite a different matter.

Firm 41 (Type 3): an executive observed that, in theory, it was easy to imagine companies shopping around for the best incentive, but in reality this did not happen. Companies went where the need and the market existed. They must have a certain market location. "Incentives are just an added bonus, with the exception of Ireland," he added. The firm had not invested in Puerto Rico, despite attractive incentives, because of transport and infrastructure deficiencies.

Firm 42 (Type 5): "In my twenty years in international operations," observed an executive, "I've never seen a collection of incentives which would have caused me to recommend a project that depended on those incentives. We do not turn our backs on what is available, but no investment is recommended because of incentives."

Firm 43 (Type 7): an executive stated that the firm had located in southern Italy as a result of the incentives that had been offered. However, they had not been "properly implemented," meaning that the firm had not received what had been promised.

Firm 47 (Type 3): according to one executive, the company paid "zero attention" to tax incentives anywhere. It did not rely on their permanence. "Philosophically, the firm does not feel that it needs them if it is competitive," he added. Management had not found that it would locate any place because of tax considerations. In fact, "We are not sure that we understand a lot of foreign tax arrangements. For example, in Latin America the letter of the law means less than the interpretation of it."

These observations accurately reflected the general tenor of the comments heard about the impact of host government incentives on decision making, and they did not seem to be associated with company type. It was clear that most firms did include "up-front" incentives—that is, those committed by a host government prior to the actual execution of an investment project—in their financial analysis. Other incentives, which were essentially promises to be delivered later were heavily discounted, if counted at all. Tax holidays came in this category. Most executives echoed the notion that incentives did not turn a bad project into a good project. The economic justification of an investment had to stand on its own. One observation bears repeating. In estimating the viability of a particular incentive, management was well advised to evaluate its rationale. If it did not make economic sense in terms of host government interests, then it was unlikely to last long. For example, would incentives of a continuing nature survive a change of government? Topping managerial scepticism in this regard was the comment from an executive in a Midwest firm when asked if promise of import protection in exchange for local manufacture was an attractive deal. He responded that the situation in Latin America could change so quickly that no one could keep up with it. There were always reasons for incentives, he went on. "Even upper Wisconsin offered certain incentives for locating plants there," and with that he shook his head in apparent bemusement.

Corporate experience with specific types of host government incentives—subsidies, tax reduction, market protection, import quotas, guarantees, and government procurement—sheds some light on both their frequency and effectiveness.

Subsidies

Fifteen firms reported 29 cases in which government subsidies had been received. We counted as a subsidy any input priced below the market. Both the United Kingdom and Ireland had been particularly generous, as well as Spain in certain cases. Subsidies in one form or another were reported from Australia, Bahrein, Belgium, Brazil, France, Ireland, Malaysia, Mexico, Saudi Arabia, Singapore, Spain, the United Kingdom, and West Germany. These had taken the form of:

Training allowances in Belgium, Ireland, Spain, and the United Kingdom

Grants for capital equipment in the United Kingdom

Subsidized energy in Australia, Mexico, and the United Kingdom

Commitment to cover early-year losses in Spain

Land grants in Spain

Grants for local research and development in France and the United Kingdom

Subsidized raw materials in Bahrein, Saudi Arabia, and Mexico

Grants for buildings in Ireland, Malaysia, Singapore, and the United Kingdom

Subsidized capital (either below market price or fixed at rate) in Brazil, West Germany, Ireland, Saudi Arabia, and Singapore

Subsidized export financing in Belgium, Brazil, France, Mexico, and the United Kingdom.

All together, there seemed to have been seven projects that had materialized when and where they did by reason of government subsidies, five in the United Kingdom and two in Ireland. It will be noted that subsidies were not a common form of incentive among Third World countries. The reason, we suggest, is that a direct subsidy to a foreign-owned firm is a politically vulnerable use of public funds. And, if given prior to an investment commitment, such a subsidy would have to be accompanied by some sort of performance bond. We encountered no such cases.

Export incentives, in the form of extended long-term export financing at a below-market rate, were somewhat an exception to the general management attitude regarding incentives. These were reported from a number of countries and in some instances had contributed to decisions to produce locally to be able to qualify for the export finance. There were two instances in which this factor appeared to have been critical, both in the United Kingdom, although the availability of such finance facilities had been contributory to several other investment decisions. One firm reported that Brazilian export financing—8 percent for ten years—had been a factor in its decision to produce in Brazil. For another, the availability of favorable export credit facilities would determine whether it got further involved in South Korea and Japan.

Tax Reduction

Executives in virtually all of the firms mentioned one or more experiences with various forms of tax incentives, either in the form of reduction or total exemption from import taxes (tariffs) and/or revenue taxes. In some countries, tax incentives had been contingent upon achieving specified export levels, as in Brazil. In others, Mexico for example, firms had received tax credit for exports. In a number of cases, tax incentives were clearly not critical, as for one company looking at the Ivory Coast. The corporation's tax department had not even been consulted. Another firm had generally not been able to take advantage of tax concessions, with one exception. It had taken over a plant in Brazil, and with it had come some special tax benefits. In some instances, specific company experience was revealing.

Firm 7 (Type 4): the company had looked for some years at Southeast Asia and finally seized upon Malaysia. An executive observed that the duty-free import of equipment had made the project more viable.

Firm 18 (Type 2): an executive referred to reduced import duties on certain goods as "fallout benefit" accruing to overseas investment.

Firm 22 (Type 4): as part of an overall joint venture arrangement in Yugoslavia, the firm had been allowed to import, duty free, the product, which was eventually to be produced locally, for a six-month test marketing. This test, according to one executive, was to be completed before the firm made an irreversible commitment. Indeed, a successful market test had probably been critical to the subsequent investment.

Firm 33 (Type 6): as part of a major investment project in Spain, the government had waived all duties on the import of equipment. In context, this incentive had probably not been critical.

Firm 48 (Type 5): a concession in the form of low duties on raw materials and capital equipment had been given by the Egyptian government. In this case, the concession may have been decisive.

In analyzing our interview data, we came up with only two cases in which the waiving of import duties had possibly been critical. In most cases, it was not the imposition of import duties that concerned management, but rather the inability to obtain unambiguous guarantees that the firm would be able to purchase foreign exchange and import licenses for imported materials to keep a local plant running.

Many cases of tax holidays or reduced taxes on earnings were recorded. Such were reported out of Belgium, Brazil, Egypt, France, Ireland, Malaysia, Mexico, Morocco, Peru, Saudi Arabia, Singapore, Spain, Thailand, and the United Kingdom. Several firms, which had already decided on expansion of capacity within the EEC, had opted for Ireland specifically because of the tax incentives offered. When an executive in one firm (which had been exempted from Irish taxes for 15 years) was asked what the company did with its tax-exempt profits, he replied that it tried to employ them elsewhere but that, in fact, most of them were remitted directly to the United States. It was difficult to see how the firm had really benefited. Another company had located in the United Kingdom, where it had received a number of incentives, a tax holiday among them, but the holiday had clearly not been of major concern. Another had received tax incentives in Spain, which, according to one executive, meant that the company could reinvest its profits uneroded by any taxation. That seemed, in the total context, important. Another firm had invested in tree farms in Brazil, in part because of a 30 percent tax allowance for tree planting. The Mexican government had bestowed a tax incentive on one firm, specifically because it had located in a priority-incentive zone, plus granting it a per-head tax credit for hiring people from the zone, which could be used as an offset against the value-added tax. In Morocco, as mentioned in another section, the government had given a firm a tax holiday and had then criticized it for making an unreasonable profit. Management pointed out that it was precisely because of the tax holiday that the enterprise had been so profitable and that the government ought to impute the tax so that the long-term profit level could be derived. One wondered why the firm had not done so itself without prompting.

One firm had initiated an expansion in Belgium, in part because of tax relief. The government of Thailand had given another firm a ten-year partial tax exemption which, however, had nothing to do with the decision to invest, according to one executive. The same firm had received a scaled tax holiday in Peru—100 percent exemption for the first five years, 50 percent for the next five, 25 percent for a final five. After a change in government, the firm had become uneasy about publicity this tax deal was getting and voluntarily relinquished it. One firm had chosen Singapore as an investment site partially because of tax benefits. Already mentioned was the special admissions' tax rebate that a U.S. film producer received in France, which could be applied only to the cost of production within the country. It had felt compelled to invest in local production as a result.

A number of executives agreed that foreign tax holidays on income were of very limited value to their respective companies by reason of the U.S. taxation of worldwide income, subject only to credit for foreign income and wealth taxes actually paid. Corporations based in countries taxing only domestic income, or with very low tax rate on foreign-source income, had a distinct advantage. As the executive of one major U.S. corporation observed, "Tax benefits are of no great help to us for the simple reason that we want to repatriate profits as soon as possible, which means that they will be taxed anyway." A benefit was derived only by firms, such as the one reported above in Spain, that wanted to increase its local capital base by reinvesting local profits (it was not planning to remit profits to the United States for many years) or that were in a deficit tax credit position.

However, special credit to be applied against local, nonincome taxes was of universal appeal. For example, one firm reported employment credits in Spain, which could be applied against social security tax liability. In Mexico, one firm had received an employment tax credit applicable against the value-added tax. In Brazil, another firm reported having taken advantage of the special tax deal for investing in the northeast, whereby funds that would otherwise have been paid in local taxes could be invested without being subject to tax.

During the course of our study, some form of tax incentive was reported from 19 countries (number of instances are given in parenthesis): Belgium (2), Brazil (3), Egypt (1), El Salvador (1), France (1), Ireland (4), Ivory Coast (1), Korea (1), Yugoslavia (1), Malaysia (4), Mexico (1), Morocco (1), Nigeria (1), Peru (1), Saudi Arabia (1), Singapore (1), Spain (1), Thailand (2), and the United Kingdom (3). Of these 31 instances, tax incentives may have been critical to investment in 8.

Market Protection

More effective than either subsidies or tax incentives was border protection. Typical was an executive's comment about his firm's investigation of a project in Nigeria. Management realized that if Nigeria were to open its borders to competing imports, the operation would be destroyed because of its inefficiency. In Mexico, the same firm had been promised protection from competing imports. At the time of our study, neither project had been negotiated. Generally speaking, according to one executive, his firm anticipated that a market for developing countries would be cut off by government action to protect those firms manufacturing within it. Therefore, in order to protect a good market for developing countries, it was necessary to manufacture locally. The purpose of another firm in going into a major venture in Yugoslavia had been very simply to capture more of the market. Protection had been assumed. However, a high barrier could produce the opposite result. An executive noted that a high tariff had encouraged substantial smuggling in Colombia, so much so that his firm's investment there had been jeopardized. High tariff countries such as Venezuela, Peru, and, to some extent, Chile had in fact reduced their tariffs as a result of this problem. For another firm, in Brazil, tariffs were important if they exceeded 5 or 6 percent. Below that, they really made no difference because economies of scale were of such overwhelming importance. For another firm, Malaysian protection given against imports from Eastern Europe had been of signal importance, apparently overriding all other incentives. A chemical firm was in Brazil, according to an executive, primarily for the large market, well protected by tariffs. Tariff protection was the only thing that made one firm's Australian venture successful. In at least one case, the South Korean government had given protection for a new enterprise, but only until it had judged that the fledgling industry was strong enough to survive competition. Another firm had rejected a South Korean project specifically because the government had not been prepared to place

tariffs on competing products. The main incentive for a firm in
the Ivory Coast had been the imposition of an import duty over 100
percent ad valorem. When the duty had been raised to this level,
a local license arrangement had followed. One of the conditions
laid down by still another firm for an investment in Ivory Coast
had been that the industry be closed to any further competition.

For one corporation, the protection of the Argentine market
had led to local production, although admittedly on an inefficient
scale. Recently, the level of protection had been substantially reduced, and the firm had been badly hurt. An executive used this as
an example of the danger of depending on such artificial devices as
market protection. A number of firms cited investments that had
been made in anticipation of continuing tariff protection but had
later suffered by reason of government failure to protect the market. Fifteen cases were reported from 12 countries: Argentina (1),
Australia (1), Brazil (1), Chile (1), Ivory Coast (2), Malaysia (1),
Mexico (1), Yugoslavia (1), South Korea (3), Nigeria (1), the
Philippines (1), and Singapore (1).

Import Rights

One form of incentive, infrequently used but effective when
it was, had to do with granting an import license or quota to the
investing firm. By selling product in the market while the investment was being made and the plant being readied for operation, a
corporation could both finance part of the project from the proceeds
of the sales and familiarize the market with the product to be
manufactured locally. The Yugoslav government had permitted
one firm, in anticipation of the finalization of its investment commitment, to test market the relevant product for six months. The
investment was contingent upon satisfactory results. Another firm
in a Yugoslav project had been permitted to sell to the joint venture
during its initial years. An executive in one firm reported a corporate policy of deliberately tying a license arrangement (this
firm was not interested in investing overseas) with an up-front
order, and it had done so successfully in Taiwan. Finally, the
Spanish government had given a machine-building company a quota
to import finished machines until the company's new plant was
ready to produce. It is our feeling that this form of incentive
could be very important, and the cost to the host government relatively modest. Yet, we unearthed only these four instances in
which it had been used.

Guarantees

Specific host government guarantees with respect to such matters as the availability of exchange for the remittance of earnings, right to import essential materials, and opposition to expropriation surfaced infrequently during our interviews. Executives in only a handful of companies made specific mention of such guarantees, although they were implicit in much of what others said. Ideally, the first condition one firm would look at, according to one executive, was the availability of guarnatees for the import of the necessary raw materials. An executive in a second company virtually reiterated this view. He would prefer to have the host government "invite us in, and, of course, give the necessary raw material guarantee." Another firm reported that both Greece and Kenya had given guarantees of foreign exchange for essential supplies on an ongoing basis. An executive in still another firm mentioned that his management would insist on the guarantee of dividend repatriation without difficulty, a requirement reiterated by spokesmen in several companies.

However, the absence of such guarantees seemed to have blocked only one investment. This had to do with proposed investment in Turkey. The firm had turned away when it realized that a guarantee for foreign exchange with which to import essential supplies would not be forthcoming. In some instances, of course, this guarantee was implicit in the agreement that a firm could retain all or a certain percentage of its export earnings ("retention rights") for the purchase of imports and repatriation of earnings.

Government Procurement

Another effective but apparently rarely used incentive is the promise of host government purchase of the product of a local plant. For example, one firm had been promised preference on government contracts in South Korea were it to produce locally. Another had allegedly made a commitment to a joint venture in Mexico in order to hold its position as the preferred supplier to the government. An executive in a third firm expressed regret that the company was not producing in Canada because of a tendency by the Canadian government to direct procurement to local firms. The company was in the business of manufacturing special purpose machine tools. Finally, one division of a large conglomerate had invested in Norway in a machine-manufacturing venture with no expectation of profit on the venture. The point was that another division of the parent was involved in North Sea oil exploration.

The manufacturing investment was felt to be a necessary commitment in order for the parent to get an exploration block. But again,
only four instances of the promise of government procurement (or
largesse, in another area) were reported. In three of the four
cases, the maneuver had probably been a contributing factor—if not
the preeminent one—in inducing foreign investment on terms acceptable to the host government.

    Table 4.3 recapitulates the reported experience with incen-
tives of the six types described here. In aggregate, there were 85
instances mentioned by executives in discussing recent investment
decisions; in 28 of these, they may have been critical (33 percent).
The most effective, although the numbers are small, were the grant
of import rights and the promise of government procurement.
Host government guarantees simply were not reported because they
were assumed in most instances. For example, where Overseas
Private Investment Corporation investment guarantees had been
used, there had to have been an underlying host government guarantee.

    Executives in different firms reacted in a variety of ways when
pressed for judgments as to host governments performance requirements and incentives. One, in a high-technology company, said
very bluntly that the firm would not accept any incentives that placed
requirements on the company on the grounds that such would be "the
tail wagging the dog." Management determined how to run its business, not a foreign government. Another high-technology firm had
been asked to make an employment commitment in Puerto Rico and
had refused. When asked why, an executive responded, "Until we
are actually in the country, we do not know how it will grow."
Asked whether the commitments demanded by governments had
ever killed a project, an executive in an automotive firm said that
he had never heard of such an incident, adding "not even Chrysler
in Taiwan when there had been a lot of restrictions imposed."
With respect to the requirements imposed on his own firm in
Spain, the fact that all of the agreements had been approved at the
ministerial level had made management somewhat more comfortable.
A spokesman for a large food processor said that he knew of no instance where one country had preempted investment over another
because of better incentives.

    It is important to note that our interviews made it clear that
host governments made no effort to differentiate between corporations
that had behaved well elsewhere and those that had not. Good behavior is defined here in terms of demonstrable sensitivity to local
need and fulfillment of performance requirements imposed. We
became aware of only one government that had employed independent

TABLE 4.3

Instances Reported of Investment Incentives
by Country and Nature of Incentive

| Country | Incentives | | | | | |
	Subsidies	Tax Reduction	Market Protection	Import Rights	Guarantees	Government Procurement
Argentina	—	—	1	—	—	—
Australia	1	—	1	—	—	—
Bahrein	1	—	—	—	—	—
Belgium	2	2	—	—	—	—
Brazil	2	3	1	—	—	—
Canada	—	—	—	—	—	1
Chile	—	—	1	—	—	—
Egypt	—	1	—	—	—	—
El Salvador	—	1	—	—	—	—
France	2	1	—	—	—	—
Ireland	3	4	—	—	—	—
Italy	1	—	—	—	—	—
Ivory Coast	—	1	2	—	—	—
Malaysia	1	4	1	—	—	—
Mexico	3	1	1	—	—	1
Morocco	—	1	—	—	—	—
Nigeria	—	1	—	—	—	—
Norway	—	—	—	—	—	1
Peru	—	1	—	—	—	—
Philippines	—	—	1	—	—	—
Saudi Arabia	2	1	—	—	—	—
Singapore	2	1	1	—	—	—
South Korea	—	1	3	—	—	1
Spain	3	2	—	1	—	—
Taiwan	—	—	—	1	—	—
Thailand	—	2	—	—	—	—
Turkey	—	—	—	—	1	—
United Kingdom	6	3	—	—	—	—
West Germany	1	—	—	—	—	—
Yugoslavia	—	—	1	2	—	—
Total	30	31	15	4	1	4
Possibly critical	7	8	6	3	1	3
Apparently unimportant	2	23	9	1	0	1

consultants to report on the global behavior of the corporations with which it was dealing. Governments were not even monitoring very carefully the fulfillment of the commitments made by corporations operating within their own territories. The point is that without rewarding those corporations with good track records elsewhere—as well as locally—by somewhat eased entry requirements and/or greater incentives, the wrong signals go out. Certainly, the executives whom we interviewed felt no relationship between the behavior of their firm in one country and how it might be treated in the next. There was no intercountry learning. Yet it would be quite simple for a government to conduct a global survey of corporate behavior. Faculty and students in graduate schools of business and management in the United States, Canada, Western Europe, and elsewhere are perfectly able to make such studies quickly and relatively cheaply, as they have done for at least one government. Corporate behavior is unlikely to be improved significantly by unenforceable rules, but corporate behavior can be influenced by rewards based on past behavior. However, if a government does not look beyond its own border, this learning process is likely to be very tedious, if indeed it takes place at all.

5

Responses to
U.S. Government
Policies and
Programs

Managers within international operations of U.S. corporations are ever mindful of the policies, laws, and regulations of their parent government. Inevitably, conversation veered in that direction, even without undue prodding. Much of it, in the U.S. tradition, was critical. Many expressed envy of support allegedly given international business by other governments. Very few gave the impression that they felt that the U.S. government was really supportive. Some spoke with restrained enthusiasm for the investment guarantee program of the Overseas Private Investment Corporation (OPIC), one or two referred to specific cases of personal assistance from U.S. officials overseas, but that was all. All other comment was critical. As one executive observed, the U.S. government should adopt a policy of working together with, rather than in opposition to, international business. "Up until recently, government officials recited a litany of what one couldn't do, but very little assistance has been forthcoming," he commented.

It should be borne in mind that what is reported here is executive opinion, not objective fact. It was not our purpose to research the realities of U.S. policies and programs vis-à-vis direct foreign investment.

The areas in which we sought specific reactions were OPIC, export credit financing (specifically, the Export-Import Bank programs), the Foreign Corrupt Practices Act, antitrust law, tax law, export controls, and other U.S. laws, regulations, and policies of concern to executives. First, we turn to OPIC.

OVERSEAS PRIVATE INVESTMENT
CORPORATION GUARANTEES

Reference here, of course, is to the three major risk cover-
ages offered by OPIC: nonconvertibility of profits, expropriation,
and loss due to war and insurrection.

By tabulating our interview data, we concluded that OPIC
coverage may have been critical for 6 firms, in at least one instance apiece. Executives in 11 additional firms mentioned OPIC
coverage in a favorable way, but it was quite apparent that the
availability of coverage had not been critical in any investment decision. In 5 other companies, OPIC coverage was viewed as being
of little value but had been used in at least 1 project by each corporation. Twelve firms had never used OPIC guarantees, and they
seemed to have no interest in doing so. Finally, we heard no mention of OPIC in 17 firms. Consequently, one can conclude that of
the 34 firms in which executives commented on OPIC, management
attitude was positive in 17 and negative or passive in 17 (see Table
5.1).

When responses were distributed by corporate types, it became clear that differences were slight. Of the total sample of 51,
exactly one-third of the responses were favorable. The split by
company type between favorable and unfavorable (including nonmen-
tion) was roughly the same except for the Type 4s, which were
slightly more favorable (7 of 12, or 58 percent), and the Type 5s,
which were somewhat more critical (10 of 16, or 63 percent). One
would have anticipated that the integrators (Type 4), with a demonstrable tendency to try for greater central control—and ownership—
would find OPIC-type backing more supportive of their needs than
would the opportunists (Type 5), with their more flexible policies
and greater ability to self-insure through geographical diversification of investment.

Some of the comments made by executives on the subject
were enlightening. One who characterized OPIC insurance as
"nice," in that it had made certain investment decisions easier,
went on to observe that one hoped that the availability of OPIC insurance never made foreign investment so easy that companies
became less conscientious about decision making.

Many executives were neutral. Characteristic was the comment by one, "If you need it, you shouldn't be there." Another commented that the availability of OPIC guarantees was not a "prime
mover," although they might assist in a marginal case. But on
second thought, he observed, the firm would not undertake a

TABLE 5.1

Management Response to OPIC Investment Guarantees by Company Type

Company Type	Availability Critical to at Least One Project	Positive Mention but Not Critical	Negative but Had Been Used at Least Once	Never Used	No Mention	Total
Type 1	1	0	2	0	0	3
Type 2	0	1	2	1	0	4
Type 3	0	0	3	5	0	8
Type 4	2	5	3	1	1	12
Type 5	3	3	1	5	4	16
Type 6	0	0	2	0	0	2
Type 7	0	2	4	0	0	6
Total	6	11	17	12	5	51

17 (6 + 11)

34 (17 + 12 + 5)

marginal investment in any event. Another firm, which had not used OPIC insurance, had not invested in countries in which the fixed investment was high enough to make the risk insignificant. Another felt that OPIC coverage was not worth the money, although the firm had coverage in a number of countries. According to another executive, his firm did not get involved in countries in which OPIC coverage would operate (which was, in fact, not quite true). Still another company had never used OPIC coverage. "A government can't take over one of our operations," an executive explained. "In such a case, we would simply stop the flow of technology."

A large Type 5 firm had recently adopted a policy of self-insuring up to a total of $5 million. Formerly, when the company had gone into small enterprises in high-risk countries, it had used OPIC coverage. But inasmuch as the corporation normally did not go into such ventures, there were few cases in which OPIC coverage had been really relevant. An executive went on to observe that OPIC screens countries with respect to political risk but that the three insurable risks that apply were fairly limited with respect to his firm's projects. He added that the comparable West German insurance available from Hermes was cheaper than OPIC. Finally, the executive observed that those cases of real expropriation of U.S. companies, in which no compensation had been paid for assets, was actually very rare.

An executive in another Type 5 firm expressed somewhat similar views. The corporation had not used any OPIC coverage. The executive, by way of explanation, cited the experience of International Telephone and Telegraph (ITT) in Chile. Congress had passed a law that had blocked any payment to ITT for assets expropriated in Chile. He observed that perhaps one would be buying something that was not actually there. Also, he pointed out, his firm did not attract political attention in that the corporation's business was "hard to define. It meant different things to different people, and hence, it had a blurred profile." Finally, the firm had never had any assets expropriated abroad. The executive went on to observe that there were not a lot of private insurance companies offering political risk coverage. The firm had not used such coverage yet, but it was considering doing so.

Some executives voiced very specific criticisms of OPIC's programs or policies. A spokesman for a Type 1 firm (a novice) reported an experience in Brazil (1973) in which an OPIC rule had allegedly tied the firm's hands concerning coverage for the repatriation of capital. Application had been made before negotiations had begun, it was claimed, but the firm had been refused coverage because the Brazilian opportunity had come upon it so quickly. Apparently it had made a commitment prior to receiving preliminary approval. He observed that the company tended to take equity for know-how, but that OPIC insisted on a significant cash contribution and, by doing so, OPIC limited what the firm could get for its know-how.

Another executive, in a Type 5 firm, pointed out that the loss of output was the real risk and that the recovery of the initial investment was only a small part of the total risk. In his judgment, OPIC had a contradictory set of objectives. On the one hand, there was the objective of reducing political risk; on the other, it was managing its portfolio of insurance on a "sound risk basis." "It seems to me," he argued, "that it should be serving a higher purpose." The availability of OPIC coverage was of obvious concern to his firm, and management was watching the per capita income restriction imposed on OPIC by upcoming legislation. It appeared that the firm would go ahead and negotiate a project in Saudi Arabia if it could obtain political risk insurance coverage. The executive knew of the private political risk market but observed that it was very limited.

In another Type 5 firm, we heard the opinion that inasmuch as OPIC had become a profit-making organization, the private sector would probably pick up this sort of business. The firm preferred doing business with the private sector, we were told. Nonetheless, it had a policy of taking out OPIC coverage whenever it was available. Currently, however, the firm evaluated each project, and the worth of OPIC insurance was carefully considered. Reportedly, the company was working with a private firm, and it was felt that its manner of doing business seemed to fit the firm's interests somewhat better. OPIC was more important for smaller firms that were taking their first plunge overseas, but that it was of very limited value to a large, geographically diversified firm which, in effect, could self-insure. OPIC was something of an incentive, opined an executive, but it was really motivated by public concern and not the "necessities" faced by a private firm. In the case of a Yugoslav project, the company had not opted for OPIC coverage. Management had felt that it was too expensive, given the risk involved.

Executives in two firms reported payoffs from OPIC coverage. The first, a Type 5 firm, had been using OPIC for a number of years and was currently reaping the benefits from its nonconvertibility coverage with respect to Zaire. A spokesman pointed out that the rules regarding nonconvertibility had been liberalized recently so that the company had not been placed in a conflict situation vis-à-vis the local government. The firm had gotten several million dollars out of Zaire via OPIC over the past two or three years. This had been a plus, admitted an executive, but the availability of OPIC coverage had <u>not</u> been critical to the original decision to invest in Zaire, nor had it been in any other decision.

The second case of an OPIC payoff was that of a Type 4 firm, which OPIC was compensating for nonconvertibility with respect to a 50 percent-owned venture in South America. An executive pointed out, however, that in his opinion there was a big flaw in OPIC coverage in that his company had delivered its blocked earnings in local currency to the State Department, which had spent them. Meanwhile the company's claim was being exhausted. The executive felt that in those cases in which the U.S. government incurred no loss, the coverage should be continued. "We have money in the country we can't get out," he observed. However, the firm would use OPIC coverage in Panama if the per capita income restraint imposed on OPIC were increased, although the firm would go ahead and expand its investment there anyway. It was clear that OPIC coverage was not considered critical by the management, although it always looked for OPIC insurance.

But OPIC had its supporters as well as detractors:

A Type 7 firm obtained OPIC insurance whenever possible. An executive considered it better and cheaper than other insurance available commercially. However, only two of six Latin American ventures were covered by OPIC. It had been unwilling to issue contracts on the other four.

For another company, a Type 5, OPIC was "key" in certain areas—the "only viable insurance" and sometimes a "balancing item." An executive observed that other sources of insurance were more expensive, and they excluded war and insurrection risk. The firm had recently obtained OPIC coverage for an Egyptian venture.

A Type 4 firm had used OPIC in some cases, and it had constituted an important element in persuading management that the risk in certain projects was tolerable. It had had OPIC coverage for its Iranian operation but had not needed it!

Management in three firms used OPIC coverage essentially, it seemed, to satisfy their top managements. In the first, a Type 7, we were told that availability of OPIC-type of government-backed guarantee was critical in that the board insisted on OPIC coverage of any developing country investment.

In the second firm, a Type 5, OPIC coverage had been very valuable over the years, claimed one executive, although it was less important currently than in the past. It had provided "a comfort level for the board." He obviously felt that OPIC insurance had never been of critical importance but that it had been very useful in situations where the overseas climate had been virtually unknown to management. It had been perceived as a way of reducing risk and was still useful to that extent.

In the third firm, likewise a Type 5, the executive responsible for negotiating with OPIC stated that the company would never go into a new investment without OPIC insurance—that is, where it is available. It was felt by management to be critical where political risks were perceived, particularly with respect to inconvertibility or expropriation. An executive observed that all investment projects had to go to a top-level management committee for approval and that it was unlikely to approve an investment without "OPIC blessing." The firm would not go into a country with very high risks even for high rewards but would be willing to take moderate risks by insuring them, an executive explained. In the 1960s, the corporation had insured just about every investment it had made, but currently its insurance coverage was much more limited—only in Nigeria, Egypt, and Sudan.

Management of a Type 4 firm felt that OPIC insurance was worthwhile and had used it for nearly all investments. In some cases, an executive believed, it had even been a critical factor. All policies were reviewed each year, and from time to time, the coverage was changed.

So it went pro and con.

Despite that fact that a number of the companies included in our sample were in a position possibly to profit from OPIC's bid bond guarantee program, we came upon only one instance in which the guarantee had been used. This was by a relatively small Type 2 firm. Management considered the guarantee to be important with respect to becoming involved in large projects, particularly those in Eastern Europe and the Middle East. Otherwise, an executive reported, the company had not used OPIC coverage.

The bottom line of our research in this area is that only six projects surfaced that might not have gone ahead in the absence of OPIC, which is not to say that there had not been others. But it was possibly significant that executives in 17, or 33 percent, of the 51 sample firms failed to mention OPIC guarantees or claimed that it had never been used by their respective firms; an additional 17 (or 33 percent) gave generally negative responses.

EXPORT CREDIT FINANCING

The alleged noncompetitiveness of export financing offered by the U.S. Export-Import Bank had driven some firms to off-shore procurement and, in some cases, to foreign production. This factor had been critical, we were told by executives in one firm, in the decision to expand manufacturing facilities overseas for hydroturbines. In another case, a firm had been sourcing out of its United Kingdom plant rather than from the United States in order to take advantage of better export finance terms in the United Kingdom. An executive in the same firm referred to an important sale being negotiated with Poland. The only government willing to give export credit for a sale to Poland, according to him, was the United Kingdom. He went on to observe that the West German government was very conservative with respect to its export financing and did not offer good terms to a lot of countries. He then mentioned a large project in Turkey, which the U.S. Export-Import Bank had turned down, but which the United Kingdom was considering. He felt very strongly that if the United States were to indicate that it would meet the competition "everybody would settle down and stop competing on export credit terms." Another firm was in the position of possibly losing a large Peruvian order for heavy machinery because of noncompetitive export financing terms for a U.S. export. An executive in another firm simply said that insofar as his management was concerned, "the Export-Import Bank is out of business." He referred to the loss of a $50 million order from South Africa in a project designed by a U.S. engineering company that had specified U.S. equipment. The order had gone to a U.K. supplier. A spokesman for a heavy machinery manufacturer cited the case in which the firm had been buying equipment for a recent project in Spain. Export-Import Bank financing had been sought, and rejected, on the grounds that the Spanish investment was tantamount to exporting jobs and that the firm should build the plant in the United States. The argument that a European competitor was entering the United States and hence the U.S. company should go into Europe and compete in its home markets had been rejected by the bank. An executive pointed out that, at the same time, the bank had been financing sales to a very large industrial complex in Saudi Arabia, some products of which would undoubtedly compete with U.S. exports. He failed to see the distinction. An executive in a chemical company observed that the lack of export support by the U.S. government sometimes forced U.S. firms into foreign investment. The offshore purchase of equipment for a large industrial project in Yugoslavia had been triggered by inadequate Export-Import Bank financing. The same had been true for a South Korean project.

The same tune was sung in many firms. Of the 51 companies, critical comment with respect to U.S. export financing was heard in 11. Three others reported that they had never used Export-Import Bank facilities. One other had used the bank but considered its operations to be unimportant insofar as the firm was concerned. Procurement for at least 12 major foreign projects had been directed to overseas suppliers by reason of noncompetitive export financing offered by the United States.

In addition, executives in four firms had criticism of Export-Import Bank procedures. Although his company would use the bank if it were to build a new plant overseas, an executive observed that bank procedures "were a bit of a pain." In a competing firm, an executive said that he was "a fan of the Bank," although occasionally critical of it. "Sometimes it is very bureaucratic." Although he did not feel that the bank was deliberately favorable to large companies as a matter of policy, he observed that, in fact, smaller companies often did not feel able to fight projects through the bank's bureaucracy. This last point was corroborated by an executive in another firm who commented that with his company's product line (food products) it had been difficult to export large enough quantities to qualify for Export-Import Bank coverage. A fourth firm had used Export-Import Bank financing for a large African project, but an executive implied criticism by stating that it was highly desirable for the bank to have a stable policy. It was quite clear that a significant number of executives felt that the United States had a serious problem in the export-financing area.

FOREIGN CORRUPT PRACTICES

Opinion varied substantially concerning the impact of U.S. law and practice with regard to illegal payments overseas. Executives expected its provisions to be modified (which, of course, they were in November 1981). Executives in nine companies reported that business had been lost; in eight, that it had not; and in one that the law had, in fact, been helpful.

For example, an executive in a Type 1 firm observed that his company would have been in one particular Middle Eastern country if it had not been for the U.S. law. "It ties our hands," he commented. "We see the Germans and French going in and doing things we cannot do in selling inferior technology." He felt that the United States was trying to change well-established practice, an effort that was "stupid."

In another, a Type 2 firm, an executive claimed that the U.S. law was a disincentive to the extent that it was almost not worth being in business outside the United States. This attitude had arisen from an experience the firm had with its Belgian subsidiary. And in Brazil, the firm had a small problem in importing a few thousand dollars worth of instruments. Customs had required the usual small bribe. He felt that the management's time and trouble expended over such trivial situations was completely out of proportion to their importance.

An executive in a Type 5 firm said that he could cite many instances of lost business due to the U.S. law. Although the corporation was a "very straight company," these losses had hurt. The company had not even provided product (which was a consumer durable) to foreign government officials, whereas it has been noted that in Uruguay, for example, government officials were using a particular competing European product, which could not be imported legally into the country. This company even feared the activity of its distributors and required that they sign statements to the effect that they were not engaging in any acts that were illegal under U.S. law. Another firm, a Type 1, had been selling overseas principally to private contractors, largely Italian and French, which had contracted for the construction of large projects with governments. Although the company spokesman really did not care to comment on the subject further, business had been lost, he claimed, by reason of the illegal payments' law.

For another, a Type 5, the U.S. law had been a serious disadvantage when the firm had been in the turnkey business. Management strongly suspected that a contract awarded to a French company in Colombia had been gained by bribery.

Due to the U.S. law, a Type 5 firm, had confessed to having paid several hundred thousand dollars in questionable payments over a five-year period. But many things had been included, an executive observed, that had not really been bribes, such as contributions to political parties in countries in which such contributions were perfectly legal. Apparently, management had been having some qualms with respect to the military in Indonesia, which the executive described as very difficult. The firm had tried to reduce the spread between the company price and that which intermediaries charged the government. In any event, management did not believe that the take was going to individuals, but rather into military pension funds. He observed that of all the countries in which he had had experience, Indonesia had probably been the worst from the point of view of corruption, although the Philippines had not been far behind. Management's principal worries with respect to the U.S. law had to do with what constituted an illegal act, the criminal penalties, and the jurisdictional problems between the Justice Department and the Securities Exchange Commission. The U.S. law had also lost a Type 2 corporation business, an executive explained, because distributors occasionally asked the corporation to establish external bank accounts, which it could not—and did not—do. For an executive in another firm, a Type 3, restrictions on illegal payments were seen basically as "a pain in the neck," commented an executive. The effort to monitor the system had been costly, although he did not feel that any business had been lost because of the U.S. law. However, he added, the company had spent a lot of money proving its innocence.

And finally, for a Type 5 firm, although it was very difficult to identify business that had been lost because of the U.S. law, an executive explained, the corporation did tend to shy away from certain countries, such as Indonesia, in part by reason of the law.

Executives in five different firms minimized the effect of the law because of a company code of ethics in force long before the law. An executive in one of these companies, a Type 4, admitted that the U.S. law had caused the firm to lose some business, but it had been "a minimal headache." He added, "I have been in international business 20 years and have never taken or given a bribe." In the second firm, a Type 5, we were told that inasmuch as the company had a very strong commitment against engaging in anything doubtful, the U.S. law had not been a major constraint. Asked about the problem of corruption, an executive in the third firm (a Type 5), responded that the company had had no problems because the company was very conservative. Anyone caught involved in any illegal transaction would be fired. "This is probably one of the most lily-white companies I've ever seen," he observed. The fourth firm, a Type 4, had refused to invest in Korea on the grounds of excessive government corruption, an executive stated. The corporation was an honest company, he said, and refused to pay bribes. According to an executive in the fifth company, a Type 3, the U.S. law had been nothing more than an "administrative annoyance." He noted, "The firm had a code of ethics long before the law." He then went on to mention the problem of "nationalized distributors" overseas, where corruption was the order of the day. Where this had been the situation, the firm had found a local intermediary.

Appointing "nationalized distributors" was one avoidance mechanism. A second was described by a spokesman for a Type 4 firm. For the past several years, the company had opted only for minority equity interests in overseas ventures, plus control via five-to-ten year management contracts. Hence, the U.S. law did not affect the firm, once the management contract had expired. This last clause was added, it seemed to us, almost as an afterthought.

In contrast to all of the foregoing comments, an executive in a Type 5 firm saw the U.S. law as a guideline and, on occasions, possibly helpful. He did admit to a "small problem" with the law's reporting requirements. It should be pointed out, however, that executives in 34 of the 51 sample corporations chose not to address the issue at all. We felt that omission was significant in that each interview was focused on problems arising out of intervention by both host and parent governments.

Over all, one came away with the distinct feeling that the U.S. law on illegal payments was not generally a cause of a significant amount of lost business overseas, except for certain countries in which corruption was seen to be particularly pervasive.

ANTITRUST LAW

Executives in only five firms came up with specific negative examples of the impact of U.S. antitrust law. An executive in a pharmaceutical firm observed that implementation of the law had been such that even exclusive licensing was sometimes vulnerable. "We do it very cautiously," he pointed out. A number of Swiss companies had joined together, he claimed, in putting up a jointly owned plant in Uruguay to satisfy the market on the grounds that only one plant was necessary for such a small market. U.S. companies could not enter into such a venture, he observed. The Japanese and West Germans were doing the same thing, he claimed. Similarly, for a large chemical producer to join a major competitor overseas in a joint venture would be very dangerous, according to an executive in a second firm. His company could not form a consortium to set up a joint venture in Saudi Arabia. In another case, because the firm had only a 50 percent interest (and, hence, lacked unambiguous control) in a foreign joint venture with a non-U.S. competitor, the corporate legal staff had approved. Another firm had had a 50-50 manufacturing joint venture in Europe with one of its principal European competitors, but it was perceived as risky. However, the arrangement had never attracted any antitrust fire. Another firm (food processing) had run afoul of antitrust law when it tried to buy an existing processing plant abroad, which was to be used for selling into the U.S. market. An executive noted that if the company had wished to build an entirely new plant—a "green field operation"—then the U.S. law would not have applied. Nor would it have applied if the acquired business had not been used for selling in the United States.

The absence of other discussion of U.S. antitrust law led one to the conclusion that, by and large, either it was not considered a serious impediment and/or U.S. business had learned to live with it. Of course, the increasing use of 50-50 and minority-owned joint ventures abroad perhaps had reduced the antitrust risk.

EXPORT CONTROLS

On occasion, U.S. export controls had interfered with the course of U.S. business overseas, but not in a major way. One firm had been subjected to pressure because its minority-owned venture in Spain had received an order for equipment from Cuba. Inasmuch as the U.S. firm held control via a management contract, it had felt compelled to go to the U.S. government and apply for an export license. The Spanish government had seen no reason, an executive explained, to clear an agreement between the Cuban and Spanish governments with the U.S. government. The problem had not been resolved. Meanwhile, the firm anticipated a similar situation in Mexico. For another company, the U.S. embargo on shipments of U.S. grain and grain products to the Soviet Union announced in January 1980 had a serious negative impact on sales and earnings. A second firm had likewise suffered by reason of the recent post-Afghanistan sanctions against the Soviet Union. An executive noted that several projects had been dropped from the Soviet plan because the sole source of the relevant technology had been the United States. He explained that he had found that a number of the Soviet foreign trade organizations preferred to purchase from Europe and Japan. The company also reported delays in obtaining export licenses. Its product was industrial machinery. Still another firm reported that export licensing was not a problem currently, for the simple reason that its trade with the Soviet Union had dried up entirely. An executive felt that the reason was that the Soviet relationship with the United States was such that it would no longer buy the firm's products. It had been the premier supplier to the Soviets of special purpose industrial equipment. Management required that the U.S. government give a guarantee that an order could be completed, the executive explained. Normally, given the firm's type of product, an order required up to two years to fill. Of course, he went on, the U.S. government was in no position to give such a guarantee, and the Soviet Union simply could not take the risk inherent in ordering from the firm when it could buy comparable equipment elsewhere. The Soviets were afraid of another political crisis that would bring about sanctions and orders not to ship, even though commitments had already been entered into.

The major concern of another firm relative to export controls had to do with security. For example, an executive pointed out, for its high-technology products, export licenses for sale to the Soviet Union would not be given. And, there could be problems with respect to the People's Republic of China as well, he observed.

An executive in a chemical company pointed out that if export controls, relative to environmental impact, were really applied to the chemical industry, the company would be pushed into offshore sourcing in minority-owned plants, that is, into manufacturing enterprises that the firm did not control unambiguously. In the pesticide area, he stated, there had been a few "abortive attempts" to control exports felt to be environmentally harmful, and the firm had had "to be quick on its feet to prevent enforcement." He agreed that in some cases there might be solid rationale for controlling exports on the basis of environmental impact, but, he claimed, some things were beginning to be banned on the basis of emotion rather than scientific evidence. He then mentioned the fact that the firm was manufacturing overseas a particular pesticide that had been banned by the United States, although "there was no scientific basis for so doing." The host government (an industrialized country) had been sufficiently "rational," according to the executive, to realize that there was no scientific basis for proving environmental damage and had approved local manufacture.

The only area in which firms expressed serious misgivings over export controls generally was with respect to the People's Republic of China. There was great uncertainty about what would or would not be permitted. Changes in policy and, hence, inconsistent export rules were feared.

TAX LAW

It would serve no useful purpose to open up a full discussion here of the complexities of U.S. tax law with respect to the taxation of foreign-source income. Indeed, few executives spoke at length of U.S. tax problems. However, a few did mention specific aspects. An executive in a large, diversified manufacturing firm reported that his office spent an undue amount of time on tax problems, and he cited specifically the law and regulations regarding the allocation of research and development expenses to foreign-source income, which thereby reduced the foreign tax credits it could take against its foreign-source income. The result, according to this executive, was that the firm did not get full recognition of its research and development expenditures.* He then pointed out that because of the sheer complexity of U.S. corporate taxation, it was very costly for the company to monitor what it was doing and satisfy all of the requirements.

Another aspect had to do with the difficulty U.S. firms faced in utilizing foreign tax holidays. A number of executives were well aware of the fact that Japanese and European competitors were

---

*No mention was made of the fact that from August 13, 1981 to August 13, 1983 all expenses for research and development conducted in the United States could be allocated entirely to United States-source income.

often in an advantageous position in this regard. If a parent government did not tax foreign-source income, or taxed it only at a very low rate, or recognized the tax-sparring notion (whereby foreign taxes waived by a host government could be credited against parent government taxes), a firm was in a very much better position than one based in the United States. We invariably queried executives, when the subject of tax holidays came up, how their firms profited from such holidays. The general response was "not much" or that they were of "marginal consequence." One executive reported that inasmuch as his firm was in excess foreign tax credit position, it could apply credits to the stream of income generated by a project for which it enjoyed a tax holiday. To that extent, it gained, but not because of the tax holiday as such, although some of the income that would otherwise have been taxed away locally could then be repatriated to the United States and protected from U.S. taxation via the application of excess foreign tax credits generated elsewhere.

Another firm had entered into an investment plan in Spain, whereby a series of enterprises were to be constructed over several years' time. For a variety of reasons, the Spanish government had given the firm a tax holiday on earnings for a number of years. The result was that the firm began to receive untaxed earnings which, by reason of the ongoing nature of the project, could be reinvested within Spain. The company gained an amount equal to the interest it would have had to pay on the funds, which it otherwise would have had to pay to the U.S. Treasury, so long as it did not remit earnings from the Spanish operation. In this case, that appeared to have constituted a substantial gain and a factor in the decision to go into the Spanish project.

Asked how the U.S. government might help an international business firm, one executive responded by making reference to the prohibition under U.S. tax law to setting up a reserve for political risk. He explained that such a reserve could be set up only with after-tax funds, although one could buy insurance, the premiums for which were tax deductible costs. He felt, however, that a U.S. corporation should be permitted to set up a reasonable reserve with before-tax income and thus self-insure.

Many executives commented negatively on the way in which U.S. expatriate employees were taxed but realized that corrective legislation was in process. At least one had felt compelled to subsidize all expatriate employees by reason of the U.S. personal income tax. According to an executive, it cost the corporation about $150,000 per expatriate per year, in part because of the U.S. tax law. But, he went on, inasmuch as the corporation had a pretax policy to divest itself of expatriate employees to the fullest extent possible, the U.S. tax had really no impact on the corporation other than increasing costs. Executives in the majority of the 51 corporations echoed this view. For example, one firm had no U.S. nationals working overseas. An executive admitted, however, that the tax imposed on expatriates had speeded up the achievement of this goal, that is, the denial of employment for U.S. nationals overseas. One executive, a West German National, pointed out that the West German government did not tax him on his U.S. salary.

Although a number of firms reported Domestic International Sales Corporations (DISCs), executives in only two firms mentioned them as major contributors to their export business. One executive observed that the DISC had been important in his firm's willingness to expand its export operations. However, an executive in another firm more into manufacturing overseas than that just cited explained that it was difficult to separate DISC income from that used for other purposes and, hence, it was almost impossible to qualify DISC income for the construction of plants. In another firm, an executive observed that DISC helped but only to a limited extent.

Closely associated with the availability of the DISC option, plus mounting pressure on firms to engage in barter and various forms of compensation trading, was the fact that at least four firms had purchased or organized international trading companies. Two others had utilized the trading facilities of the Japanese general trading companies, and one had set up a joint-venture trading company in an Eastern European country to facilitate barter trade. Clearly, the need to organize in order to accommodate barter trade was widely felt. Some firms were responding actively. Any modification of U.S. law to facilitate the organization of trading companies would be welcome, though executives who expressed themselves on the subject were skeptical about the scope of the current congressional initiative.

DOMESTIC REGULATIONS

As the executive in one automotive firm pointed out, there are regulations in overseas markets as well as the domestic, but many governments showed a greater understanding than did the United States of the time required for major changes in such a complex industry. He suggested that the domestic industry would welcome the same degree of cooperation as shown by the European and Japanese governments toward their respective automotive industries. It had been argued, of course, that inasmuch as the more economical, small car had been developed in the more congested foreign markets before the U.S. industry had done so, it had been easier for the foreign manufacturers to comply with U.S. requirements. This lead, according to one executive, bestowed a two-year advantage on foreign suppliers.

There was also much concern expressed in the pharmaceutical industry and, to a lesser extent, in the chemical over the impact of domestic regulation. It was pointed out that over the past decade or so, the time required to satisfy government regulations for obtaining approval to market a new drug had lengthened from two years to an average of eight. The result had been not only delay in securing a return on investment in research and development, but also lost years of patent protection. Another management estimated that the usable patent life on a new pesticide could be as short as 8 to 10 years as compared to the full patent life of 17 years. Patents had to be applied for early in the regulatory process to protect proprietary rights and often were issued well in advance of market approval.

There was some suggestion that, as a result, certain research and development had been removed from the United States to foreign laboratories;* so, likewise, had initial production inasmuch as foreign government regulations prior to market introduction were sometimes less time consuming. Any unnecessary delay between development of a commercially viable product and the beginning of a stream of earnings could be very costly—and constitute an impediment to research. The present discounted value of the anticipated earnings stream was simply too low, given the displacement in time of that earnings stream.

OTHER U.S. LAWS, REGULATIONS, AND POLICIES

We asked open-ended questions to plumb executive thoughts with respect to U.S. laws, regulations, and policies that had an impact on the manner in which their respective firms conducted business internationally. Some of the executives' responses were not entirely expected; others were more predictable.

In the first category was a statement by an executive in a large food processing firm. He reported that there had been discussion within management about the impact of U.S. foreign policy

---

*Of possible significance was the fact that 16 of the 51 sample corporations reported at least some research and development activity in 18 countries outside the United States.

on international business. Apparently, some interest had surfaced in these discussions in getting the company to push for the recognition of the economic origins of problems in Central America and the realization that these problems had not arisen simply because of Castro's involvement. It was felt that the United States needed to admit that something should be done about the appalling social conditions in Central America. "All one hears about," the executive concluded, "is military assistance and virtually nothing about assistance to ameliorate the economic conditions in those countries." Management obviously felt that U.S. foreign policy was creating a difficult environment for U.S. business operating in the region, which this firm was.

An executive in an automotive firm commented on the apparent unwillingness of the U.S. government to support U.S. firms overseas. For example, when one of the executives being interviewed had been in Uruguay recently, he had found that he was competing for sales with the European and Japanese embassies, rather than European and Japanese companies. Even press releases from these embassies, he said, had supported their respective companies' interests. He then cited a case in India. The government had put out a tender for the establishment of a 100,000-vehicle plant. A number of companies had been on it from the beginning, such as British Leyland and French Renault. Each had put together a package, with their respective government's support, that the U.S. firm simply could not match. Another executive then gave a Pakistani example. The French government had contracted to put in a nuclear plant, and part of the package had been an involvement by a French auto manufacturer to sell or establish a plant in Pakistan. There was, an executive observed, "great need for a coordinated approach by government and business."

In another firm, we heard words of caution about mixing political and economic policies. An executive gave as an example the human rights posture of the U.S. government, a view repeated by executives in several firms. This particular executive said, "The U.S. Government should realize that we need the export business and work toward alliances, or at least not adversary relationships."

The final comment in one interview was that there was no long-term national commitment in the United States in support of international business. Executives cited the low-rate, long-term capital made available by some foreign governments for the construction of plants to manufacture for export. They lamented the fact that the U.S. government had no comparable program. It seemed agreed that it was virtually impossible to qualify DISC income for that purpose.

The spokesman for another firm observed that as a result of a U.S. decision to go along with a U.N. resolution on limiting the production of a particular medicinal drug to certain countries, which had forced the company to close down a plant overseas (without any compensation), management had become disgusted with trying to adhere to U.S. government policy and would no longer do so unless it coincided with sound business practice. The company tried to be "patriotic" but could not "if it costs that much." He then referred to congressional hearings, then underway, in respect to direct foreign investment. Apparently, he said, these related to the charge that one of the principal inhibitions to international trade and investment was the requirement imposed by foreign governments that foreign investors satisfy an export commitment. He obviously did not agree; he felt that the U.S. government itself was a large part of the problem.

In another company, we heard the story of a proposal that had been made by the firm to a Middle Eastern government. According to an executive, the proposal had made good sense from the point of view of both the host government and the corporation. The U.S. Agency for International Development (AID) had then entered the picture by saying that it would sponsor the project. First, however, AID would have to make a study to determine the feasibility of the venture, though the company had already made an extensive feasibility study, which it offered to AID but was refused. AID said that it needed to get a neutral study made and consequently employed an outside group that had never done anything similar before. It was still in the study stage six years later. Meanwhile, the company had walked away from the project. "We had no time to mess with it further," the executive concluded.

AID had been instrumental, however, in marketing the product of another firm, which had developed a "weaning food" for Third World countries. The product, used specifically by weaning children and lactating mothers, could be produced at a fraction of the cost of milk and contained a high carbohydrate, high protein concentrate. Because of the much-publicized Nestlé baby-food experience, the company had been very reluctant to push the product, although it had sold some in Lebanon via pediatricians. But the threat of adverse publicity when the Nestlé business exploded stopped even this. More recently, the product (which was only produced in the United States) had been sold through AID. The product had not been approved for sale in the United States, a process that would have taken four to five years. An executive opined that the product would be very appropriate in a country such as India. The product for sale in Lebanon had been packaged specially by the firm for AID and contained instructions and ingredients in Arabic as well as English. The present distribution through AID was apparently targeted to six countries, which remained unnamed. Several interesting aspects emerge from this experience. First, the company had developed the product specifically for the Third World and then had been so intimidated that it had withdrawn from the market. Second, AID had taken up its distribution though the product had not been approved for sale in the United States. Third, the fact that AID had been purchasing the product meant that it had to be manufactured in the United States. The firm had wanted to develop manufacturing facilities in several places in the Third World.

It so happened that the principal researcher and one of his associates had just completed a month of interviewing 50 executives, at various levels in perhaps 30 Japanese corporations, immediately prior to commencing interviews in the United States in conjunction with the present study. The contrast between the two sets of interviews was remarkable on one score. In not a single Japanese interview did we hear one word of criticism of the Japanese government. When pressed on the point, Japanese executives simply said that they found no basis for criticism, that they felt that the government was doing as well as it could. There seemed to be no sense of "we" and "they." One felt no area of conflict. Japan was Japan and everyone—business, government, labor, the general public—were all in the same boat. As can be concluded from the preceding pages, in the U.S. interviews we heard much criticism of the government, and very little sense of common interest came through. It was an adversary relationship. It was assumed that objectives differed.

6

Conclusions

In Chapter 3, management's response to the policies and practices in 14 developing countries was discussed. However, we tabulated observations relative to 28 additional countries, which were either developing countries of relatively minor interest or among the developed industrial countries. (In this latter category, we placed Bahrein, Kuwait, the United Arab Emirates, and Saudi Arabia because of their oil wealth and different set of needs.) Observations relative to these 28 are reported in Appendix A. In addition, the 51 sample corporations reported one or more affiliates in 28 more countries, thus bringing the overall total on which some information was collected to 70. Although the affiliates from this latter group of 28 were included in the various tables in the text, no executive comment was recorded regarding them. In addition, there was some minor comment made about 9 other countries in which no investment was reported: Algeria, Angola, Bolivia, Haiti, Hungary, Israel, Libya, Tunisia, and Zambia. Licenses or other forms of contractual relations were mentioned with regard to 3 of these (Angola, Bolivia, and Tunisia), as well as 7 others about which no mention was made during the interviews (Aruba, Denmark, El Salvador, Nepal, Poland, Syria, and Yemen).

One of the interesting results to emerge from the data on affiliate distribution was the heavy concentration in a relatively few countries. Of the 11 Type I countries, 4 (Belgium, West Germany, the Netherlands, and South Africa) were reported to have 74 percent of all affiliates reported in that group. Of the 16 Type II countries, the top 4 countries (Australia, Brazil, France, and the United Kingdom) claimed 70 percent of the affiliates. If one adds a fifth, Italy, the percentage rises to 77. The one developing country in the group,

146

Brazil, accounted for 16 percent. The 4 most popular of the 35 Type III countries (Canada, Japan, Mexico, and Spain) were home to 60 percent of the affiliates in that group. Add 2 more, Argentina and Venezuela, and the percentage climbs to 71 percent. Among the Type IV countries, 2 (India and the Philippines) claimed 58 percent, but neither had as many as 20 affiliates. And of the 2 Type V countries, Yugoslavia was named in 71 percent of the cases, but again the number was small (7). So, of the total 899 affiliates reported from all 70 countries, the first 15 countries listed above (Types I-III) accounted collectively for 625 affiliates or 70 percent of the total. Included were only 4 developing countries (Brazil, Argentina, Mexico, and Venezuela), which reported a total of 142 affiliates, or 16 percent of the total. For all 46 developing countries in which affiliates were listed, the total was 357, or 40 percent of the 899 reported affiliates. If one then subtracted those developing countries with over 10 affiliates each (the 4 listed above, plus Singapore, Costa Rica, Taiwan, Colombia, Malaysia, South Korea, India, and the Philippines), 34 developing countries were left with 114, or 13 percent of the total between them. In other words, the investment in over half of those countrids in which affiliates were reported was trivial.

Table 6.1 combines the data on reported affiliates for all five corporate types. We can see that of the five affiliates of Type 1 corporate parents, one (20 percent) was located in a Type I country and four (80 percent) in a Type II. If we compute a table on such a basis, we derive Table 6.2. The significant aspect of the distribution in Table 6.2 is that it is roughly the same across the five groups of countries for all but corporate Types 1 and 7, the novices and mavericks. However, if we eliminate from the data all developed industrial countries, the pattern changes somewhat (see Table 6.3). These data distributed by percentage of affiliates, according to the classification of their parent corporations, across country types yield the array shown in Table 6.4. Now we see that the affiliates of Type 2 firms (learners) tend to be concentrated in countries with emphasis on incentives but with few entry controls in place, that is, in Type II countries. (Since only a single Type 1 affiliate was reported in a developing country, Brazil, no conclusion can be drawn about that corporate type, at least from the data here.)

Type 3 firms (builders) tend to concentrate in countries with entry screening plus incentives, the Type III countries. The pattern for the Type 4 parents (integrators) and Type 5 (opportunists) looks very similar although with a slight shift in the latter case toward the Type III countries. But none of the differences among Type 3, 4, and 5 firms were sharp. The Type 6 corporate parents (retrenchers) show a shift toward the less open Type IV countries.

TABLE 6.1

Distribution of Reported Affiliates by Classification of Corporate Parents across Country Types

Corporate Type	Country Type					Total
	I	II	III	IV	V	
Type 1 (novices)	1	4	0	0	0	5
Type 2 (learners)	8	5	15	1	0	29
Type 3 (builders)	21	37	37	4	0	99
Type 4 (integrators)	33	71	73	9	2	188
Type 5 (opportunists)	75	170	228	26	5	504
Type 6 (retrenchers)	3	2	7	3	0	15
Type 7 (mavericks)	9	26	21	3	0	59
Total	150	315	381	46	7	899

TABLE 6.2

Percentage Distribution of Reported Affiliates by Classification of Parents across Host Country Types

Corporate Type	Country Type				
	I	II	III	IV	V
Type 1 (novices)	20	80	0	0	0
Type 2 (learners)	28	17	52	3	0
Type 3 (builders)	21	37	37	4	0
Type 4 (integrators)	7	38	39	5	1
Type 5 (opportunists)	15	34	45	5	1
Type 6 (retrenchers)	20	13	47	20	0
Type 7 (mavericks)	15	44	36	5	0
Total	17	35	42	5	1

148

TABLE 6.3

Reported Affiliates in Developing Countries by
Country Type and Classification of Parents

Corporate Type	Country Type					Total
	I	II	III	IV	V	
Type 1	0	1	0	0	0	1
Type 2	1	2	3	1	0	7
Type 3	4	7	14	4	0	29
Type 4	7	16	36	7	2	68
Type 5	7	54	116	24	5	206
Type 6	1	1	2	3	0	7
Type 7	1	18	17	3	0	39
Total	21	99	188	42	7	357

TABLE 6.4

Percentage Distribution of Reported Affiliates in
Developing Countries by Classification of
Parents across Country Types

Corporate Type	Country Type				
	I	II	III	IV	V
Type 1	0	100	0	0	0
Type 2	14	29	13	14	0
Type 3	14	24	48	14	0
Type 4	10	24	53	10	1
Type 5	3	26	56	12	2
Type 6	14	14	29	43	0
Type 7	3	46	44	8	0
Total	6	28	57	12	2

The similarity in affiliate distribution for Type 3, 4, and 5 firms could emerge for several reasons:

1. The classification of corporate parents is not meaningful;
2. The classification of host country investment policies is not meaningful;
3. The total number and distribution of affiliates accumulated over the years may not relate to a corporation's present structure, attitudes, and policies;
4. Host country investment policies make little difference with respect either to attracting or repelling foreign investment.

Although one might quarrel with our classification of both corporate parent and host country investment policy in certain cases, we would maintain that the questionable cases of classification are limited, and even if they were shifted there would be very little difference in the general outcome. Admittedly, we may have caught a certain number of the corporate parents at the point of transition from one corporate type to the next. We were aware that the structures, attitudes, and policies of certain divisions of some corporations were in one stage of development, for example, of a Type 5 nature, but that the rest of the corporation was in the Type 3 or 4 mode. This inconsistency was particularly apparent where the corporate parent verged on being a conglomerate, with each major division organized somewhat differently relative to its foreign operations, and each with a different history. These differences were particularly great, one suspected, for corporations that had grown via acquisition.

The reason for the failure of a less well-defined pattern to emerge probably has much more to do with the third explanation above. That is, our classification of corporate types tends to be sequential in time, but data relating to affiliates are cumulative. For example, firms typically move from Type 1 to Type 2 to Type 3, etc., with the exception of the Type 7s (mavericks), which stand by themselves and are out of sequence by definition. This means that we should have concentrated on the distribution of newly organized affiliates to be able to compare those marginal in time, rather than the cumulative historical distribution. However, our data fell short of this refinement. It is suggested that if we were to compare corporations on the basis of affiliates formed exclusively within say, the last five years, the differences would stand out much more sharply.

In fact, the experience reported by executives in the 51 sample corporations compels one to conclude that the explanation for the similarity of affiliate distribution among Type 3, 4, and 5 firms lay largely in reason number 4 above; that is, host country invest-

ment policies make little difference with respect to either attracting or repelling foreign investment. Certainly, the evidence collected led to the conclusion that neither the imposition of investment
requirements nor the granting or withholding of investment incentives had resulted in either repelling or attracting investment to any
significant degree. In that the interviewers were searching specifically for investment projects that had been blocked by the imposition
of performance requirements or stimulated by incentives and came
up with such few instances of either was revealing. For example,
only 33 instances of blocked investment by reason of the imposition
of performance requirements surfaced in the study. All together,
some 124 instances were reported (as against 707 reported investments made in those countries in which one would expect to encoun-
ter performance requirements, that is, in Type III, IV, and V countries). But 19 of these requirements that allegedly blocked investment were due essentially to the reservation of certain sectors for
locally owned firms, thereby leaving only 15 cases of projects rejected by reason of the imposition by host governments of specific
performance requirements.

The explanation is, of course, that many of the requirements
(those relating to ownership, employment, local content, and training) pushed in the direction in which a foreign firm was already inclined. The only requirement causing problems of a serious nature
was that relating to exports, but even there we found only four instances in which an investment project had been rejected clearly for
this reason. No executive interviewed voiced strong feelings on the
subject other than related to the export requirement. And even then,
several indicated that the pressure for exports was perfectly under-
standable. Finally, there was much reason to suspect that performance requirements had been evaded in a significant number of
cases by one means or another.

Much the same could be said of investment incentives, and
for the one country in which incentives had been peculiarly attractive, Ireland, there were serious second thoughts reported in some
quarters about the wisdom of having responded. In any event, of
the 85 instances in which incentives were mentioned specifically, in
only 30 cases did they seem to have been critical to the investment.
The most effective—and probably least costly—incentives were sel-
dom reported. These were the permission to import the finished
product either to test a national market for a given period of time
and/or the right to import the finished product during the establishment of a local plant. The second was the promise of procurement
by the host government in event of local production. It seemed that
specific government guarantees relating to such matters as market
protection, foreign exchange availability, and immunity from ex-

propriation or nationalization* were heavily discounted by management and rarely a critical element in an investment decision. Executives were very wary about relying on any nonmarket factors unless they were subsidies made available at the start of a project. But, for reasons already discussed, it is probably politically unacceptable for the governments of developing countries to offer undisguised subsidies to foreign corporations. The inescapable conclusion is that most incentives were largely ineffective; investment would have taken place in their absence.

In the total context of our many discussions, it did seem that the most effective approach would be an explicit host government reward to corporations which had demonstrated in the past—locally or elsewhere—their responsiveness to government policy and national interest, plus consistency of policy. By reward is meant preferential treatment vis-à-vis other foreign firms, such as legally designating such firms to have the same status as those that are locally owned.

One might argue that it was the relatively larger size of the Type 5 firms that appeared to make them somewhat less apprehensive about countries with less liberal investment environments. And, indeed, the mean size of Type 5 firms, as measured by 1980 annual sales, was substantially larger at $14 billion ($7 billion if one eliminated the two largest and two smallest). The figures should be compared with the mean size of Type 4 firms, $3.7 billion ($3.1 billion if one eliminated the largest and smallest); $4.3 billion for Type 3 firms; $1.6 billion for Type 2; and $1.0 billion for Type 1 firms. Type 6 firms (the retrenchers), of which there were only two in the sample, registered a mean of $5.6 billion; and the Type 7 firms (the mavericks), of which there were six, registered $3.9 billion. But would relatively greater size tend to lead to the more tolerant opportunist mode, or would the corporate policies and attitudes consistent with that mode tend to lead to greater size through more rapid growth? The direction of causality could not be determined from the data. What was possible, however, was that one effect of the more restrictive investment policies imposed by Type IV and V countries was a tendency to inhibit entry by the smaller firms. Presumably, the larger firms could tolerate more easily the added costs and risks inherent in government intervention. But, as already noted, the difference in the numbers was small, which meant that

---

*As used here, expropriation refers to a taking over of assets by a host government with or without compensation, and nationalization to the forced spinoff of ownership to local nationals.

differences in size could not have been a significant factor except possibly at the very lowest end.

The smallest company in our sample, with annual sales at around $50 million, had no overseas operations. This firm, a successful manufacturer of specialized industrial machines, had not expanded abroad despite competitive pressure to do so. In our 1956-59 study, this management had expressed no interest in overseas production; in 1981 it did.

The other relatively small firm included in our sample, with annual sales of about $150 million, had foreign operations only in Brazil and the Netherlands. Management had actively considered Mexico, Singapore, and Taiwan because of competitive pressure, but somehow the firm had not moved. Decision making tended to be highly personal and investment driven by personal interest. A third corporation on the small end, with annual sales of $350 million, was manufacturing in Canada, the United Kingdom, and Sweden, with licenses in India and Taiwan (possibly in South Korea as well if a negotiation underway in 1981 were successful). Also, negotiations with the People's Republic of China were reported. All of these moves had been made subsequent to our 1957-59 survey. What seemed to differentiate these firms most sharply was the reported level of exports as a percentage of total sales. The figures were about 50 percent for the smallest, 43 percent for the next, and only 17 percent for the largest, which was the firm moving most actively into foreign production. Apparently, the first two firms had been able to compete to date fairly effectively from the United States, but not so the third. All three were producing technically sophisticated industrial equipment, and all were relatively labor intensive. Depreciation as a percentage of net sales was between 1.5 and 2.5 (the exact number for one firm was not known because it published no financial statements). These measures were on the low end. Net property and equipment per employee was between $1,500 and $2,000, again on the low end. This finding suggests that among the smaller firms, governments interested in stimulating investment should target, not those with a relatively large and stable export market, but those that have lost exports or are unable to gain an export market from their U.S. base.

The aggregate ownership data also lead to some interesting insights. From the aggregate data, we can conclude that the encouragement in Type III and IV countries to restrict—or spin off—foreign ownership has been at least partially effective (see Table 6.5). In such countries, 50 and 46 percent, respectively, of all reported affiliates in which ownership was specified (368) were owned less than 100 percent by the U.S. parent. In fact, 43 percent were owned either 50-50 or on a minority basis. But, as pointed out earlier, in the highly restrictive Type IV countries, many wholly owned affiliates remained—54 percent to be exact of those for which ownership was reported. This suggests evasion of host country policy in a fairly massive way (see Table 6.6).

TABLE 6.5

Distribution of Affiliates by Ownership and Country Type

| Country Type | Ownership | | | | | |
	100 Percent	Majority	50 Percent	Minority	Unknown	Total
Type I	104	6	11	12	17	150
Type II	186	29	24	32	44	315
Type III	165	24	45	93	54	381
Type IV	22	4	4	11	5	46
Type V	0	0	0	7	0	7
Total	477	63	84	155	120	899

TABLE 6.6

Percentage Distribution of Affiliates
by Ownership and Country Type

| Country Type | Ownership | | | | Less than Wholly Owned |
	100 Percent	Majority	50 Percent	Minority	
Type I	78	5	8	9	21
Type II	69	11	9	12	31
Type III	50	7	14	28	50
Type IV	54	10	10	27	46
Type V	0	0	0	100	100
Total	61	8	11	20	39

Note: Data are calculated on the basis of affiliates of known ownership.

The fact that we picked up no really negative comment about the policies pursued by Type V countries, but many regarding Type IV countries, tends to reinforce the finding that a consistent, clearly enunciated policy that is relatively devoid of corruption in its application is the ideal—plus attractive underlying economic conditions, of course. The degree of restrictiveness of that policy seems to be relatively unimportant.

The question finally arises, of course, what can and should a parent government do to stimulate a more equitable distribution of world wealth and income in terms of policies that might push private sector skills, technology, and capital in the direction of those countries most desperately in need of such inputs. Significantly, the sole U.S. government program cited in any interview during the course of our study as supportive of international business was the investment guaranty program of the Overseas Private Investment Corporation. But even there, as previously reported, judgment had been divided—favorable in 17 corporations, critical in 17, nonuse in 12, and no comment in 5. Even so, it appeared to us that OPIC coverage had been critical to at least 1 project each in only 6 firms, favorably mentioned but not critical in 11 others. Executives in 17 other firms reported use in one instance but were generally critical of OPIC for a number of reasons, including its allegedly conflicting objectives and high cost. Several spoke of comparable private insurance. In general, however, executives felt that the U.S. government was basically unfriendly to international business, and they were unable to explain that official posture except in terms of political expediency. The public image of international business was unattractive for a variety of reasons.

One came away from these conversations with a sense of the general bewilderment of executives in many companies. In their view, the United States was a business-based society. Yet, despite much rhetoric about world development, the U.S. government provided very little guidance, leadership, and support of the flows of U.S. skills, technology, and capital that could fuel that development. Given the full panoply of U.S. government policies—export financing, foreign corrupt practices, antitrust, export licensing, and taxation—spokesmen for virtually all 51 of the sample corporations saw obstructionism and added cost vis-à-vis foreign competitors.

According to the vice-president and treasurer of a large conglomerate, which we classified as a builder (Type 3), the future of international business lies more in the service sector than manufacturing. He insisted that the statistics indicated that the international transactions of services were growing more rapidly than the international flow of goods or direct investment. Although few executives explicitly recognized such a trend, the apparent shift in policy

directions of their respective firms did. Between 8 and 10 of the
51 sample corporations had either established international trading
companies themselves or had entered into some variety of relationships with the large Japanese general trading companies. There
seemed to be a rapidly increasing interest in various forms of international contracting for technical, managerial, and marketing
skills. In an uncertain world, the ability to shift sources of product
was reassuring, but to be locked into fixed manufacturing assets that
one owned was much less so. Wholly inadequate research has been
done in respect to the international movement of services, including subcontracting and various forms of countertrade, and the governmental policies and institutions needed to support such relationships. The era of relatively cost-free international data flows, of
flexible production tooling, the miniplant, and the international
technical service and trading company is upon us. The obsession
that both public policy makers and private researchers in the international business area have had with equity-based systems should
be redirected more to the contractually based systems.

Appendix A

Note on
Management Responses Relative to
Developed Countries and
Those Developing Countries of
Relatively Minor Interest to Management

TYPE I COUNTRIES

Belgium. Eighteen firms reported 19 investments (15 100 percent owned, 1 majority owned, 1 50–50, 1 minority owned, and 1 unspecified). One firm mentioned a plant expansion initiated by reason of tax relief and training grants. In the final analysis, the site had been narrowed down for economic reasons to Belgium, the Netherlands, and France. The choice among the three had been dependent on the degree of government incentives offered. Overall view: favorable.

Netherlands. Seventeen firms had invested in 20 ventures (11 100 percent owned, 3 50–50, 3 minority owned, and 3 unspecified). Only 1 firm reported a negative experience. One of its plants had been severely damaged by fire, and the firm had applied to the local municipality for a permit to rebuild. The permit had been given, but no assurance that an operating license would be granted. (The national government intervened only with respect to employment.) An executive admitted that the plant would be located in the heart of the town and that it was "not the best neighbor" by reason of dust and smell, plus a fear of explosion from one of the chemicals being used in the process. The executive felt that a number of people wanted the firm out and that the community "was in fact playing games with the company." The upshot was that the firm had been forced out.

South Africa. Seventeen firms had invested in 28 ventures (13 100 percent owned, 2 majority owned, 1 50–50, 5 minority owned, and 7 unspecified). Two others reported licensees. One of these latter had been producing via a local licensee for a number of years, both for the local market as well as for Zambia and Zimbabwe. The advantage was lower labor cost. For this firm, a manufacturer of mining equipment, the greatest market outside of the United States, Canada, and Mexico was southern Africa. There were tariff problems in South Africa in that preferential treatment was given to locally manufactured equipment, and the firm's competitors were in the market. Another firm, as a matter of corporate policy, did nothing in South Africa. A third was in a mining and manufacturing venture, the U.S. firm owning a minority interest. Attractions for the company had been the fact that the venture had been 60 percent debt financed, and there was the possibility of a management contract. The government had approved the deal partly, it was felt by the U.S. management, because the venture was to be located in one of the black homelands. Homes for the employees were built on the site with financial help from the government. Reaction from its U.S. shareholders had been mild, but an executive speculated that the problem would now be more serious and would represent a serious disincentive if the investment had been subject to more recent decision. Overall view: caution.

West Germany. Thirty-three companies had invested in 45 operations (36 100 percent owned, 1 majority owned, 4 50-50, 3 minority owned, and 1 unspecified). One service-oriented firm had run into restrictions, but there was no indication that these had constituted discrimination against foreign business. Another firm reported a concessionary loan to locate a facility in Berlin. A third reported that West Germany was the one case where the government was seeking to attract investment, specifically of that firm, and was prepared to offer incentives. But, an executive added, "It would not have made any difference; we would have gone in anyway, because we wanted to be there." Overall view: No critical comment came out in any of the interviews.

TYPE II COUNTRIES

Australia. Twenty-seven companies in 52 ventures (25 100 percent owned, 14 majority owned, 2 50-50, 7 minority owned, and 4 unspecified). One firm reported that it had encountered neither bribery nor pressure for payments, but there was "a ton of bureaucracy." No incentives had been offered other than subsidized energy, which the firm felt could be a trap. It had refused a low-price energy contract for fear that retaliatory action might be taken later

in the form of a penalty price. A second firm had been able to negotiate a tradeoff of exports in return for a lower local content requirement. It had been permitted to reduce its local content by 7.5
percent for an increase in exports equal to the same amount. For
this firm, incentives had been important; they had been plugged into
the financial analysis. Compliance with the conditions specified—
export percentage and local content—had been carefully monitored
by the government. Performance guarantees were seen as precon-
ditions for all incentives. No incentives had been offered to another
firm other than subsidized power. The same firm reported that
transfer prices had to be approved by a governmental agency. Overall view: no serious problems. Incentives were linked to performance. Two firms had withdrawn for unspecified reasons.

Bahrein. One firm reported a single, minority-owned venture. Natural gas, made available at a "good price," had been the
inducement.

Chile. Three firms reported five operations (four 100 percent
owned and one majority owned). One had been intervened in Chile
and, as a result, had filed an OPIC claim. Shortly thereafter, the
government had changed, and the company had been asked by the
new regime to return, whereupon the firm had withdrawn its claim.
The Latin American manager in a food processing company stated
that his "priorities are in Chile and Venezuela." Chile was selected
because he felt that it was politically safe, gave promise of a good
return, and had a good market with growth potential. Another company had been caught in Chile by a change of rules. To have a viable
industry of its type required a duty spread of about 30 percent.
Overall view: favorable.

Costa Rica. Five firms reported ten ventures (eight 100 percent owned, one majority owned, and one 50-50). Only one executive spoke directly to a Costa Rican operation. He was critical of
the "irresponsible economic policies" of the government, for example, inappropriate price controls that prevented "reasonable profits."
The company, a food processor, had gotten into an agricultural type
development with the government, which owned a minority share.
Allegedly, the government had dragged its heels very badly and had
to be prodded—an executive used the word "threatened"—to get it to
produce its share of the investment. No incentives had been offered,
and no performance guarantees imposed. Overall view: cautious.

Ecuador. Four companies reported five enterprises (four 100
percent owned and one majority owned). One of these firms had

invested because of a government threat to ban further imports.
The firm had entered, but the promised tariff protection never materialized. The firm was operating a high-cost plant competing with
low-cost imports, the result of which was that it was generating
little if any profit. Overall view: skepticism of government commitments.

France. Twenty-four firms reported 43 operations (26 100
percent owned, 1 majority owned, 6 50-50, 3 minority owned, and
7 unspecified). Two firms in the service area reported discrimination enforced against them. One of these, which had a motion picture subsidiary, operated a production facility in France to recap-
ture the tax paid on motion picture admissions, which was possible
up to the cost of the negatives for a motion picture filmed in France.
However, to qualify, the film script had to be approved by the French
government, and no deviation was permitted. There was no money
"up front," only return via admissions after the film was made. Another executive explicitly classified France as having a hostile environment for U.S. business. Executives in two firms frankly admitted management prejudice against investing in France and, in
both cases, that prejudice was cited as a reason for investing elsewhere. Another, which had a manufacturing plant in France, was
very cautious about expanding it. Management felt that it had been
compelled to invest in France because of French product regulations,
although they were probably contrary to European Community regulations. The firm had been told that it would get a better price review for its products (which were under price control) were it to engage in certain local research and development activities. It was
reported that another firm had been "blackmailed" into local research and development by "a massive tax threat." The result of
the government pressure was that the firm would not invest further
in France. Several executives felt, in one way or another, that the
French government was inhibiting international trade within the
European Community by a number of its policies. For still another,
the French government was said to have been very helpful in arrang-
ing a joint venture with a local company that had been in deep financial trouble, but it had insisted that the U.S. company not take a
majority position. Finally, a computer manufacturer had wanted to
build a plant in France but had been blocked in doing so by the French
government, apparently out of fear that the firm would compete too
strongly with a local firm. Overall view: highly discriminatory in
favor of local firms.

Ireland: Ten firms reported 12 investments, all wholly owned:
3 Type 3s, 7 Type 4s, and 2 Type 5s. Many company spokesmen,

who were generally very skeptical with respect to the value of country incentives, not infrequently cited Ireland as unique. One firm (Type 3) observed that incentives were just an "added bonus—with the exception of Ireland." In another firm, government incentives and grants were not included in feasibility studies and an executive referred specifically to Ireland. But executives in a large pharmaceutical firm (Type 4) said that in the case of both Puerto Rico and Ireland, the incentives were so great that the firm definitely recognized that they were different. The company would not have gone into either area in the absence of those incentives. In still another firm (Type 5), a consumer products manufacturer, executives observed that it manufactured abroad only in two circumstances; first, to protect a market from which it was being excluded by government action; and second, when the incentives for manufacturing locally were so great that they attracted management attention. The only two examples of the latter, to which reference was made, were Puerto Rico and Ireland. Managers in a chemical firm (Type 5), did not move into projects merely because of local incentives. Asked specifically about Ireland, they observed that it was, in their judgment, trying to persuade companies to invest there when it really was not economic for them to do so, although in some industries, perhaps pharmaceuticals, it was probably "okay." But if one were talking about an auto industry, for example De Lorean, it was open to considerable doubt. Doubt was also expressed about the wisdom of intercountry competition that such incentives as those offered by Ireland tended to induce. An electronic firm executive, when queried about an ideal government investment incentive program, replied that he would like to see a country make a statement to the effect that it "wanted to be the Ireland or the Singapore of that area." It was clear that the Irish program was seen as ideal by some executives but as an uneconomic trap by others. Some felt that inasmuch as Ireland was being integrated into the European Community, it would be compelled to reduce the level of its incentives to that approved by the European Community.

Of the 10 companies reporting manufacturing ventures in Ireland (all 12 of which were 100 percent owned), 7 discussed some of their motives and expectations in so locating. Executives in 3 other firms gave their reasons for rejecting Ireland as a site. The following comments are from the 7 firms investing in Ireland:

Firm 1 (Type 4) reported that its Irish project had been EEC motivated. The Irish government did offer incentives, it was pointed out, but these incentives had not even been reflected in the capital proposal made to management, having been mentioned only in a footnote. In calculating the return on investment, a typical tax factor had been used. The trouble was, we were informed, that tax laws could be changed easily and, hence, it was not justifiable to launch a business venture on the basis of a special tax situation. The Irish project included the construction of three plants and the expansion of a fourth. These were world-scale plants, but the expectation was that business in Europe would grow to take all of the production. In fact, this had happened, and Europe was currently taking 95 percent of the Irish output. Ireland was, one executive claimed, simply the best business site. He then went on to point out how sensitive the Irish government had been to company needs. An example was assistance given in training cost accountants in a local junior college. He also cited the easy accessibility of high-ranking government officials and recalled an appointment he had with the Irish minister of finance. It was a two-hour appointment, the principal purpose of which was the desire of the company to discuss the importance of maintaining the Irish exchange rate within the European "snake." It was on the verge of being overvalued, thereby making export difficult. An adverse change in the rate could close the plant, he told the minister. Subsequently, the Irish devalued their currency.

Firm 6 (Type 5) felt that it needed to source closer to a major customer in West Germany. It felt that it had to source within the European Community and opted for Ireland, specifically because of the tax incentives offered. The company was not required to pay any Irish taxes for 15 years. It had been "a very profitable little enterprise." It employed only some 250 people.

Firm 23 (Type 4) was given a five-year tax holiday, but it appeared that it had been the location that had been critical. The company felt compelled to produce within the EEC, both to supply the European Community and market in certain African markets. Prior to the decision to go into Ireland, an exhaustive six-month survey had been made covering all of Europe and Africa. An alternative had been Zaire, but that "fell out early in the process." It was clear that it had been the Irish incentive package that had pulled the firm in, once it had made the decision to produce within the European Community or one of its associated countries.

Firm 25 (Type 5) had been drawn into Ireland precisely because of the incentive package. As one executive put it, "The incentives in these two countries [Puerto Rico and Ireland] were so great that they draw you into the country." He felt that one advantage over other countries was that the incentives in these two cases were very specific.

Firm 36 (Type 4), for which the Irish incentives had been critical to a decision to invest there, was concerned that neither its Puerto Rican nor Irish plants become what an executive called "runaway plants" and start to ship their output into the United States at a cost lower than the domestic cost of production. In order to avoid this, the company was, to use the words of the spokesman, "maintaining a proper balance of investment in the high incentive countries."

Firm 41 (Type 3) had gone into Ireland to serve the market and only after it had assured itself that the necessary level of production could be maintained. However, the incentives were important, and Ireland was probably the one place to which the company had been attracted by the incentives. A company spokesman spoke enthusiastically of the capital grants, tax holiday, and training subsidies. The tax holiday was a total exemption until 1990 and then taxation at a 10 percent level for the next 10 years. The Irish incentives were described as "being almost too good to be true." Among other things, the Irish government was leasing a plant to the company on terms that meant that it would have the use of $1 million worth of plant and equipment for a total cost of about one-quarter of that amount and with payments spread over five years. Before making its final commitment, Firm 41 representatives spoke to executives in other companies with Irish operations and learned that there was no cause for concern. The level of local skill was all that was required. One executive summarized the experience by saying that the Irish government had been extremely flexible and cooperative. Decisions were easy to get and rapid—"unlike the United Kingdom," he observed. The Irish had approached the company some years before and maintained continuing communication until the firm invested. One executive observed that the Irish ran their incentives like a business. He felt that the investment would repay the Irish in about two and one-half years, in terms of employment and other benefits. He observed, further, that such incentives as the firm received were important in two ways: first, their effect on cash flow; second, their qualitative characteristic (by that he was referring to tangible evidence of a government's favorable posture vis-à-vis the firm). He got the impression that the Irish knew what they were doing, and helped the firm cut through the red tape. "It was like one-stop shopping," he said. In the final analysis, however, there were serious misgivings within management about the Irish operations. One executive admitted that the firm would like to close it down since the market had not developed. However, this would be too embarrassing for many reasons, both internally and externally. It also would require repayment of its grants.

Firm 51 (Type 3) appeared to have had a very favorable experience in Ireland. One executive observed that Ireland was a very attractive entry into the EEC. He specifically mentioned the tax incentives and the educated work force. He did feel that the productivity of Irish workers might have been lower than originally assumed and also that the infrastructure and transportation to the rest of Europe were problems. The basic consideration, he opined, should be whether the investment made good economic sense. In this case, the market already existed, but he questioned whether the capacity of the Irish plant was really justified.

These final notes of skepticism were reflected more forcibly in opinions expressed in three other firms:

Firm 13 (Type 2) had no operation in Ireland. Queried as to the reason, one executive said that his firm had not considered Ireland seriously, in part because of a serious scarcity of the highly skilled labor required. The grants and subsidies were simply not sufficient to make up the disadvantages of locating in Ireland which, of course, had no domestic market. (It might have been significant that Firm 13 already had three plants in the European Community, all in West Germany.)

Firm 31 (Type 3) had looked at Ireland very closely. However, as one executive explained, the incentives were not great enough to overcome the difficulties. It was a good source of technical people, a good place for a multinational group to live, and an environment where you could expect good productivity. It was not, however, a particularly good place to get customers into. In any event, he observed, Ireland was getting fairly saturated with industry.

Firm 37 (Type 5) had likewise looked at Ireland as an investment site but at least temporarily had rejected it. The problem was that the company had substantial facilities in several other European countries and, consequently, a technical basis for expansion, a basis that it lacked in Ireland. Hence, it had not been responsive to the various grants and incentives offered by the Irish but with which the firm was fully familiar.

The interesting point to note is that even though the Irish incentive package was acknowledged by those with experience to be among the more attractive in the world and was coupled with some economic advantages, no Type 1 or 2 firms had been lured into Ireland and only two Type 3 firms. One might have expected that, given the extraordinarily favorable conditions offered, more of these firms would have been attracted. The conclusion that one can draw is that even under the best of circumstances, government incentives are really effective with respect only to those firms that have reached the point at which management perceives the advantages—and has the capability—of integrating international operations. After all, an Irish plant would be justified primarily on the basis of other national markets its products might reach advantageously. Such planning and market integration implies a control capability in the parent firm that is uncharacteristic of Type 1 and 2 firms.

Even among Type 3 firms, relatively few have the capability of controlling an internationally integrated operation. They are still thinking primarily in terms of producing overseas either for the local market, in this case, the Irish, or for import into the United States. One of the Type 3 firms had expected business to develop sufficiently in the area to justify the investment. It had not, and management would really prefer to close down the operation. Currently, it was serving as a world source for a certain product, but one got the impression that the U.S. management was distinctly uneasy about this situation. The other Type 3 firm investing in Ireland also had doubts about the wisdom of the investment. A spokesman questioned whether the capacity of the plant was justified, given excess capacity in its continental European plants (Spain, West Germany, and the United Kingdom). Significantly, a Type 2 firm, which had looked at Ireland and desisted, was worried about adequate labor skills and the nonexistence of a local market. By contrast, a Type 5 firm resisted the Irish attractions, which management was fully familiar with, simply because it already had substantial operations in five other European countries and, if expansion were needed, it would be cheaper to build onto existing facilities. Another Type 5 firm was not in Ireland simply because corporate decision makers did not give much weight to government incentives, which they saw as being transient in their impact. This was a firm that was relatively capital intensive (depreciation on a percentage of sales was 6.9 percent, which meant that only 2 of the 51 firms had a higher percentage). Only 1 capital-intensive firm had been a satisfied investor in Ireland, but it was not clear that its Irish facility actually embodied capital-intensive processes. Firms were skittish about making capital-intensive investments in relatively small markets, whatever incentives might be offered.

All together, there were only five firms (three Type 4s and two Type 5s) that seemed unambiguously enthusiastic about their respective Irish ventures. Problems relating to deficiencies of the infrastructure, labor skills, transportation, and communication seemed to erode many of the benefits derived from the incentive package. It seemed that many companies, at first enthusiastic about the subsidized, English-speaking Irish source for the European Community market, were having more sober second thoughts. The real question now was whether Ireland could keep the investment that it had attracted.

Italy. Eighteen companies had invested in 25 undertakings (18 100 percent owned, 1 majority owned, 3 50-50, and 3 unspecified). One firm had withdrawn; it had made an investment in southern Italy some years before, receiving several incentives in the process which, according to one executive, had not been implemented properly. Another reported a "nice fit" between a recent Italian acquisition and the rest of its business. There had been no government intervention. An executive in a third firm said that his company would not invest either in Italy or Libya under any circumstances. In fact, he personally would not even travel in those countries. An electronics manufacturer, in scouting possible plant sites in the European Community, had concluded that it did not "feel comfortable" in Italy. People were getting "their knees shot off," one executive explained. The timing was wrong, he felt. Overall view: caution.

Ivory Coast. One firm reported a 100 percent-owned subsidiary; another, a license. A third had been negotiating actively. A condition laid down by the third firm was that the market be closed to any further competition. Four competitors were already in the market or had gained permission to enter. The point was that the government had been requested to close the market and lock out further competition. An executive felt that the tax incentives, which he expected might be offered, were not critical. The firm had not even alerted its tax people. The company was proposing to set up a local holding organization, the ownership of which would eventually revert to the U.S. firm. Meanwhile, the U.S. company would not be responsible for any debts if the enterprise failed. For another company, the main incentive had been the existence of an import duty. Tax holidays were of little importance. When the Ivory Coast raised the duty to over 100 percent, it precipitated a license with a local manufacturer. The firm would not consider direct investment at the present. Management felt the economy was in a bad way, and there was a problem of political succession since the incumbent president was quite elderly. Overall view: worry about depending on government intervention to protect the market.

Portugal. Four firms had undertaken 100 percent-owned ventures. One had given serious consideration to manufacturing in the country in the early 1970s but had desisted. The main problem, at that time, had been the lack of an appropriate site and poor telecommunications. Also, the firm had been warned by other U.S. companies that the government was less stable than it might appear. Would the firm reconsider that decision now that the government had undergone change? An executive felt that it was a possibility, but that there were no present plans to invest there. A second firm had also looked at Portugal in some detail. It had had a local licensing arrangement, and the licensee had offered its business to the U.S. firm. In response, management investigated the political climate, regulations and risk, incentives, economic conditions, profit controls, currency stability, foreign investment legislation, the "texture" of the country, and the structure of the market. The outcome of the preliminary investigation was that the investment was deemed not worthwhile, that the price was too high. The project had been dropped. Overall view: lack of enthusiasm.

United Kingdom. Thirty-eight corporations had invested in 75 ventures (53 100 percent owned, 2 majority owned, 5 50-50, 1 minority owned, and 14 unspecified). Executives in 5 firms spoke specifically of the attraction of U.K. export credit facilities. As an example, an executive in one observed that among the great advantages in operating in the United Kingdom was its international competitiveness, thanks to a government subsidy to banks for export financing, which was given to exporters almost automatically at subsidized rates. One firm had invested in a plant in the United Kingdom after a company team had checked out a number of different countries and wound up getting offers of very attractive incentives from the United Kingdom. These incentives, according to one executive, had been important. And, as construction had begun, the project had been enriched with additional incentives—which had led to an expansion of the project over that initially contemplated. In the final analysis, the firm had received subsidized financing, tax holidays, guaranteed utility rates, and training allowances. Other factors of importance were trainable labor, infrastructure support, a substantial domestic market, and entry to the EEC. In the case of another company, government grants for capital equipment had been critical in the building of a manufacturing facility. An engine manufacturer had several plants in the United Kingdom, the first of which had been started up in the early 1970s. An executive observed that the British government had really made the decision for management, in that the plant had become available at a bargain price by reason of the bankruptcy of a British company. The plant was in a semidepressed area and hence was subject to receiving "second-level" incentives from the government. The firm had gone to the U.K. Ministry of Industry and negotiated a grant to help finance the plant's expansion. An executive felt that this grant had been critical. Another grant had been received for increasing a second plant to economic scale. Management had found people in the Ministry of Industry "pragmatic," in that they had recognized that a subsidy was needed if a firm were to invest in the United Kingdom under present circumstances. "No one would have invested there in the last five years without a grant," an executive added. He felt that the grants were given not only for the purpose of adding jobs but also to prevent the loss of jobs. He then mentioned a major expansion of a

third plant and he observed that, basically, the U.K. government
had built this plant for the firm and then had leased it at a "very
good rate." A food processor had received a standard "tax grant"
that was described as "substantial" and available to anyone in
Leicester. "But," an executive added, "it didn't influence anything; the company would have invested anyway. Adequate transport facilities were the critical factor. The decision was made on
a business basis." An electronics firm, after it had determined
that expanded manufacturing in Europe was necessary, had looked
at the top three sales countries: West Germany, the United Kingdom, and France. The United Kingdom had been selected, finally,
by reason of market potential and the degree of government support,
nationally and locally. One of the sectoral programs, with regard
to research and development and technical transfer, provided grants.
There had also been an attractive tax incentive. Asked why the firm
had bypassed the development regions in the United Kingdom and
associated incentives, an executive responded that this was to have
been a large facility with a significant research and development
component. The company had wanted a place where professionals
would live comfortably. It was already operating in Scotland, and
it had looked at Manchester. The point was that there were always
reasons for the regional grants. In any event, such grants, as a
percentage of the total investment over time, were not that great.
The site that was selected seemed ideal. There were good universi-
ties close by, and it was easily reachable from Heathrow. Also,
the location was such that customers could get to it easily. The
point was emphasized that the incentives given by the U.K. government had not been really critical to the investment decision. Another firm, a metal processor, had invested in a plant in Wales.
Executives mentioned area cash grants that had offset some of the
natural disadvantages of locating in nonindustrialized areas. For
example, that part of Wales in which the firm had located lacked an
industrial tradition. This factor had been of importance for a con-
tinuous process plant in which three shifts are employed. It had
been difficult for people to adjust to a lifestyle involving a 24-hour
operation, and it had taken the firm "five years of difficult times"
to get people adjusted. Cash grants had been fairly significant in
selecting the location, but possibly less so than a power contract,
which was clearly at a subsidized rate. Finally, an investment
equipment manufacturer had acquired an English company very
cheaply as a vehicle for penetrating the European market. The
plant had been technically attractive in that it was highly automated.
The U.K. government had given its approval very easily and seemed
happy to have the U.S. firm acquire the plant, inasmuch as it was
threatened with bankruptcy. The acquisition had "made a big splash

in the British press," and all of it had been positive, an executive told us. No government assistance had been received. Overall view: impressive array of incentives, at both the national and regional level, without any specific performance requirements. No resistance to foreign takeovers of ailing plants.

TYPE III COUNTRIES

Argentina. Eleven firms reported 19 affiliates (16 100 percent owned, 2 minority owned, and 1 unspecified). One firm had proposed that it be a party to a local manufacturing facility to satisfy the local content requirement for the supply of heavy machinery to a government project. Another had declined an investment due to concern about social and political unrest. A third company had been hurt by the relaxation of protection, which was cited as an example of the danger of depending upon such artificial devices as government protection of a market. Another firm had developed a major manufacturing enterprise out of blocked funds arising out of the sale of another local subsidiary. Overall view: not attractive. Incentives were not likely to make a difference. One firm had withdrawn.

Canada. Thirty-three companies reported 97 investments (49 100 percent owned, 4 majority owned, 3 50-50, 9 minority owned, and 32 unspecified). Executives in three firms looked at Canada as basically hostile to U.S. business. One said that government regulations there sent him the message that U.S. business was not welcome. An executive in a fourth company reported that the government had talked to his company from time to time about the desirability of 25 percent Canadian ownership, but nothing had happened. An executive in another corporation, a Type 3, expressed concern over the separatist activities in Canada and the possibility that the country might end up as three different nations. This concern had apparently slowed the firm's expansion in Canada. In still another firm, it was noted that its Canadian venture had been unable to compete with local firms because of its inability to buy new timber licenses. Consequently, the firm was making no new investment. But another management wished it were in Canada because of a tendency for the government to direct procurement to local firms as well as to receive government subsidies (which were not defined). Finally there was a Type 5 corporation that recently had acquired a Canadian firm, only to have the government exert pressure for a commitment to spin off ownership. The company had been obliged to give an employment guarantee, which it had not been able to live up to. The government would probably do nothing; the firm was a very small operation and would probably be overlooked. In another sector, the restaurant business, the same corporation had found it impossible to secure a license to operate. An executive commented, "It may turn out that Canada is just as difficult as Mexico." Overall view: there seemed to be gathering animosity across the border in both directions.

Colombia. Ten companies reported 15 ventures (8 100 percent owned, 1 majority owned, 3 50-50, 2 minority owned, and 1 unspecified). One executive reported that no further increase in capacity would be authorized for his firm without export and employment guarantees. The latter was not a problem, but the former was, in that the company was already producing in many markets. Another strongly suspected that a contract awarded to a French company by the Colombian government for a majority industrial project had been awarded on the basis of bribery. The investment of a chemical producer had been heavily dependent upon a 35 percent import tariff. However, the high tariff had encouraged smuggling to such an extent that it had jeopardized the investment. But if the tariff were reduced too much, it would be necessary to close down the plant. Executives in another firm reported that the government required that 30 percent of the output of its local plant be exported. The exports would be quite unprofitable, and the parent firm felt this requirement to be unacceptable. Overall view: inconsistent implementation of policy, sometimes unreasonable requirements.

Egypt. In our sample, we came across just one firm (48, a Type 5) with an affiliation in Egypt, a majority-owned venture in the light consumer goods industry. Two others had given serious consideration to Egyptian ventures (Firms 12 and 17, all Types 4 and 5, respectively) but had decided not to go ahead. Another actually reached negotiating stage (Firm 42, a Type 5) but then withdrew. Two others (Firms 22 and 28, Types 4 and 5) had Egyptian licenses but no investment. One was currently negotiating (Firm 25, Type 5). Executives in six firms discussed their Egyptian interests in some detail:

Firm 4, a Type 4 machinery manufacturer, had looked very closely at a project in Egypt. It developed that the chairman had become very much interested personally in the country and had kept coming up with ideas to get the company involved. The management, however, had simply not seen a market in Egypt for the product to be manufactured there. As one executive commented, the main problem was the bureaucracy, which "makes it damn near impossible to get anything done. " He then referred to the Coca-Cola situation. It had been reported to him that Coca-Cola had tried to bring in a special seed for an agricultural project to which it had committed itself as part of the price for its entry into the market. Coca-Cola was told at the last moment that it needed another kind of license for importing the seed, whereupon the Coca-Cola representatives were alleged to have said, "Okay, but be certain that the seed is well protected while we are negotiating for the other license. " The license was promised in a day or two. In fact, it took 17 days to go through the bureaucracy, and then Coca-Cola found that the seed had not been stored under cover as directed and was probably ruined. The executive told this story as an example of the ineptness and inefficiency of the Egyptian bureaucracy. He went on to comment that Sadat was undoubtedly doing what was right but that his efforts were really being subverted by the bureaucracy. Somebody had suggested that the company offer to bring a group of Egyptian industrialists to the United States for training. This executive argued, however, that what was needed was to bring bureaucrats for training, although he was uncertain whether appropriate training would be available in the United States. The point was that the firm's Egyptian project never got off the ground.

Firm 12 (Type 4) likewise had an Egyptian project that had not been undertaken, despite careful study. The reasons given were the nonavailability of a suitable local partner and a currency problem. The firm had been unable to secure a government commitment that raw materials could be imported without restriction, a commitment that management felt to be absolutely essential. A further point was that there were two small local firms, in the same line of business, which opposed the entry of the much larger U.S. firm. A U.S. executive pointed out that his company had no desire to take over the two Egyptian firms, the latter's product being of poor quality. It had been the experience of the firm elsewhere that governments rarely revoked a guarantee of foreign exchange with which to import raw materials or to remit dividends. Credit for this was given to the firm's local partners. For this reason, management looked for local partners who were influential, were good business people, and had an "awareness of their situation and the right connections. " Asked what the Egyptian government could have done in this case to make the situation more attractive, an executive admitted that he really did not know. Part of the problem was that his firm had not been exactly credible on its own in that it lacked a local partner. He did feel that the attitude required from the Egyptian government was one of "Yes, we want you. " The firm would still not go into Egypt without a local partner.

Firm 17, a Type 5 chemical producer, had looked at Egypt very carefully and had a continuing interest, but by reason of the impossible bureaucracy and the inability to get anything done, Egypt had been "put on the back burner."

Firm 22, a Type 4 food processor, would have preferred a joint venture project in Egypt, but only a licensing arrangement "had been permitted." An executive observed that the economic situation in Egypt was, in his view, excellent; the country had become a net exporter of oil, and there were substantial revenues coming in from the widened Suez Canal. But he felt that public statements, to the effect that Egypt welcomed investors, differed from the fact; it was really very selective about whom it allowed in. The only need it had for foreign capital was in the high-technology area. At the time, the import duty on the firm's products was about 75 percent. Sales were about $1 million, largely due to the expatriate population. It was this 75 percent duty that was forcing the company into local manufacture. All raw materials and packing materials still had to be imported but at a significantly lower rate of duty. The only way to enlarge the market, management concluded, was by local manufacture.

Firm 25, a Type 5 manufacturer of consumer products, was currently negotiating an Egyptian project. We were told that the project had arisen as a result of an Egyptian government decision to impose a duty to protect a competitor who had set up in Egypt. The U.S. firm was already in the market, and it desired to protect its position. Management concluded that local manufacturing was the only alternative. The proposal was that the Egyptian enterprise be wholly owned by the U.S. firm initially, but that its ownership would be reduced to 65 percent after five years and thereafter remain constant at that level. The effect of various incentives had been calculated to determine which alternative would bring the greatest return on investment. The site had been selected by the Egyptian government. Management felt that new manufacturing equipment would be inappropriate for this investment, and it expected to use reconditioned machinery. Permission to use this machinery was being sought in the negotiation. An executive noted that the firm had been able to obtain OPIC political risk coverage for the venture.

Firm 42, a Type 5 animal feed producer, had looked at projects very recently in Nigeria and Egypt. When asked why Egypt was chosen, an executive responded, "We keep in touch, and Egypt has always been one of the countries on our list largely because it has a lot of customers." He explained that after the Sadat government emerged and made a major peace effort with Israel the environment had become somewhat more favorable. Also, Sadat had made a major effort to attract foreign investment. One of the key executives in the firm was a member of a business group at which Sadat had appeared seeking private investment from the United States. Having operated for many years in Europe and the Middle East, observed this executive, the territory was more or less familiar, and "so we decided to take a look at it." Sadat had been promising less red tape and a reduction of the foreign exchange risk. Although Sadat was a dedicated man, according to this executive, the effort to attract investment had not been successful. There is an entrenched civil service, and "regardless of what the boss wants, there are some things the boss can't get." Corporation representatives went to Egypt and "tried to walk a bunch of things through bureaucracy, attempting to get certain assurances. They failed." The local production of raw materials was found inadequate, and the firm could not get assurance that import permits would be forthcoming. Also, the company took a look at the producers of animal products and found that a monumental task in organization and training was called for, which was well behind the capabilities of the company. He added that a few companies were sticking with Egypt, but he felt that most were simply not willing to make the effort. The upshot was that the company worked on the project for six to nine months before calling it off.

Firm 48, a Type 5 producer of consumer goods, was the only 1 of the 51 that had a facility actually operating in Egypt. According to one executive, the firm considered this to be a relatively risky investment, given the potential for war in the area. On the other hand, management had felt that everything was moving in the right direction. The firm had had a trading company in Egypt for some years and, consequently, had local support for the venture. The only competition was one highly inefficient local producer. The executive stated that the company had received some 200 incentives with respect to lowered duties on imported raw materials and equipment, assurance that there would be free access for personnel, the first long-term (six years) loan negotiated by a U.S. firm in Egypt, a five-year tax holiday, and no price control. He pointed out that the plant would almost certainly run at a loss for the first two years, but that the subsequent three-year profit could be important. The work force, an estimated 1,700, was reported to be excellent, and the plant had already reached 95 percent efficiency relative to world operations.

It was clear that Egypt was in no condition to impose performance requirements. Very little direct foreign investment was moving in, largely because of the time and effort—and cost—of getting any sort of commitment out of the bureaucracy, plus the political leverage of Egyptian business firms that feared the competition of foreign firms producing within the country. It should be noted that only Type 4 and 5 firms had demonstrated any interest, and they had done so only because of the personal interest of a key executive and/or the threatened loss of the market. Promised incentives were seen to have been given only marginal consideration by management, possibly because there was no confidence that such incentives would in fact be fulfilled by the Egyptian government.

Greece. Three firms reported three investments (two 100 percent owned and one majority owned). One had invested in a food processing plant. Exporting from the United States in the long run, management felt, would not be as profitable as producing particular products in Greece. The membership of Greece in the EEC had been assumed. Some impetus had come from the International Finance Corporation (IFC) in the form of partial financing. The IFC had also introduced the firm to the Greek Development Bank which, likewise, had taken some equity and provided debt. At the time, management had narrowed down possible sites for the proposed investment to Spain, Italy, or Greece. The right growing conditions for the produce the firm planned to process were important. It was already in Italy but not in the south where the produce would have to be grown. In Spain, financing had not been so readily available. Also, it was felt that Spain was further away from EEC membership. And, in neither Spain nor Italy had the firm been impressed with the local producers. Finally, the Greek government agreed to permit the duty-free import of capital equipment. The firm ended up holding a 50 percent equity interest, the IFC 10 percent, the Greek Development Bank 40 percent. The IFC was in the process of selling its share to the firm (which had the right of first refusal), a development approved by the government. The transfer of equity, however, was not critical; the firm had been satisfied with 50 percent. Overall view: reasonable.

Jamaica. Five firms reported six enterprises (two 100 percent owned, three minority owned, and one unspecified). One had withdrawn from a joint venture after having recorded losses year after year. An executive observed that it had seemed impossible to hire and retain competent people. Whenever the firm trained someone, that person tended to leave the country. He felt that the underlying antibusiness posture of the government had been reflected in many of its policies. The upshot was that the firm had opted to close its plant shortly before a recent election. Management had feared the outcome, which might result in the company being trapped in the country. The executive who had made the decision observed, "I did not want to send helicopters down there to take whites off the roof of

the building. " He felt that, in fact, the firm should probably have
withdrawn earlier. Another company was in partnership with the
government. An executive reported the relationship as having been
very constructive. Management, he reported, was much less concerned about political stability in Jamaica than many outside ob-
servers. Overall view: extreme caution.

Japan. Twenty-four corporations had invested in 60 enterprises (5 100 percent owned, 2 majority owned, 16 minority owned,
and 21 unspecified). One reported that it was helping to write the
regulations in Japan that would apply to its type of business, which
was of a service nature. It was of interest to note that 2 U.S. firms
had entered into offshore joint ventures with Japanese firms, 1 in
Canada and 1 in the Philippines. And another had provided technology in return for a 50 percent equity in one of its 8 Japanese affiliates, all with different Japanese companies. Some years later,
under pressure from its partner, the U.S. firm had sold 80 percent
of its interest. An executive observed that the longer a joint venture born of technology lasted, the more the resistance mounted.
He felt that the firm had been successful in Japan because it let the
Japanese management run the business its own way. An industrial
instrument manufacturer had considered manufacturing in Japan via
a joint venture. The reasons for not going ahead were the uncertainty that it would bring additional sales, the problem of achieving
adequate volume (and, hence, lower cost), and the fact that the firm
had a very strong distribution system in Japan and was not aware of
having lost any sales. Another firm, a tire and rubber producer,
had a general policy of transferring its technology only to majority-
owned companies, but an exception had been made in the case of
Japan. Its technical agreement had been entered into shortly after
World War II, in part because of encouragement by the U.S. government, which was trying to stimulate Japanese development. The
Japanese company manufactured a product bearing the U.S. name
for delivery back to the U.S. company, for sale both in Japan and
abroad. A firm in the service industry attributed a significant
amount of its success in Japan to a particular member of the Diet.
An executive, with much humor, described his visit to the United
States. One of his first questions, despite his advanced age, had
been "Where are the girls?" Overall evaluation: great respect and
awareness (and envy) of the close, mutually supportive ties between
government and business.

Kenya. Only four ventures were reported for Kenya, one
wholly owned (a Type 5), two majority owned (one Type 3 and one
Type 7), and one minority owned (a Type 5). But in only one inter-

view was Kenya really discussed, and that was in Firm 15, a food processor. As part of the entry price, it had agreed to train a certain number of local people. An executive observed, however, that the company had been glad to do it; it would have done so anyway. No other performance guarantees could be recalled. In this case, the firm was operating affiliates in 11 countries, including Kenya. Another firm, in the automotive field, was involved in a 49 percent-owned assembly plant. Another, a manufacturer of consumer goods, had established a wholly owned manufacturing facility in 1973. A second consumer goods firm was operating a 63 percent-owned manufacturing enterprise. The absence of comment led one to conclude that important problems had not emerged, either upon entry or subsequently, and that the market was not such as to attract attention. The one investor was classified a Type 7 (a maverick) because it was a conglomerate and really did not fit any of the categories. Although it reported only 11 operating affiliates abroad and a relatively small percentage of international sales, it was involved in other international activities in the service area, and its overseas involvement went back at least 50 years.

Morocco. Three firms reported three 100 percent-owned enterprises. An executive in one observed that his firm had enjoyed a tax holiday, but because of the government's socialist orientation, it had displayed very obsolete notions of what constituted an appropriate return on investment. The firm had faced price control, and when it asked the government for a price change, the response had been that the firm was making enough money. Management then tried to point out that precisely because of the tax holiday the operations had been very profitable and that the tax should be imputed to derive the long-term profit level. It was important, he observed, to determine what a government felt to be a reasonable return on investment. What guidelines was the government following? Also, does the government have a record of giving incentives and then taking them away, which this executive obviously felt had happened in Morocco? Another company had been interested in participating in a mineral development, about which the government had been approaching a number of firms. The government wanted to own the operation or, at least, retain a majority position. It had also spoken to the Soviet Union, which allegedly had frightened many firms. An executive noted the French orientation of the country, which gave rise to animosities. He opined that it would be better if a developing country asked for a foreign proposal rather than dictate terms. The outcome had been that the firm had withdrawn from contention. An executive in a third firm reported Morocco as a bad example of government signals to foreign business. Apparently, management had been giving it some consideration. The executive pointed out that smuggling existed on a wide scale, even within the army. In addition, the government had demanded that a certain percentage of product be exported, which the firm felt to be un-realistic. A further point was the tradition and competition in France. He felt that the government had very little credibility be-cause of its inability to control the smuggling. Overall view: nega-tive, due to the charge of discrimination in favor of the French and the unrealistic demands imposed.

Nigeria. Many of the companies (nine) in our survey had con-sidered investment in Nigeria, but only three (two Type 4 and one Type 5) reported three affiliates in the country: one majority owned, one minority owned, and one of unspecified joint ownership (prob-ably minority). The general attitude seemed to be one of extreme caution. Executives in three of the investing firms presented their cases:

Firm 1 (Type 4) had a 40 percent-owned distribution company in Nigeria. It was currently struggling with the idea of manufactur-ing locally. Under the law, an executive observed, it could own 60 percent of a local plant. The problem was that if Nigeria were to open its borders, any effort to manufacture locally could be de-stroyed. Management was also worried about Nigerian politics for, the executive noted, "if they ever get their backs up about South Africa" they might close down local firms that also had operations in South Africa. For this firm, the South African market was too attractive for it to consider withdrawal. The executive observed that the role of the Nigerian government in the firm's investigation had been negative, although it did offer the possibility of closing off competitive imports. Also, even with a 60 percent-owned manufac-turing company, one could not assume that the Nigerians would, in fact, invest something equal to 40 percent in value.

Firm 12 (Type 4) expected to have a very recent investment in Nigeria operational in the near future. The firm had been ap-proached by the owner of a partially West German-owned brewery who was felt to be an excellent potential local partner. In addition, the firm had obtained a government guarantee with respect to the transfer of dividends. No other commitments had been made in either direction. Incentives had played no part in the investment decision.

Firm 48 (Type 5) had been manufacturing in Nigeria about two years. The reason was that management had seen a market of 100 million people, one sizable, sophisticated competitor already producing in the market, and a fairly stable country. Its partner was a government-owned enterprise. An executive noted that there was a formal government policy, in writing, relative to foreign investment, which he regarded as a strong positive factor. He felt that the time had been right for investment in the country, both politically and economically. This company was not involved in a high-technology type of manufacture, and the products were for mass consumption. The banking facilities were found to be adequate and, indeed, 70 percent of the investment was in the form of local debt. The government position, with regard to the technical service fee, remittance of dividends, and availability of foreign exchange for essential imports were all satisfactory.

Four other companies (one Type 3, two Type 4, and one Type 5) had demonstrated positive interest in Nigeria, but had failed thus far to make any move. Firm 3 (Type 3) had intended to manufacture several products locally, but problems had arisen when it looked at costs. Nigeria was recognized as a very significant market, but management had been put off by the high cost of the facilities and the inadequacy of the ports. In short, it did not see adequate profit from the "grass roots" development it had planned. Even so, options had not been closed, and the firm was actively studying other ways of entering the market. An executive stated that it was strict business considerations that had discouraged the firm; repatriation of profits had not been seen as a major problem. Import duties, however, were perceived as a difficulty. Firm 4 (Type 4) had likewise spent time looking at Nigeria. According to one executive, "There is a hell of a market there. We've got a man there studying how to get into the market. It is just a difficult environment." He went on to observe that it was hard to secure trained people and the type of management needed in a place like Nigeria. Another, Firm 22 (Type 4), was already licensing and selling in Nigeria but wished to set up some sort of local company. The manager for African market development, who is located in the United Kingdom, had responsibility for studying the profitability of a joint venture. One of the firm's principal preoccupations had been the limits on royalty repatriation. Thus the firm was driven to consider a joint venture where the firm's maximum shareholding would be 40 percent. No details had been worked out; it was still in the exploratory stage.

Firm 32 (Type 5) was faced with a problem. The Nigerian government had given licenses to four firms in its industry to manufacture locally. The company had tried to get one of the licenses but had failed. An executive felt that all four of the firms had been based in Europe. Everyone else had been locked out by this move. By the time the firm had heard of the Nigerian move, it was really already too late to make a bid. He expected Kenya to go the same route. The firm was watching developments there very closely.

Contrast this latter attitude with that of the management in Firm 38 (Type 5), a chemical producer, which explicitly did not consider any country in Africa to have a market large enough to justify an economically sized plant. Asked if Nigeria could do anything to make its case more attractive, an executive replied that possibly it could do so with some sort of regional arrangement that would enlarge the market. Asked about the ownership requirements in Nigeria, he said that the firm greatly preferred 100 percent ownership if the investment were in the production of its own products. He did observe that the firm might get involved in a related business, in a joint venture or even on a minority basis, and he cited its entrée into the Brazilian market as an example. Obviously, the firm had not looked closely at Nigeria and did not expect to do so.

On the other hand, the management in Firm 42, a Type 5 food processor, expected that in the future it might invest in Nigeria, but not at the time of our interview, since management felt that the administrative infrastructure was simply not present in Nigeria. Also, the country lacked basic transportation, storage, and distribution facilities. In addition, there was a land tenure problem. An executive cited problems with hotels, ports, and permits to get expatriates into the country to work. He then referred to the ownership requirements, that is, to the Nigerianization of enterprises. He also observed that one had to deal with the old tribal relationships and that key managers were at a very high premium in Nigeria. He suggested that there was no question as to the intent and good will of the top leadership, and he felt certain that these problems—or many of them—would eventually be resolved. The modernization process was going slowly because the administrative services could not keep up. By the time one put all the costs into the picture, he observed, it would obviously be better for Nigeria to import the firm's type of product. The Nigerian leadership understood this, he said, but it was counting on other things to happen. "The headlong rush to modernization," he went on, "really left no room for us. Our company is not in the business of making deserts bloom—or the jungles, as the case may be. The company is not in land development, although there has been some discussion within the corporation about the desirability of its joining, or organizing, a syndicate to get into land development." He felt that the corporation had wisely opted to stay out of that business because it was not the sort of business that it did best, which was food processing. The firm's business was really better adapted to entry midway in development, not at the start. He concluded by saying that both Egypt and Nigeria were still on the firm's list and that he expected that one day the corporation would be operating in both.

Firm 49, a Type 7 food processor, had looked at a small project in Nigeria but had not really considered it seriously. This had been a situation in which a group of private Nigerian investors had been prepared to invest in a plantation type crop in Nigeria and had approached the firm to participate with capital and expertise. An executive listed the reasons for turning the project down: the firm did not need an additional source of the particular product involved (although, admittedly, there was a local market) and there was fear of the "corruption aspect" of doing business in Nigeria and concern about the stability of the country.

Executives in three other noninvesting firms emphasized negative aspects of the Nigerian investment climate. One in Firm 14 (Type 5) referred to another firm in the same industry that had made an investment in Nigeria on the basis that the border would be closed to competing products. Subsequently, it had discovered that the border was not being kept closed. The result had been the loss of a good share of the market due to its inability to compete. This example was cited as a principal reason for not giving Nigeria close attention. An executive in Firm 10 (Type 5) used Nigeria as a bad example of a country arbitrarily limiting the number of foreign employees. He felt that the Nigerians were localizing the work force entirely too fast and in far too arbitrary a manner; "it was detrimental to their ultimate good," he noted. Management had assumed a negative posture. Finally, a spokesman for Firm 30 (Type 2) simply viewed Nigeria as an unattractive place in which to invest.

As can be readily seen, much of the comment has a negative or critical ring. Executives felt, almost without exception, that the local ownership and local employment restrictions imposed by the Nigerian government were not acceptable, given the lack of administrative support, the disorganization of the market, local corruption, and uncertainty about political continuity. Only a handful of Type 4 and 5 firms saw Nigeria in a sufficiently attractive light to qualify for investment. Mexican regulations, which in some regards were even more rigorous, were accepted with less criticism and drove away less investment because many executives tended to see Mexico in quite a different light.

Spain. Nineteen firms had invested in 26 ventures (12 100 percent owned, 2 majority owned, 3 50-50, 4 minority owned, and 5 unspecified). One had withdrawn. Some firms had passed Spain by because of uncertainty as to its entry into the European Community. One reported that it had been very successful despite problems. The government had provided some tax incentives, with the result that U.S. taxes could be deferred, thereby permitting the company to use its untaxed earnings as a way of financing the project.

The firm had also received a government grant, in return for locating the plant in a less developed area, plus employment credits in the firm of credits applicable against social security taxes. The latter had been given on the basis of the increase in employment created by the project. Another reason for selecting Spain had been the absence of price controls. The fact that Spain might become a member of the EEC had not been important, inasmuch as the plant had been designed to supply domestic demand only. No performance requirements had been imposed by the government. For another firm as well, a prime incentive for a Spanish investment had been to get into the Spanish market but also to supply a particular product to southern Europe. Also important had been the incentives offered by the government with respect to grants of land, provision for training, and others. The analysis had been launched in 1977 on the assumption that Spain would enter the EEC. An electronics producer had come out differently. After an admittedly superficial study, management had concluded that the market was not yet large enough. Management in a machinery-producing firm had reacted positively when approached by the Spanish government to buy an ailing Spanish venture. Negotiations had taken about a year. What was the reason for the interest in Spain other than an admitted personal connection? The desirability of developing a large manufacturing venture in Europe, that is, within the EEC, which would lead to the rationalization of the firm's other operations on the continent. The upshot was that the firm took a 35 percent equity position, plus management control via a six-year management contract and an option to increase its equity up to 65 percent. The Spanish government had made the deal more attractive by agreeing to cover all losses for the first three years, waive all duties on the import of capital equipment, and provide a quota to import the product into Spain until local production was underway. The firm had also received the "standard training grants" from the government. Finally, the 90 percent local-value-added rule had been lowered to 70 percent. The principal interest of the Spanish government had been in maintaining employment at the ailing facility, and the firm had committed itself to maintain employment at the existing level. It had also committed itself to export a certain amount into Europe. Management was well pleased and fully expected to develop a large, efficient, and internationally competitive plant. OPIC coverage would be used for major new investments the firm planned. The firm saw negligible political risk. One serious problem had arisen; the Spanish government saw no reason the firm should acquiesce to a U.S. government policy not to sell to Cuba. An executive in another firm reported what was alleged to have been a clear case of discrimination against foreign business firms. An executive observed that only foreign companies, which were not well informed about local tax practices, paid the full assessed taxes. One might claim that this difference was not important, he observed, but it really acted as a kind of discrimination against the foreign firms. Overall view: general enthusiasm; although the government had imposed various performance requirements, no criticism was heard.

Turkey. Two firms reported as many ventures, one 100 percent owned and one unspecified. Another had withdrawn. A truck manufacturer reported that it had given the country very serious consideration as a site for manufacture, but management had reacted negatively to the export and local context requirements imposed. It was also worried about the political situation. The result had been the tabling of the project. One of the things that had attracted the firm's initial attention had been a move by the Turkish government to permit the purchase of so-called consolidated debt paper at full value for local investment purposes. Previously, it had been discounted on the market at approximately 30 percent. A second firm had gotten halfway or more into the construction of a manufacturing facility in Turkey when the government had changed the ground rules, and the facility was never completed. No further details were offered. Another firm had a plant in Turkey and, because of the foreign exchange situation, had been forced to spend its own foreign exchange for imported materials to keep it going. Finally, management had served notice on the government that it would not continue to do so. The blockage of earnings might, however, push the firm into an entirely new line of business, oil exploration, for which blocked funds could be used. If the firm were involved in this activity, permission would be given to remit earnings in dollars—assuming that it found some oil. Overall view: profound disillusionment; as one executive observed, "U.S. industry has probably lost a fortune in Turkey."

Zaire. As might have been anticipated, one heard very little interest in Zaire. Only one firm (Type 5) reported a wholly owned manufacturing facility. It had been operating a plant in Zaire under a special convention with Zaire government for the past ten years. The agreement included a cost-plus arrangement that permitted the firm to make a given amount of profit in addition to cost, and that was where the product price was supposed to be set. When the government later introduced a general price control law, it was argued successfully by the company that the convention superseded the law. An executive observed that the government had been "very happy" with the firm and that visitors to the country were invariably shown the plant, which is alleged to have been the only foreign plant to have operated nonstop over recent years. The reason for the firm's original interest in Zaire was that it was the only Black African country, other than Nigeria, that could conceivably support a plant. The executive admitted that it had been profitable largely due to OPIC's convertibility guarantees, which had, however, been exhausted. The result of that situation was that the government had asked management to provide a long-range plan about how the firm's blocked earnings might be used. There were really no exportable products other than coffee, and the export of that product, management felt, would involve the firm in illegal operations. The point was that, in many instances, coffee was exported illegally because its price was controlled, as was the percentage of foreign exchange the exporter might retain. Therefore, much of the coffee was allegedly exported under false invoices specifying that the coffee was of lower quality than in fact was the case. This practice meant that there were offshore payments to the exporter into a foreign bank account. The firm had not wanted to get involved in this sort of business. A principal customer in Zaire had been a foreign exchange earner with permission to purchase foreign exchange for operating purposes. The firm sold to this customer only if he were willing to give the firm some portion of his foreign exchange license. An executive said that the only alternative to finding exports or someone who wanted local currency would be to invest in fixed assets locally, such as real estate. The firm had done so but felt that it had reached the limit.

Obviously, the foreign investment policies of Zaire were not really relevant because of the serious financial straits in which the country found itself.

TYPE IV COUNTRIES

Algeria. No investments were reported, but one firm (Type 5) reported that the government had called for tenders with respect to an engine and truck program to which the firm was currently responding.

Saudi Arabia. Four firms reported on as many ventures (one 50-50, two minority owned, and one unspecified). One was currently negotiating, and two others were considering initiating negotiations. One had begun negotiating with the Saudis in the mid-1970s, when there had been talk of the firm's involvement in a large industrial complex. The firm's original interest had been stimulated by the desire to obtain a secure supply of oil at a more stable price. Entitlements to oil were given at the time of investment as a form of government incentive. Originally, the deal had taken the form of an entitlement to 1,000 barrels of oil per day for each $1,000 of investment. More recently, this amount had been reduced to 500. In the absence of such an arrangement, the firm would not have been interested in going into the project. There was also a tax holiday, plus the provision of infrastructure for which the project would pay, but at a subsidized rate. Fifty-fifty ownership and a time limit on the joint venture (which, however, was renewable prior to expiration) had been involved. Whether the tax incentives would be of value for the firm was a question still being studied by the firm's tax people. An executive observed, "We like to get things up front because it minimizes our formal commitment and exposure. A tax holiday is only worthwhile if you make a profit." A specified percentage of the product would be earmarked for internal Saudi use. The firm would be committed to give equal sales effort to selling the joint venture's product and of wholly owned plants located elsewhere. How would the Saudi government monitor this equality of effort? An executive said, "You could argue that, logistically, the product had some economically justified marketing areas, such as the Middle East, Western Europe and Asia." He did admit that there were some suspicions that the firm would not treat the joint venture fairly. Another executive observed that on a scale of one to ten the investment climate of Saudi Arabia would rate about five, and that of Yugoslavia about nine. Another firm had very recently entered as the minority partner in a Saudi venture. Two reasons were cited: the need to develop service facilities for equipment already installed, and the fact that the competition had already established a joint venture. Still another, a chemical producer, was not in Saudi Arabia because its products were "too far down stream" to be related closely to those being produced locally. An executive then observed that it had gotten a raw material break in Brazil, and if Saudi Arabia offered the same sort of deal, local manufacture might become more attractive. Finally, a metal processor reported an attractive agreement in Saudi Arabia relative to the supply of energy, plus significant finance on attractive terms (long-term debt at a fixed interest rate). Overall view: great interest but concern about the fulfillment of government commitments.

Appendix B

Interview Outline

Promise of confidentiality and copy of final study published by Overseas Private Investment Corporation, if desired.

1. Scope of international operations (relative importance of foreign sales, profit contribution)
   1.1 Age (year of first FDI)
   1.2 Geographical
   1.3 Relationships (re ownership, contractual)—preferences?
   1.4 Products
   1.5 Functions (assembly, manufacture, procurement/extraction, marketing only)

2. Structure of company
   2.1 Export oriented (that is, export department)
   2.2 International (that is, international division)
   2.3 Multinational (by region, product, function, or a mix)

3. Where are FDI decisions really made?
   3.1 Initiation
   3.2 Final approval

4. In reference to three FDI decisions within the last five years (one negative, two positive—one of which is deemed by the company as not living up to expectations)
   In each case:
   4.1 How did the project arise? Was the initial stimulation external or internal?
   4.2 Why was the company initially interested in the project?

4.3   Why was this particular country selected? (Were other countries considered for this project?)

4.4   What was the evaluation process? What factors were taken into consideration? (Note any evidence of role of personal interest on the part of key executives.)

4.4.1   General political-economic climate (political risk, that is, expectation of discontinuities of costs/returns that could not be anticipated)

4.4.2   Host government incentives (note particularly any reference to performance requirements)

4.4.3   U.S. government programs and policies (political relations, OPIC, tax, antitrust, other)

4.4.4   Access to a market

4.4.5   Access to raw materials

4.4.6   Access to cheap labor

4.4.7   The competitive situation

4.4.8   To gain a portfolio effect (via risk diversification)

4.4.9   Access to capital

4.4.10 Other factors mentioned

5.   The respondent's general opinion of the impact of host government investment incentives, and attitudes toward performance requirements specifically.

6.   The respondent's general opinion about the impact of U.S. programs and policies.

7.   Can a developing country government intervene in such ways as to induce a greater inward flow of foreign corporate resources—technical, managerial, and financial—than could otherwise be expected? How?

List of preferred countries:

Hong Kong	Kenya
Ireland	South Korea
Egypt	Malaysia
Philippines	Mexico
Yugoslavia	Nigeria
Liberia	Venezuela
Singapore	Zaire
Brazil	Peru
Taiwan	Indonesia
Thailand	Sri Lanka

Index

Government procurement, 122–25, 152, 169

Grandfather clause, 54, 98

Great Britain (see United Kingdom)

Greece, Development Bank of, financing by, 174–75; guarantees in, 121; investment in, 174–75; investment in, by corporate type, 69, 70; investment re, cited in, 62; tax reduction in, 174

Guarantees, 122, 152, 177 (see also Private Overseas Investment Corporation)

Guatemala, 69, 70

Guinea, 69, 70

Haiti, 146

Holland (see Netherlands)

Honduras, 69, 70, 106

Hong Kong, affiliates in, 29, 30; classified as Type 1, 27 (n.*); incentives in, xiv; listed as promising, 19; performance guarantees in, xiv; Singapore picked over, 27

Hungary, 146

Import Rights, 41, 87–88, 121, 152

Incentives, government procurement, 122–25; guarantees, 121; import rights, 121; market protection, frequency of, 121; market protection, responses to, 120–21; responses to, 108–24, 164–65; subsidies, frequency of, 116, 123–24; subsidies, responses to, 116–21; tax reduction, frequency of, 120; tax reduction, response to, 117–20; typology of, 108 (see also Overseas Pirate Investment Corporation;

also, individual countries

India, Das article on, xii; disinvestment, 72; expatriate employment, 103; export requirements on, 95–96; foreign government support in, 143; government pressure by, 14, 15; investment concentration in, 146; investment in, by corporate type, 92, 81; license in, by small firm, 153; ownership related to exports in, 96; ownership requirements in, 72, 98, 99, 100 (n.*); patent protection in, 72; performance requirements in, 109; work permits in, 72

Indonesia, arbitration in, 76; subsidized loans in, 77; capacity licensing in, 75; classified as Type 4, 27 (n.*); contract manufacturing in, 76; corruption in, 77; employment requirement, 73–74; expatriate employment, 103; export requirement in, 76, 96 (n.*); flag carrier requirement in, 76; International Finance Corporation as: investment, by corporate type, 73, 77, 81; investment in, reasons for, 73–77; investment in, rejected, 77; investment incentives in, response to, 73; investment level requirement, 105; investment requirement in, 74; ownership in, 73–74, 75, 76, 77, 99, 100; performance requirements in, 109; pioneer status in, 77; previous study in, 27 (n.*); seen as alternative to Singapore, 19; tax holidays in, 77; training requirement in, 76, 103, 107

removal of, 112, 159, 169,
180; Singapore, in, 112, 121;
Taiwan, in, 107; Venezuela,
in, 107, 120
"Maverick" firms, 24, 148, 149
Mexico, classified as Type 3, 27
(n. *); corruption in, 64; development zones in, 57; export
financing in, 58, 62; export
requirement in, 57, 58, 59,
60-61, 62, 63, 96 (n. *), 96;
exporting firm, 60-61, 94;
government procurement, 122;
incentives in, 124; incentives
in, response to, 56-65, 110;
investment concentration in,
146, 153; investment in, by
corporate type, 56, 65, 69,
70; investment in, reasons
for, 56-65; investment in, re-
jection, 64; listed as promising, 19; local and content requirement in, 60-61, 62, 64,
104; market protection in, 120,
121; multiple plant problem in,
62; negotiations, delay in, 65;
ownership in, 56, 57, 58, 59,
63, 64, 65, 98, 100, 102; ownership related to exports, 95,
98; patent problem in, 64; performance quantities, response
to, 56-65; performance requirements in, 109; personal
interest stimulates investment
in, 14; previous study, in, 27
(n. *); price control in, 57, 63;
priority incentive zones in, 58,
117; production level requirement, 106; protection of local
industry in, 107; protection
offered in, 64; research and
development reported in, 106;
restricted areas in, 59; seen
as unfriendly, 20; subsidies
in, 115, 116; tax reduction in,

116, 118, 119; U.S. export
controls and, 137
Morocco, export requirement in,
95 (n. *); incentives in, 124;
incentives in, response to,
investment in, 176-77; investment in, by corporate
type, 69, 70; ownership requirements in, 100 (n. *), 102;
performance requirements in,
109; smuggling in, 177; tax
reduction in, 117, 118, 119,
176
Multinational corporations, decline of, xviii (n. *); defined,
5; included in sample, 5, 7;
pressures on, 11-12

Nationalization, 152
Nepal, 146
Netherland Antilles, xiv, 28
Netherlands, affiliates in, 29,
30; disinvestment in, 157;
incentives in, xiv; investment
concentration in, 146, 153;
investment in, 157; performance requirement in, xiv
New Zealand, 31, 46, 47, 96
(n. *), 106, 109
Nicaragua, 69, 70, 105, 106, 109
Nigeria, corruption in, 180;
classified as Type 3, 27 (n. *);
employment guarantee in,
105; expatriate employment,
restrictions on, in, 61, 103,
108; guarantee for dividend
repatriation, given by, 177;
incentives in, 124, 177; interest in, 172; investment in,
177-80; investment in, by corporate type, 69, 70; investment rejected in, 62, 63;
local content requirements in,
103, 104; market protection
in, 120, 121, 177; OPIC

About the Author

RICHARD D. ROBINSON is Professor of International Management, Alfred P. Sloan School of Management, Massachusetts Institute of Technology. He has written and lectured extensively about international business, management, and economic/political development. Recent publications include International Business Management: A Guide to Decision Making; National Control of Foreign Business Entry: A Survey of Fifteen Countries; Foreign Investment in the Third World: A Comparative Study of Selected Development Country Investment Programs; and The Internationalization of Business: An Introduction to the Practice and Study of International Business Management.

Dr. Robinson holds a Ph.D. in International Business from the Alfred P. Sloan School of Management, Massachusetts Institute of Technology, and an M.B.A. from the Harvard Graduate School of Business Administration.